MONOGRAM PICTURES PRESENTS

Educational Pictures

2823

"THE SPICE OF THE PROGRAM"

SECOND

THE BEST OF THE Bs

A Citadel Press Book

Christmas , 1996

Dear Jack,
 Thanks for being such a good
friend and customer and an outstanding
film buff.

Sincerely,
John Cocchi

FEATURE

BY JOHN COCCHI

Published by Carol Publishing Group

Dedicated to THE COOPERATIVE FILM SOCIETY AT JOE'S PLACE

1967-1982

And to the two who made it possible,

JOE JUDICE AND CHRIS STEINBRUNNER.

(front cover) Dick Purcell in *Captain America*; Lew Ayres and Florence Rice (top right) in *Panic on the Air*; John Derek and Carolyn Craig (bottom right) in *Fury at Showdown*.
(back cover) Robert Livingston and Heather Angel (top left) in *The Bold Caballero*; Jane Wyman and Ronald Reagan in a publicity photo; Charles Gemora (in gorilla suit) and Phillip Terry in *The Monster and the Girl*.

Copyright © 1991 by John Cocchi

A Citadel Press Book
Published by Carol Publishing Group

Editorial Offices
600 Madison Avenue
New York, NY 10022

Sales & Distribution Offices
120 Enterprise Avenue
Secaucus, NJ 07094

In Canada: Musson Book Company
A division of General Publishing Co. Limited
Don Mills, Ontario

Citadel Press a registered trademark of
Carol Communications, Inc.

Queries regarding rights and permissions
should be addressed to: Carol Publishing Group,
600 Madison Avenue, New York, NY 10022

Manufactured in the United States of America

DESIGNED BY LESTER GLASSNER

Carol Publishing Group books are available at special discounts
for bulk purchases, for sales promotions, fund raising, or
educational purposes. Special editions can also be created to
specifications. For details contact: Special Sales Department,
Carol Publishing Group, 120 Enterprise Ave., Secaucus, NJ 07094

10 9 8 7 6 5 4 3 2
Library of Congress Cataloging-in-Publication Data

Cocchi, John.
    Second feature: the best of the Bs/ by John Cocchi.
    p. cm.
    "A Citadel Press book."
    Includes index.
    ISBN 0-8065-1186-9:
    1. Motion pictures--California--Los Angeles--History. 2. B films--
California--Los Angeles--History. I. Title.
PN1993.5.U65C58   1991
791.43'0973-dc20   90-21525

STEPIN FETCHIT *in* Miracle in Harlem (*Screen Guild 1947*).

ACKNOWLEDGMENTS

Thanks to all the companies that made this book possible:
Academy Pictures, Ajax, Allied Artists, Almi, Ambassador-Conn-Melody, American International, Atlantic, Avco Embassy/Embassy Pictures, Banner, Beacon, Big 4 Joseph Brenner, Bryanston, Burroughs-Tarzan, Cinema 5, Cinema Shares International, Columbia, Commodore, Compass International, Continental, Crown International, DCA (Distributors Corporation of America), DeLaurentiis, Eagle-Lion, Equity, Eureka/Jewell, Falcon Pictures, Filmgroup, First Division, G & H Productions, Goldsmith, The Samuel Goldwyn Company, Grand National, Hallmark/ Kroger Babb, Hollywood Pictures, Hollywood Productions, Independent-International, Invincible, Lippert, The Lutheran Church, Majestic, Manson Distributing, Marcy, Mascot, Mayfair/Action Pictures, McLendon Radio Pictures, MGM, Monogram, New Century/Vista, New Line Cinema, New World, Parade, Paramount, Pathé, Robert Patrick Productions, Peerless, Pine-Thomas Productions, Platinum Pictures, Plymouth Productions, PRC (Producers Releasing Corporation), Realart, Reliable, RKO Radio, Hal Roach Productions, Rochelle Films, Sack Amusement Enterprises, Screen Classics, Screen Guild, William Steiner, Tiffany-Stahl, Troma Team, 20th Century-Fox/Fox Film Corporation, United Artists, Warner Bros./First National, World Wide, B.F. Zeidman, *and to* Republic and Universal, the two consistently fine producers and distributors of B product.

Thanks to those whose generous allowance of material and information helped immeasurably:

Mary Atwood, Alan Barbour, David Barnes (Supreme Video), David Bartholomew (Theatre Collection at Lincoln Center), Eric Benson, Richard Bojarski, Eddie Brandt (Saturday Matinee), Janet Chandler, Larry Cohn (*Variety*), Bob Dahdah, Diana Gibson (Rosemary Schropp), Alex Gordon, Herb Graff, Pierre Guinle, Ron Harvey, Ed Hulse, Richard Koszarski (American Museum of the Movie Image), Audrey Kupferberg (Edelman), Ed Maguire, Leonard Maltin, Howard Mandelbaum (Photofest), Richard A. Mayfield, Doug McClelland, Missy McMahon (Martha Pappas), Norman Miller, James R. Parish, Bill Perry, George Sherman, Sam Sherman (Independent-International), Marion Shilling, Eric Spilker (Spilker Film Company), Jean Sullivan, Lou Valentino, Tom Weaver, Maurice Zouary (Movietronics)

Personal thanks to:

Barbara Barondess, Verna Hillie, John Beal, Louise Campbell, Esther Ralston, Philip Trent, Valerie Allen and Candace Hilligoss.

Special thanks to:

William K. Everson, an inspiration for any film writer. Allan J. Wilson, the best editor any writer could have. Mark Ricci of The Memory Shop, for making it all possible. My late uncles, Frank Valluzzi and Arthur and Ralph Cocchi, whose memory and belief in me will always be cherished. And to my parents, John and Rose Cocchi, who sustained me, as always.

ESTHER RALSTON *In* The Spy
Ring *(Universal, 1938).*

CONTENTS

PAUL KELLY *at 20th Century-Fox,*
1935.

INTRODUCTION

You could say that I've been a lifelong film buff (having been born in the year regarded as the best ever for films). Although loving all types of films, I have a particular fondness for the B feature. The first one I can remember seeing was *Swamp Fire* in 1946, on a bill with a reissue of Disney's *Dumbo* (1941). Yes, in those days, double features were the norm, especially in the neighborhood theaters. My section of Brooklyn, Bay Ridge, boasted movie houses in all directions. By the late Forties, television began causing the demise of the smaller revival houses and eventually most of the bigger theaters. Of fond memory are the Stanley, Electra, Center, Coliseum, Bay Ridge, Shore Road, Harbor, Sunset, Vanity, Dyker— now supermarkets, banks, shopping centers and the like. Still in operation and now multiplexes are the Alpine and the Fortway.

Television, while ending one outlet for old pictures and B Product, created another. Being among the first generation to grow up with TV, I was able to see many of the films which were the staple of the early years of the medium. The summer of 1950 was the happiest of my life. Because of my allergies, I was sent from the family's summer home to stay with my maternal grandparents, dear old Rocco and Kate Valluzzi. They lived with their unmarried children just one block from my home. At every possible opportunity, I was allowed to watch old movies on TV. From constant viewing came an appreciation of the B, not overlooking the frequent trips to the local theaters.

When I reached my twenties, I discovered that there were others out there, film buffs as dedicated as I. New York is a major center for movies and it was a great pleasure to find film societies in some unlikely places. The late Jim Acito, a well-known film dealer, was in the business of showing and selling 16mm prints. From him, I purchased my first features, initially *Wild Horse* (1931) with Hoot Gibson. That was in early 1962, just a few months before Hoot's death, which made the film of even greater sentimental value. A favorite from early TV, *Alias Mary Smith* (1932) with Blanche Mehaffey, was another purchase.

Although the cost of 16mm prints was relatively minimal, it became apparent that you could actually make a bit of money by starting your own film society and showing your prints to fellow buffs. On a less mercenary and more important level, you could share your films with them and often have them reciprocate by doing the same. Before 1962 was out, I had started showing films in my basement. Shortly thereafter, the LeMetro Cafe in New York City offered an outlet. It was there that we ran the best attended film program with

MARY BRIAN *in* Charlie Chan in Paris *(Fox 1934).*

REGIS TOOMEY *in* The Light of Western Stars *(Paramount 1930).*

JANE DARWELL *in* The Great Gildersleeve *(RKO Radio 1942).*

FAY WRAY *in* Navy Secrets *(Monogram 1939).*

REX BELL *in* Crashin' Broadway *(Monogram 1933).*

WENDY BARRIE *in* A Girl With Ideas *(Universal 1937).*

PORTRAIT GALLERY

which I've ever been associated, all 12 chapters of the Republic serial *Adventures of Captain Marvel* (1941), then considered rare. Over a hundred people saw that show, which was arranged through the services of a very good friend, Chris Steinbrunner of WOR-TV. He had his own film group, running features and complete serials.

After two years in the service (our side), I returned home and participated in further film showings, at the Grand Central YMCA. It was there that Chris arranged a meeting with Joe Judice, a master electrician and carpenter who loved B features, Westerns and serials and had quite a collection of prints. He had the idea of converting his workshop into a movie theater and wanted me to help with the programming. In January of 1967, The CoOperative Film Society at Joe's Place, his address at 403 West 40th Street in Manhattan, came into being. For members, we drew upon the buffs we knew from the other film groups. Most of us were friends at that point and new ones were made on a regular basis. At first, we rented some films; then, since many of the members had their own film collections, we ran privately-owned prints, weekly.

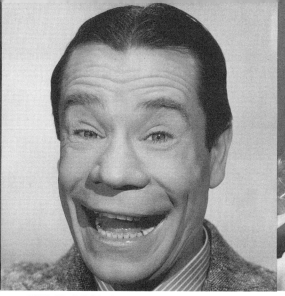

CKIE COOPER *in* Gangster's Boy *Monogram 1938*).

JOE E. BROWN *in* Joan of Ozark *(Republic 1942)*.

ONSLOW STEVENS, *in* Life Returns *(Universal 1935/Grand National 1938.)*

ARREN HYMER *in* Desert Justice *(Atntic 1936)*.

FERN EMMETT *in* Burning Gold *(Republic 1935)*.

BRODERICK CRAWFORD *in* Undercover Doctor *(Paramount 1939)*.

OF STARS

Within the first few years, a policy of programming evolved. Since the major films were constantly being shown at other revival houses or on TV, we played the less familiar material. Naturally, B pictures and Westerns were common. Complete serials would be shown in one evening, sometimes running to five hours or more. Since the films were usually short and I realized that many were available, we generally ran triple features. Even when we had occasional programs of A features, there would often be three films on the bill. Some of the best ever made weren't normally shown. We may have been the only film club in existence to have had only one (nonpaying) customer for *The Day the Earth Stood Still* (1951) and to have no one sit through *Dead End* (1937)—we cancelled the latter and closed up early that night. I'd often thought that this was one group which would prefer to see Don "Red" Barry in *Red Desert* (1949) rather than Antonioni's film of the same name. We finally did show the Barry Western and it was disappointing.

The Thanksgiving of 1969 proved to be a crisis time for me. I had lost my job as well as my girlfriend and was in danger of losing the club. Chris stepped in and arranged for us to

VALERIE ALLEN *at Paramount, 1959.*

CANDACE HILLIGOSS *in* Carnival of Souls *(Herts-Lion International 1962).*

BARBARA BARONDESS, *screen test, 1932.*

LOUISE CAMPBELL *at Paramount, 1937).*

PHILIP TRENT *in* Bombay Clipper *(Universal 1941).*   VERNA HILLIE *at Mascot, 1934.*

obtain a city charter so that we could stay in operation. Also, I found a better job and quite a few other girlfriends. That better job was with *Boxoffice* magazine, for which I was a reporter-movie reviewer for the decade of the Seventies. As for the club, I felt it was a good place to lose a girlfriend, once you'd brought her there (as I seemed to be in the habit of doing). With new movies on the job and old movies at the CoOp, what could be better for a buff?

With the Eighties came new problems—the city had taken over the apartment building in which the club was housed and was demanding higher rent. Unbelievably, we were paying just $40 a month for years. Professor Richard Brown of The New School, for whom I was then working on a free-lance basis, intervened and kept the raise in rent down to $75. That was just about all we could afford, as the club always operated on a self-sustaining basis. The end came in December of 1982 when Joe decided to move to Puerto Rico, taking his collection with him, and the city saw fit to increase the rent to $500 a month.

For awhile, we had screenings at other locations after the club was unavailable. Mary Atwood, then Orlando, generously donated her appartment, as did Miriam Raiken, who married one of our members, Roger Kolb. There were celebrity screenings at New York hotels with Barbara Barondess, Ann Corio and Verna Hillie. We wound up at the apartment of our former projectionist, Bobby Everroad. It was at his place, in mid-1987, where we finally ended the long run of The CoOp. Since we'd lost Joe's Place, it had been spasmodic showings at best.

In the club's heyday, we had occasional celebrities in attendance. Filmmaker Sam Sherman, head of Independent International Pictures, was a member; later film producer Jon Davison attended once or twice. Such performers as Lanny Ross, Bob Allen, Valerie Allen and Barbara Barondess came; Louise Campbell attended with daughter Missy

JOHN BEAL *in* We Who Are About
To Die *(RKO Radio 1936).*

McMahon; old-time filmmaker Denver Dixon was brought there by old friends Sam Sherman and Bob Price. Alan Barbour and Al Kilgore, Dick Bann, Larry Quirk, other historians, were occasional visitors. Two of the best books ever written about films were researched in part at the CoOp. One was Doug McClelland's *The Golden Age of B Movies* (Charter House, 1978)—apologies for using so many of the titles he includes. Another was Leonard Maltin's *The Great Movie Shorts* (Crown, 1972)—he dedicated the book "To the Gang at Joe's Place," possibly the only time a film group was ever singled out in that fashion.

The reason why this book is dedicated to The CoOperative Film Society is that the group was unique in its time. Also, many of the films covered were first shown at the club. Some of the later writings come from my time with the trade papers *Boxoffice* magazine and *The Film Journal* or research for American Movie Classics. I'm happy to report that the former premises of the club, located near the Port Authority building, is now serving a useful purpose. After five years of decayed vacancy, it became the Clinton Housing Development Company. We hadn't intended to make history with the club. And we didn't. With the help of this book, the spirit will live on.

As early as 1912, feature films were being produced in the United States. With this development came the creation of the B. That is, a lower budgeted feature designed to make a quick return on production investment. The advent of double features some years later made the B a longtime staple of moviemaking. Called quickies, programmers, second features or just B films (as opposed to A, or major, pictures), they were to a great extent a necessary part of the motion picture industry. Major companies would make B pictures in order to have product for their release schedules. Many great talents were connected with these films, often at the beginning—or the end—of their careers. Some filmmakers and talents, however, never rose above the level of the genre and spent decades in turning out such product.

Poverty Row was the name given to the Hollywood area in which many of the producers-distributors had headquarters or studios. Gower Gulch was the designation for the locale in which the Western movies were produced. For years, New York was also a film production center. Quality was often sacrificed for quantity, but occasionally a gem emerged. It may be true that no one ever set out to make a bad movie, but quite a few turned out that way. Today, producers tend to avoid the B designation while admitting to making a low budget feature. Of course, that could mean anything produced under a cost of $10 million. In the old days, that amount could have financed dozens, even hundreds, of quickies.

This book is an attempt to present just a bit of that rich history. The entries include many of the very best B films ever made and a few of both the worst and the indifferent ones for contrast. The reader will see how B films were influenced by A pictures and by each other, plus how they influenced A product as well. Talent which had a beginning in Bs and went on to greater things are mentioned, as well as those who never went anywhere and some who had once been great. The thousands of silent B features are impossible to evaluate, due to the vast numbers which were made, their total unavailability (many don't exist anymore) and the lack of involvement on the part of all but the most informed film historians. In short, no one ever heard of them.

All entries are personal choices of the author, who has seen every film discussed. All or most exist in one form or another, or did within the author's lifetime. The exclusion of a film may be due to several factors: I don't consider it a B; I didn't like it or have nothing new to say about it; or simply, I just haven't seen it. That should answer, "How could he leave out—?" On the other hand, the question, "How could he include—?," can only be explained as a matter of taste—good or bad. In the compilation of the book, it was decided to restrict entries solely to American-made films (certainly no other country can lay claim to having made Bs on such a volume) and even to eliminate a few which were made in part outside of the country. All of this, of course, should explain what's in and what's out. Also, a lack of titles from the 1980s reflects an inability to view many of the worthy possibilities. Plus, of course, there's the fact that, as they say, "They just don't make them like that anymore."

And so, we begin with a pictorial history of the B feature....

WANDA McKAY *in* The Royal Mounted Patrol *(Columbia 1941).*

LINDA STIRLING *at Republic, circa 1946.*

ROBERT SHAYNE *in* Criminal Lawyer *(Columbia 1951).*

HORACE McMAHON *in* Roger Touhy, Gangster *(20th Century-Fox 1944).*

BONITA GRANVILLE *in* The Truth About Murder *(RKO Radio 1946).*

ANN CORIO *in* The Sultan's Daughter *(Monogram 1943).*

LILA LEEDS *in* Wild Weed
(Eureka/Jewell 1949).

SHELLEY WINTERS *in* South Sea Sinner
(Universal-International 1949).

JACK HOLT *in* The Arizona Ranger
(RKO Radio 1948).

JANE WITHERS *in* Danger Street
(Paramount 1947).

STEVE ALLEN *in* Down Memory
Lane *(Eagle-Lion 1949).*

LOUISE ALLBRITTON *at Universal, 1945.*

NOEL NEILL *in* Smart Politics
(Monogram 1948).

ADRIAN BOOTH *in* The Sea Hornet *(Republic 1951)*.

RUTH WARRICK *in* One Too Many *(Hallmark/Kroger Babb 1950)*.

JOAN BENNETT *in* Highway Drag-net *(Allied Artists 1954)*.

MARA CORDAY *in* The Giant Claw *(Columbia 1957)*.

LISA GAYE *in* Drums Across the River *(Universal-International 1954)*.

JUDY CANOVA *in* Carolina Can-nonball *(Republic 1955)*.

GEORGE O'HANLON *in* Bop Girl *(United Artists 1957)*.

ANN HARDING *in* I've Lived Before *(Universal-International 1956)*.

WILLIAM CAMPBELL *in* Man in the Vault *(RKO Radio 1956)*.

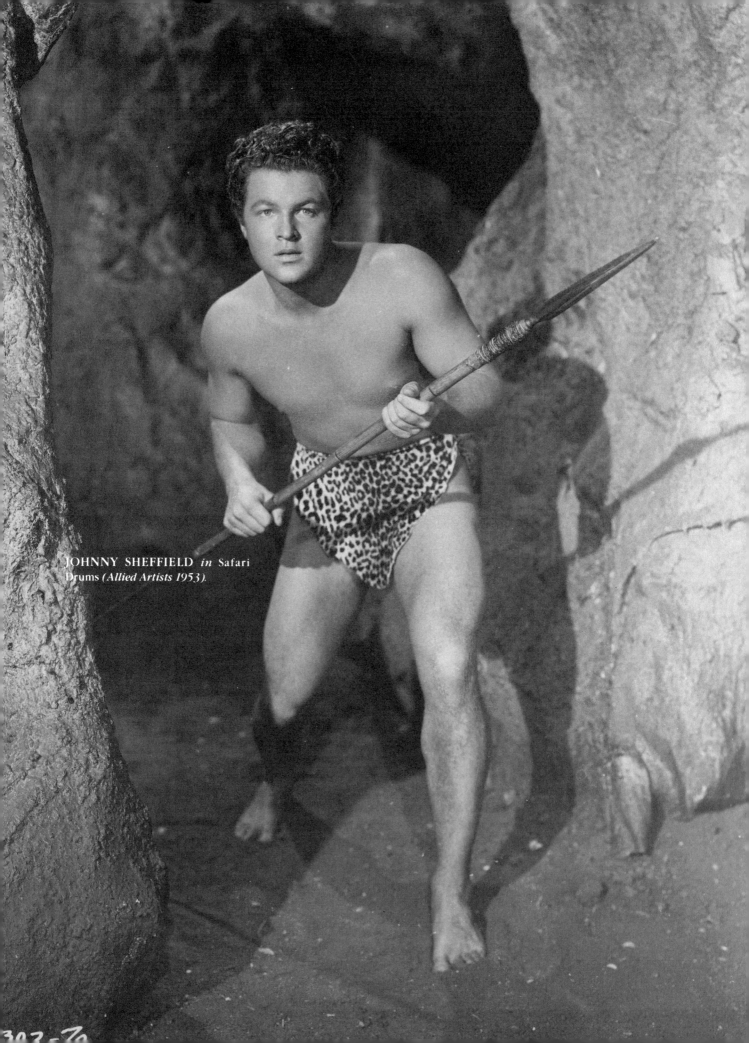

JOHNNY SHEFFIELD *in* Safari
Drums *(Allied Artists 1953).*

JIM DUKAS *in* The Great St. Louis Bank Robbery *(United Artists 1959)*.

WALTER MATTHAU *in* Ride a Crooked Trail *(Universal-International 1958)*.

ELAINE EDWARDS *in* Battle Flame *(Allied Artists 1959)*.

JOHNNY CASH *in* Road to Nashville *(Robert Patrick Productions/Crown International 1966)*.

LARRY FINE *in* Have Rocket, Will Travel *(Columbia 1959)*.

MARJORIE MAIN *in* The Kettles in the Ozarks *(Universal-International 1956)*.

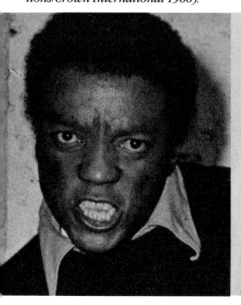

PAUL WINFIELD *in* Gordon's War *(20th Century-Fox 1973)*.

CHERI CAFFARO *in* Ginger *(Joseph Brenner 1971)*.

RUSS TAMBLYN *in* Satan's Sadists *(Independent-International 1969)*.

GEORGE KENNEDY *in* Mean Dog Blues *(American International 1978).*

GLORIA STUART *in* It Could Happen to You *(20th Century-Fox 1939).*

DIANA GIBSON *in* Adventure's End *(Universal 1937).*

STELLA STEVENS *in* Monster in the Closet *(Troma Team 1986).*

RORY CALHOUN *in* Motel Hell *(United Artists 1980).*

VALERIE BERTINELLI *in* C.H.O.M.P.S. *(American International 1979).*

CATHERINE MARY STEWART *in* Dudes *(New Century/Vista 1987).*

PAM GRIER *in* Bucktown *(American International 1975).*

CHRISTOPHER LEE *in* The Rosebud Beach Hotel *(Almi 1984).*

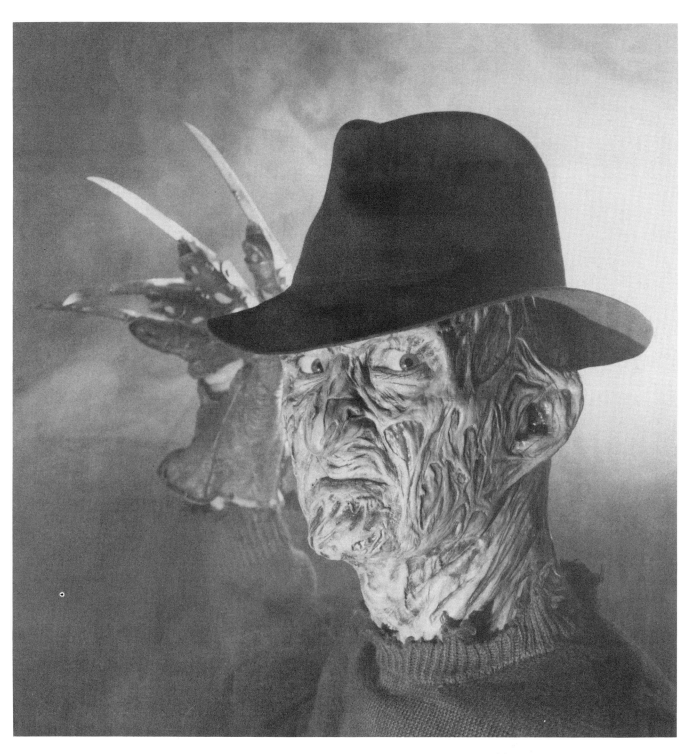

ROBERT ENGLUND *in* A
Nightmare on Elm Street 4: The
Dream Master *(New Line Cinema
1988).*

THE B FEATURE

Hundreds of programmers were produced in the silent days. A late one, Streets of Shanghai (Tiffany-Stahl 1927), featured Anna May Wong and, in Oriental makeup, Jason Robards (Sr.).

In the beginning were Bs. One of the very first, Via Wireless (Pathe 1915), provided stock footage for other films, years afterward.

Westerns were made by the dozens, hundreds. Of the talent involved with Blazing Days (Universal 1927) with Fred Humes and Bruce Gordon, only its director, William Wyler, really achieved great fame.

Before dubbing was perfected, entire foreign language versions were made of many early talkies. Indicating which in the case of Men of the North (MGM 1930) are John Reinhardt (later a director), Gilbert Roland, André Luguet and Franco Corsaro. Hal Roach took a rare directorial credit.

Shorts were a staple on the local theater's program. A popular series, "Crime Does Not Pay," offered Gertrude Michael in Pound Foolish (MGM 1939).

Serials were long popular. One of the best, from Republic's Golden Age, is Captain America (Republic 1944), starring Dick Purcell.

Action was always in demand. Doing horse falls in Buck Jones' Outlawed Guns (Universal 1935) are Cliff Lyons and Jim Corey.

Documentaries have to be considered low budgeters. Pumping Iron (Cinema 5), a 1977 look at body builders, helped launch the movie career of Arnold Schwarzenegger.

Get a top stuntman to star, as David Sharpe does in Social Error (Ajax/Marcy/Commodore 1935)…

It helped if your stars were good riders, as Dick Foran, Andy Devine and Leo Carrillo demonstrate in Road Agent *(Universal 1941), a non-series Western…*

Or hire a stuntman who one day will become a star. Don C. Harvey, Jock Mahoney in the air and Charles Sullivan in Hoedown *(Columbia 1950)...*

(Below, left)
Sign a star with athletic prowess. Sterling Hayden proves his agility and Paul Cavanagh shows his villainy in Sam Katzman's production The Golden Hawk *(Columbia 1952).*

Actresses also mix in occasionally. Judo expert Bruce Tegner and Gloria Talbott fight in Albert Zugsmith's Girls' Town *(MGM 1959).*

Car stunts have long been in vogue; this is from Texas Detour *(Cinema Shares International 1978), in which Patrick Wayne (John's son) stars as a stunter.*

Insure that the stunt double resembles the hero: John Carroll and stand-in Jack Rose on Rose of the Rio Grande *(Monogram 1938).*

The Bs were ever a spawning ground for young talent. Philip Pine and Robert Loggia, with hair, in The Lost Missile (United Artists 1958).

Not all talent stayed before the cameras, however. Blake Edwards, before going on to other pursuits, played bits in the Forties. In Gangs of the Waterfront (Republic 1945), he menaces Robert Armstrong.

Here's a young couple who alternated between A and B features at Warners. It's 1941 and they were then married: Jane Wyman and Ronald Reagan.

35

Sets could include an ambitious re-production of New York's Bowery around 1900, as in Sunbonnet Sue *(Monogram 1945).*

Makeup might entail use of a false nose, as Louis Hayward displays to Barbara Britton in The Return of Monte Cristo *(Columbia 1946).*

A reuse of a standing set. Warner Bros. recycled this one from such epics as The Charge of the Light Brigade *(1936) and* Another Dawn *(1937) for* Adventures in Iraq *(1943) with Warren Douglas, Ruth Ford and John Loder. The film itself is a remake of George Arliss'* The Green Goddess *(1929).*

For monster movies, a normal sized creature and miniature props might do, as long as they don't resemble toys. The Giant Gila Monster (McLendon Radio Pictures/Hollywood Pictures 1959).

Scars should look real. Jack Kelly notices that Mickey Rooney's doesn't, in Drive a Crooked Road (Columbia 1954).

Wardrobe can be a problem, as Brenda Joyce, Lee Tracy and Raymond Walburn find in I'll Tell the World *(Universal 1945).*

Dressing up, or cross, can be fun. Chester Morris, June Vincent, George E. Stone in Trapped by Boston Blackie *(Columbia 1948).*

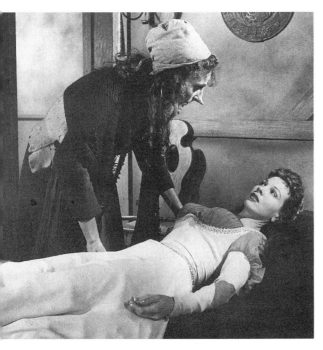

Shoot it where you can. For The Undead *(American International 1957), Roger Corman used a converted supermarket. Dorothy Neumann and Pamela Duncan.*

Trends were always welcome subjects. Panic on the Air *(Columbia 1936) with Lew Ayres and Florence Rice was a melodrama about radio.*

Location shooting can be stimulating. Marjorie Woodworth and director Hal Roach Jr. on location in the High Sierras for Dudes Are Pretty People *(Hal Roach-United Artists 1941).*

Some pictures used movies themselves as background. Eddie Nugent and Kay Hughes in A Man Betrayed *(Republic 1936).*

Being well dressed also insures publicity. Lucille Ball steps out smartly for RKO Radio in 1936.

Answering fan mail is a must. Tom Keene, 1938 Monogram Western star, looks at his. A copy of Boxoffice *magazine is prominently displayed.*

Always, ballyhoo has its place. Mary Avram and producer Sam Sherman participate in a contest for The Naughty Stewardesses *(Independent-International 1974).*

Nothing like a plug for your own product. Bud Geary, Duke Green, Ace the Wonder Dog and Tim Holt in The Rookie Cop *(RKO Radio 1939), in front of a poster for the studio's* Pacific Liner *(1938), with Chester Morris and Victor McLaglen visible.*

A rare instance of a major company release that was reissued as an exploitation feature is What Price Innocence? *(Columbia 1933) with Beatrice Banyard and Betty Grable.*

Boy and dog tales were always popular. London the dog and Buddy Hart do their thing in The Littlest Hobo *(Allied Artists 1958).*

Avoid including equipment (at left) in the shot. Sally Payne, Lynn Merrick, Joseph Allen Jr. and The Weavers (Leon, Frank, June) in Mountain Rhythm *(Republic 1942).*

An instance of a film being revised with new footage into something for the exploitation market: A Modern Marriage (Monogram 1950) became Frigid Wife (Ken Productions 1961) with an added prologue. Remaining its stars are Margaret Field (mother of Sally) and Reed Hadley.

Indie producers weren't afraid to tackle the classics, as Monogram did with Robert Louis Stevenson's Kidnapped (1948) with Sue England and Roddy McDowall.

Publicity is an important part of moviemaking. Maria Montez and Mischa Auer pose for Moonlight in Hawaii (Universal 1941).

During filming, shots should be angled so as not to take in the end of the process screen (note right). Give Us Wings (Universal 1940) with Billy Halop, Bernard Punsly, Bobby Jordan, Gabriel Dell, Huntz Hall.

Sports stars would play themselves, often not too well. Roger Maris, William Frawley, Bryan Russell and Mickey Mantle in Safe At Home! *(Columbia 1962).*

Exploitation features long endured. A later one, The Devil's Bedroom *(Manson Distribution Corp. 1964),* starred John Lupton and Valerie Allen, a woman of many careers.

Sports stories should have action. Hal Baylor, John Indrisano and Alex Nicol supply that in Champ for a Day *(Republic 1953).*

Later on, sports stars would be hired for character cameos. Mamie Van Doren demonstrates her boxing ability to Rocky Marciano, the heavyweight champ, in a pose for College Confidential *(Universal-International 1960).*

A star must learn how to relax. Drue Leyton, Alan Mowbray and Mona Barrie do it between takes on Charlie Chan in London *(Fox 1934).*

Through everything, a performer needs poise at all times. Nella Walker and ZaSu Pitts in Going Highbrow *(Warner Bros. 1935).*

IRIS ADRIAN

SPRING BYINGTON

JOHN BOLES

ROBERT ARMSTRONG

BINNIE BARNES in Gateway (20th Century-Fox 1938)

LEO GORCEY

NANCY COLEMAN *in* Her Sister's Secret *(PRC 1946)*

CLEO MOORE

C. HENRY GORDON

HIGH VOLTAGE (Pathe 1929) Directed by Howard Higgin. Of interest as one of the earliest sound films available and a *bad* one as well. The premise of a bus being stranded in Nevada snows, with the passengers seeking shelter in an abandoned church, seems solid, and the cast is certainly a good one. Yet, the attempts at action and drama fail to excite. Billy Bevan is the driver and the passengers are Detective Owen Moore and his prisoner Carole Lombard, plus banker Phillips Smalley and daughter Diane Ellis. During their snowbound layover, Moore begins falling in love with Lombard, but soon has a rival in the person of William Boyd, a derelict who turns out to be a fugitive. To liven things, unsuccessfully, comic Bevan is given several songs, and Moore—once Mary Pickford's husband—is even presented doing a number (with his back to John Mescall's camera, he's obviously dubbed). Actor James Gleason worked on the script with Kenyon Nicholson and Elliott Clawson, based on a story by Clawson. *High Voltage* has low wattage and minimum impact.

OH, YEAH! (Pathe 1929) Directed by Tay Garnett. This picture from the same studio, in contrast, is far more entertaining, combining large doses of comedy with touches of action, including a fight on a moving flatcar. Drifters Robert Armstrong and James Gleason, the heroes, arrive in a railroad town called Linda, finding romance in the persons of Patricia Caron and ZaSu Pitts at the camp restaurant. Frank Hagney and Bud Fine provide menace, and Paul Hurst is also in the cast. Making this historically important is the constant use of slang, to the point at which a foreign viewer might need subtitles to follow the dialogue. Garnett and Gleason collaborated on the script, based on the 1928 *Saturday Evening Post* story "No Brakes" by Andrew W. Somerville. Robert Fellows, later a producer associated with John Wayne, is assistant director, while Garnett, George Waggner and George Green provided the song "Love Found Me," which fits in nicely.

WHISPERING WINDS (Tiffany-Stahl 1929) Directed by James Flood. This touching drama is one of the few part talkies available, has both sound and silent sequences, and concerns a Maine fisherman, Malcolm McGregor, who marries Patsy Ruth Miller on the rebound after his sweetheart Eve Southern forsakes him for a singing career. Years later, Eve proves to be genuinely in love with McGregor, but acts indifferent for Miller's sake. Although she plays a singer, Southern has her songs dubbed and her dramatic scenes are silent. Her few later sound films proved that she had a speaking voice. Some agreeable (but unfortunately uncredited)

songs almost make this a musical and include "Listen to the Rain" and the theme "Whenever I Think of You." [With this film comes a tale as to how a print survived. In 1962, my younger brother Robert married high school sweetheart Valerie La Ferla and moved into her family's home. When her grandmother Julia D'Amico emptied a closet to make room for the newlyweds, a cache of 35mm films was discovered after having been hidden away for over 30 years. Being the family's resident movie buff, I obtained the print and managed to preserve all but two middle reels. Who knows what other films might be out there?]

THE MEDICINE MAN *(Tiffany 1930) Jack Benny goes dramatic with Eva Novak—the film is so old that Benny wasn't yet 39 (he was 36 at the time).*

THE MEDICINE MAN (Tiffany 1930) Directed by Scott Pembroke. Surprisingly, this Jack Benny vehicle isn't a comedy, but rather a straight drama with the star as a medicine man in a traveling show. At one small town, he falls in love with Betty Bronson, whose tyrannical father E. Alyn Warren beats her. Here's a good example of a comedian yearning to go dramatic and Benny proves that he can handle himself capably. Although his movie career was always the source of jokes, he really did make several fine features in the Thirties and Forties. Based on the play by Elliott Lester and adapted by Ladye Horton and Eve Unsell, this one co-stars George E. Stone, Tom Dugan and silent star Eva Novak.

NIGHT WORK (Pathe 1930) Directed by Russell Mack. Possibly Eddie Quillan's best work, as the star runs

NIGHT WORK *(Pathe 1930) Georgia Caine, Sally Starr, Charles Clary and Eddie Quillan search for a record of Douglas Scott's parentage as the boy looks on.*

the gamut in this tour-de-force, singing, dancing, acting and getting laughs, being appealing in every aspect. Although a bit convoluted, Walter De Leon's original screenplay revolves around a window dresser who cares for a nurse (Sally Starr) and an orphan (Douglas Scott). The large cast includes George Duryea (later Tom Keene), Frances Upton, John T. Murray, Robert McWade, Marjorie "Babe" Kane, Anita Garvin and Vince Barnett. Songs by Mort Harris and Ted Snyder, "Deep in Your Heart" and "I'm Gettin' Tired of My Tired Man," are most pleasant.

TODAY (Majestic 1930) Directed by William Nigh. At a time when most films were avoiding the effects of the Depression, *Today* confronted it right on. Actually, the Seton I. Miller scenario was an updating of the 1913 play by Abraham Schomer and George H. Broadhurst. Conrad Nagel is forced to work as a second hand automobile salesman after being wiped out by the stock market crash. Confident that wife Catherine Dale Owen will adjust, he soon comes to realize that she's unable to and confronts her as she slips into prostitution. Having to choose between two endings, one tragic and the other happy, producers Harry Sherman and Jack D. Trop (later connected with the Hopalong Cassidy series) cleverly included both. Here, they have James Wong Howe's crisp camerawork as an asset.

LEFTOVER LADIES (Tiffany 1931) Directed by Erle C. Kenton. Here is a good domestic drama with some unusual camerawork by John Stumar. Ursula Parrott was a popular writer of women's novels, one of whose works became Norma Shearer's 1930 Oscar-winning *The Divorcée*, and her original story for *Ladies* was adapted by Robert R. Presnell (he also functioned as a producer). Two couples are involved in divorce: Claudia Dell and Walter Byron, who part while still in love, and the sophisticated Alan Mowbray and Dorothy Revier, who couldn't care less. Dell's friendship with the tragic, aging Marjorie Rambeau (a top characterization) makes her realize her mistake. Roscoe Karns, Rita LaRoy, Selmer Jackson, Henry Armetta and Bill Elliott are also in the cast.

THE BLACK KING (Southland Pictures 1932) Produced and directed by Bud Pollard. Reissued as *Harlem Big Shot* by Sack Amusement Enterprises. Here is an hilarious all-black production (a few whites have minor parts) based on the career of Marcus Garvey, who organized a Back to Africa movement among blacks in the United States. A.B. Comathiere portrays Garvey's fictional screen counterpart, Deacon Charcoal Johnson, heading an organization of the same name and raising funds all the way from Logan, Mississippi to Harlem. Typical of the freewheeling humor is the use of Victor Herbert's "March of the Wooden Soldiers" for a procession by Comathiere, his elite troops and followers. This film (and a rather racist one at that) was made at Metropolitan Studios in Fort Lee, New Jersey, with Lorenzo Tucker, an accomplished actor-writer-producer, as an elegant attorney and Johnny Lee, later Lawyer Calhoun on TV's *Amos 'n' Andy*, as Count of Zanzibar.

TODAY *(Majestic 1930) Early Depression drama: Conrad Nagel is about to tell his self-centered wife Catherine Dale Owen that he's been wiped out financially.*

FALSE FACES (World Wide 1932) Directed by Lowell Sherman. Buffs constantly enjoy the work of actor-director Sherman, usually seen as the sophisticated cad with a self-deprecating sense of humor. Here, though, in a change of pace, he directs himself as a Chicago plastic surgeon and quack whose biggest failure in the operating room leads to tragedy. A strong cast supports—Lila Lee, Peggy Shannon, Berton Churchill, David Landau, Geneva Mitchell, Joyce Compton, Nance O'Neil, and Eddie "Rochester" Anderson. Ken Maynard, then doing a Western series for the company, has a guest bit in a night club.

FALSE FACES *(World Wide 1932) Director-star Lowell Sherman (2nd left) proves to be devious in court, as associates Peggy Shannon, Harold Waldridge and Berton Churchill learn.*

THOSE WE LOVE (World Wide 1932) Directed by Robert Florey. Adapted by F. Hugh Herbert, from the play by S. K. Lauren and George Abbott. With credentials like that, this Mary Astor drama just can't miss. One of the most effective of the none too plentiful independent dramas, with Astor as the loving wife of writer Kenneth MacKenna, standing by him from their post-World War I marriage through his affair with other woman Lilyan Tashman (another film buff's delight). For the sake of son Tommy Conlon, MacKenna returns to his incredibly patient, always forgiving spouse.

THOSE WE LOVE *(World Wide 1932) Family reunion at a new country home: Hale Hamilton, Tommy Conlon, Kenneth MacKenna and Mary Astor.*

UPTOWN NEW YORK (World Wide 1932) Directed by Victor Schertzinger. Yet another good drama from that studio, with Jack Oakie in a rare dramatic part, playing a vending machine operator who marries Shirley Grey, unaware that she really prefers Dr. Leon Waycoff (later Leon Ames). Warren B. Duff's screenplay, based on Vina Delmar's story "Uptown Woman," and Norbert Brodine's cinematography, combined with Oakie's performance, make this especially appealing. [Shown at the 1975 Hollywood Cinecon, attended by film buffs from around the country and by Oakie himself, this impressed viewers with the star's performance as well as the World Wide logo, which features a woman with two globes revolving in front of her.]

IN THE MONEY (Chesterfield-Invincible 1933) Directed by Frank Strayer. Similar but superior to Paramount's *Three Cornered Moon* (also 1933) which stars Claudette Colbert and Richard Arlen. Lois Wilson and Skeets Gallagher star in the comedy of a wacky family facing hardship because the stock which has supported them is worthless. Warren Hymer, Sally Starr, Junior Coghlan, Arthur Hoyt and especially Louise Beavers are assorted nuts in the cast. Remade as *Red Lights Ahead* (see 1936 entry).

CONVENTION GIRL *(Falcon Pictures/First Division 1934) On the beach at Atlantic City, Rose Hobart listens as Weldon Heyburn attempts to define his idea of love.*

BEGGARS IN ERMINE (Monogram 1934)
Directed by Phil Rosen. One of the best B dramas, this movie made from Esther Lynd Day's novel finds Lionel Atwill—filmdom's master villain—in a completely sympathetic role, playing a steel mill owner who loses his legs in an accident engineered by his crooked secretary-treasurer Jameson Thomas. After meeting blind peddler Henry B. Walthall, Atwill organizes a number of Walthall's cohorts via a dues-paying system. Also in the cast are Betty Furness, James Bush, Astrid Allwyn and George Hayes.

CONVENTION GIRL (Falcon Pictures/First Division 1934) Directed by Luther Reed. Comedy-drama of Atlantic City's hostesses, catering to businessmen looking for diversions from convention meetings. Filmed on location and a valuable screen artifact as a result, it contains shots of the famed Steel Pier and the Ritz-Carlton Terrace. Rose Hobart stars as the most-in-demand convention lady, beloved by casino owner Weldon Heyburn, one of the many Gable look-alikes, and Philadelphia soap manufacturer Herbert Rawlinson, playing with a straight face. Sally O'Neil, Lucila Mendez and Nancy Kelly (not the later star) are other hostesses, with Kelly performing "You Oughta Be Arrested for Breaking My Heart." Ruth Gillette sings "I've Got Sand in My Shoes," which is not the popular song of another day. Isham Jones and Orchestra and the Ned Wayburn Dancing Girls join in the musical numbers, written by Louis Alter and Arthur Swanstrom. Two surprises in the cast: Nell O'Day, seen largely in Westerns, as a young girl who nearly goes astray; and Shemp Howard, of The Three Stooges, in a non-comic role as a local petty crook. (The pressbook indicates that he was originally to have been killed, unusual for the veteran comedian.) Toni Reed, a tap dancer, is Hobart's odd-looking nephew and O'Day's love interest here. Adapted by George Boyle and Max Lief from Boyle's novel, the independent production successfully skirts any deeper interpretation of the ladies' profession.

STOLEN SWEETS (Chesterfield 1934) Directed by Richard Thorpe, filmed at Universal City. In a very satisfying comedy-drama in the rich girl-poor boy vein, wealthy but unhappy Sally Blane meets insurance man Charles Starrett on board ship and falls in love, much to the annoyance of her nasty fiancé Jameson Thomas. One of Starrett's circle of fun-loving friends, who show Blane how to enjoy life, is Blane's real-life sister Polly Ann Young. When butler Tom Ricketts greets Starrett's pals with "Walk this way, please," they imitate his bent walk. Later in 1934, Ricketts did the very same thing in Frank Capra's *Broadway Bill*, and it has since become a standard routine.

THE NUT FARM (Monogram 1935) Directed by Melville Brown. Neat spoof of independent filmmaking, as swindler Bradley Page induces Betty Alden to take the family fortune and invest in making a movie rather than buying the nut farm her husband Oscar Apfel wants. Alden's brother Wallace Ford directs the film, a straight desert epic, which proves to be a disaster at the preview, but he sees an opportunity to save the day by re-editing the movie into a comedy. Possibly based on real life, the satire also stars Joan Gale, Florence Roberts and Spencer Charters. Ford certainly knew his way around the George Waggner script, as he'd also had the lead in the 1929 John C. Brownell play from which this was adapted, along with Pat O'Brien and Natalie Schafer.

STREAMLINE EXPRESS *(Mascot 1935) Victor Jory's attempts at being an efficient valet exasperate Evelyn Venable aboard the Express.*

STREAMLINE EXPRESS (Mascot 1935) Directed by Leonard Fields. Showing no shame, producer Nat Levine credited this as an original story by Wellyn Totman, with screenplay by Fields, Dave Silverstein and Olive Cooper. It's really a year-later remake of *Twentieth Century*, the Barrymore-Lombard classic by Ben Hecht, Charles MacArthur and Bruce Milholland. This time, Evelyn Venable is a Broadway star who elopes on opening night and Victor Jory is her producer, following her aboard the crack Streamline Express and masquerading as a waiter. Ralph Forbes has virtually the same role he played in the more-famous 1934 film. Proving that to a dedicated film buff there's no such thing as a bad Mascot feature or a bad Mascot cast, this has Esther Ralston, Sidney Blackmer and Erin O'Brien Moore on board. However, Ralston wrote in 1989, "Can't remember a single thing about this turkey."

WOMEN MUST DRESS (Monogram 1935) Directed by Reginald Barker. Fashion is the passion in an

WOMEN MUST DRESS *(Monogram 1935) Sharing a domestic moment are housewife Minna Gombell and her daughter Suzanne Kaaren; drama with comic touches.*

engaging comedy-drama, produced by Mrs. Wallace (Dorothy) Reid, who wrote it with Frank Farnsworth and Edmund Joseph. Businessman Gavin Gordon forsakes dowdy wife Minna Gombell for fashion writer Lenita Lane, prompting Gombell to return to her position as a dress designer and a woman of grooming. Suzanne Kaaren is the daughter who fears that Dr. Hardie Albright, her beau, might not be Mr. Right. Zeffie Tilbury wins laughs as Gombell's pony-playing mother and Arthur (later to be "Dagwood Bumstead") Lake and Charles (later to be Jon Hall) Locher enliven things considerably as Kaaren's silly friends. Small roles are played by the winners of the International Agfa-Ansco Screen Star Contest, none of whom quite naturally ever went anywhere in the movie business.

DON'T GET PERSONAL *(Universal 1936) "I came to get some laughs," telephone lineman James Dunn informs Sally Eilers on her wedding day, although he truly loves her.*

BACK TO NATURE (20th Century-Fox 1936) Directed by James Tinling. Third entry in "The Jones Family" series is both scenic and entertaining as they travel to Yosemite National Park. Joining regulars Jed Prouty, Spring Byington, Florence Roberts, Shirley Deane, Kenneth Howell, June Carlson and Billy Mahan are Tony Martin and Dixie Dunbar. Singer Martin plays a con man who romances Deane and doesn't sing while dancer Dunbar doesn't dance, although she warbles a bit of "Sailor's Hornpipe." Robert Ellis and Helen Logan based their screenplay on Katharine Kavanaugh's characters; the Joneses, who obviously liked to travel, visited Grand Canyon in a later entry, *Quick Millions* (1939).

DON'T GET PERSONAL (Universal 1936) Directed by William Nigh. The team of James Dunn and Sally Eilers was popular at Fox earlier, and this later attempt to duplicate their success is highly entertaining. Dunn and pal Pinky Tomlin are hired to drive Sally Eilers from New York to Ohio and marriage to George Meeker. Along the way, of course, Dunn and Eilers fall in love. Tomlin and Coy Poe wrote some pleasant tunes, best of which—"An Old Fashioned Song"—has the three stars joined by elderly couple George Cleveland and Lillian Harmer in song and square dance. Jean Rogers, the beautiful heroine and Priscilla Lawson, voluptuous villainess of the great *Flash Gordon* (1936) serial, have bits.

HOLLYWOOD BOULEVARD (Paramount 1936) Directed by Robert Florey. With a cast of dozens of silent stars in featured parts and bits (see photo), this is a vastly satisfying experience for those who remember. Although the background is Hollywood, the Marguerite Roberts screenplay (story by Max Marcin and Faith Thomas) is more of an exposé of scandal magazines as a has-been actor, played by John Halliday, agrees to write his memoirs for publisher C. Henry Gordon. When daughter Marsha Hunt asks Halliday to desist for the sake of ex-wife Mae Marsh, the actor attempts to break his contract. Robert Cummings, Frieda Inescort and Esther Ralston are also featured, while contemporary stars Gary Cooper and Eleanore Whitney make guest appearances among the old-timers.

JUST MY LUCK (Corona Pictures 1936) Produced and directed by Russell Ray Heinz. Fans of silent star Charles Ray cheered him in movie houses for his few appearances in sound films. The handful who saw his only starring talkie must have marveled at its old-fashioned quality. Shot at Fine Arts Studios, the seldom-seen feature borrowed ideas from Chaplin's *The Immi-*

grant (1917) and Griffith's *Intolerance* (1916). Ray, fired from Dunn-Wright Rubber Company, is sure that his formula for indestructible rubber, called Durex, will be a success. What he endures to protect his invention forms the basis for the plot. In the cast are Anne Grey, Eddie Nugent, Snub Pollard, Mathew Betz, Beth Marion and Western villain Charles King as a kidnapper. Seen best with an uncritical eye.

RED LIGHTS AHEAD (Chesterfield 1936) Directed by Roland Reed. This remake of *In the Money* (see 1933 entry) gets more mileage, amusingly, out of the wacky family routine. Roger Imhof, a member of The Whales fraternity, invests in a gold mine and does well until the returns dry up. Lucile Gleason, for once without husband James, is the wife while Andy Clyde as grandpa shows that all good comedians can handle a bit of dramatics well. Frank Coghlan, Jr., repeats his role from 1933, while Ben Alexander, Paula Stone and a platinum blonde Ann Doran are the other family members. Western actor Addison (Jack) Randall plays the smooth operating swindler. Officially a 1937 film; the title refers not to traffic signals, but the problems facing the Imhof family.

AMATEUR CROOK (Victory 1937) Directed by Sam Katzman. Of all the Herman Brix-Victory features of 1936-37, this is the most—intentionally—funny. It doesn't depend upon the action content of the others, playing outlandish situations for laughs. Brix (later Bruce Bennett), a struggling artist, and pretty Joan Barclay (formerly Geraine Greear) steal her father's diamond from thieves Monte Blue and Jack Mulhall, encountering gas station attendant/amateur detective Fuzzy Knight in their flight. Funniest character is Edward Earle as the bucolic deputy of sheriff/justice Henry Roquemore; he repeats everything others say. A rare directorial credit for long-time producer "Jungle Sam" Katzman. Another in the Brix series, *A Million to One* a.k.a. *Speed to Spare* (1937), co-starred Joan Fontaine.

SHE MARRIED AN ARTIST (Columbia 1937) Directed by Marion Gering. The short story "I Married an Artist" by Avery Strakosch was adapted by Gladys Lehman and Delmer Daves into this disarming low budget comedy. Artist John Boles and model Frances Drake seem made for each other, but he weds Parisian designer Luli Deste (an Austrian actress in the first of her five American films). When the marriage breaks up, housekeeper Helen Westley attempts to bring Boles and Drake back together. Boles delightfully sings "Parlez-Moi

HOLLYWOOD BOULEVARD (*Paramount 1936*) Stars of the silent screen—*Top: Tom Kennedy, Pat O'Malley, Jack Mower, Freeman Wood, Roy D'Arcy, Mae Marsh, Albert Conti; Middle: Ethel Clayton, Maurice Costello, Creighton Hale, Charles Morton, Jack Mulhall, Oscar Apfel, Edmund Burns, Betty Compson, Charles Ray; Seated: Ruth Clifford, Bryant Washburn, Jane Novak, Francis X. Bushman, Esther Ralston, William Desmond, Mabel Forrest, Herbert Rawlinson, Rosemary Theby.*

GATEWAY *(20th Century-Fox 1938) In his least favorite film, Don Ameche (center) is asked to introduce Arleen Whelan to Gilbert Roland, aboard ship.*

d'Amour" (Speak to Me of Love) in both French and English, forgetting some of the words both times. In most of his Thirties films (*Frankenstein*, 1931, being a notable exception), he managed to include a song or two. [A crowd pleaser at The CoOp, where the work of Albert Dekker, Franklin Pangborn and Jacqueline Wells (Julie Bishop), all in featured roles, was always appreciated.]

THE AFFAIRS OF ANNABEL (RKO Radio 1938) Directed by Ben Stoloff. Playing an early leading role, Lucille Ball was Annabel Allison, a top Hollywood star, something Lucy wasn't yet in actuality. Working for Wonder Pictures, she gets into difficulties as a result of press agent Jack Oakie's publicity stunts. Lucy goes to jail for "Behind Prison Bars" and he's unable to free her. While posing as a domestic for "A Maid and a Man," she

is kidnapped by Edward Marr and Anthony Warde and has to be rescued by director Fritz Feld and 50 movie cops—shades of Buster Keaton. When "Maid" is changed to "The Diamond Smuggler," Ball is arrested. Funny spoof of the filmmaking business, based on Charles Hoffman's story "Menial Star." A sequel, *Annabel Takes a Tour*, released just two months later, also with Ball, Oakie, Bradley Page (the producer) and Ruth Donnelly (secretary), was almost as good.

GATEWAY (20th Century-Fox 1938) Directed by Alfred Werker. Based on Walter Reisch's story "Ellis Island" (also the film's production title), with a screenplay by Lamar Trotti. Don Ameche is a correspondent, returning to America on a ship headed for Ellis Island. Among the immigrants aboard is Irish lass Arleen Whelan, who has trouble with Mayor Raymond Walburn and jeopardizes her marriage to stuffy Lyle Talbot. Other passengers include divorcée Binnie Barnes and deported gangster Gilbert Roland. Ameche, expectedly, falls for Whelan and becomes involved in an Ellis Island riot led by deportee John Carradine. In a rich comic performance is Gregory Ratoff, who replaced Prince Mike Romanoff in the role and who also directed the second unit scenes shot on location. Fifty years after its release, Ameche stated that this was his worst film and that producer Darryl F. Zanuck had to force him to make it. Actors are often the worst judges of their careers, even in retrospect, since *Gateway* is an entirely entertaining comedy-drama-romance with melodramatic overtones. As was often said at The CoOp, "all your favorites" are featured: Harry Carey, Marjorie Gateson, Maurice Moscovich, Fritz Leiber, Warren Hymer, E. E. Clive, Robert Lowery, Joan Carol, George Chandler, Mary Gordon and former Western star Robert Allen as a straw-hatted reporter.

WIDE OPEN FACES (Columbia 1938) Directed by Kurt Neumann. Wide open faced Joe E. Brown is confronted with three formidable leading ladies in this gangster comedy—Alison Skipworth, up-and-coming Jane Wyman and Lyda Roberti. Criminals converge on Lakeside Inn, where bank robber Stanley Fields has hidden $100,000. Joe E., the soda jerk of Willow Springs who aided in Fields' capture, tries to prevent the crooks from wrecking the inn. On opposite sides of the law are such as Alan Baxter, the formidable Barbara Pepper, Sidney Toler, Lucien Littlefield and Berton Churchill. This was the last film for Roberti, a Polish singer-comedienne popular in this era; she died at 29 just a month after the film's release.

WIDE OPEN FACES *(Columbia 1938) For a Joe E. Brown comedy, Lyda Roberti is about to step out in her last film, as Alan Baxter, Barbara Pepper and Joseph Downing react.*

HEAVEN WITH A BARBED WIRE FENCE (20th Century-Fox 1939) Directed by Richardo Cortez. An interesting road odyssey, written by Dalton Trumbo, Leonard Hoffman and Ben Grauman Kohn, it served as the feature debuts of its promising leading men, Glenn Ford, 23, and Richard Conte, 25, then using his real first name of Nicholas. Ford plays a New Yorker on his way to Arizona, along the way picking up as companions hobo-professor Raymond Walburn, illegal alien Jean Rogers and rebellious Conte. They spend time riding the rails and encountering bar proprietress Marjorie Rambeau. Ward Bond, Eddie Collins, Kay Linaker, Paul Hurst and Irving Bacon are also in the running. At the time, the film was considered a good opportunity for Rogers, who seems too American to be cast as a Spanish refugee. Ford, who went the furthest in a career over the next fifty years, somehow failed to impress.

HEAVEN WITH A BARBED WIRE FENCE *(20th Century-Fox 1939) In their feature debuts are Glenn Ford and Richard Conte; the story, a road odyssey.*

OUR NEIGHBORS—THE CARTERS (Paramount 1939) Directed by Ralph Murphy. Touching comedy-drama which could have developed into a series. Small-town druggist Frank Craven faces bankruptcy when a lower priced chain store opens in his vicinity. He and wife Fay Bainter worry over how to support their large brood—Scotty Beckett, Bennie Bartlett, Donald Brenon, Mary Thomas (a.k.a. Joyce Arleen) and Gloria Carter (whose character name is the same). Well-to-do Edmund Lowe and Genevieve Tobin, a childless couple, offer to "buy" one of their children, causing the family to become even closer. [A film which raised a few lumps in the throat at the club.]

THE ZERO HOUR (Republic 1939) Directed by Sidney Salkow. Republic was unbeatable in the making of Westerns, action films and serials. If anything, this drama proves that at least one genre was beyond the studio's creative capabilities, being one of the worst ever. Broadway producer Otto Kruger and star Frieda Inescort wed despite his paralyzing accident, but years later, she falls for widower Don Douglas when both attempt to adopt little Ann E. Todd. Feeling he's in the way, Kruger commits suicide by maneuvering his wheelchair to the edge of a roof. Garrett Fort adapted the Sol C. Siegel production from his (Fort's) original story, so he's doubly to blame.

THE BISCUIT EATER (Paramount 1940) Directed by Stuart Heisler. Highly regarded drama of a boy and his dog, simple yet touching. Filmed in Albany, Georgia, it

OUR NEIGHBORS—THE CARTERS *(Paramount 1939) Meet the Carters — left, top to bottom: Fay Bainter, Donald Brenon, Bennie Bartlett; right, top to bottom: Frank Craven, Gloria Carter, Scotty Beckett, Joyce Arleen (later Mary Thomas).*

THE ZERO HOUR *(Republic 1939) A feature that lives up to its title: Frieda Inescort, Ann E. Todd and Don Douglas are involved.*

could have made a star of its lead, little Billy Lee, who gives a fine performance. The small cast includes Cordell Hickman as Billy's best friend, a black boy, Richard Lane, Helen Millard and Lester Matthews, as well as Snowflake (Fred Toones) and Promise the dog. Stuart Anthony and Lillie Hayward lovingly adapted James Street's story, which lives up to the introductory title, "… And knowing man's need of a friend, God gave him a dog." Remade by Disney/Buena Vista in 1972 with Johnny Whittaker and George Spell as the boys.

THE COURAGEOUS DR. CHRISTIAN (RKO Radio 1940)

Directed by Bernard Vorhaus. Jean Hersholt started in silent films as a villain and changed his image to that of a kindly, dedicated doctor as a result of *The Country Doctor* (1936) with The Dionne Quintuplets. Capitalizing on that was the "Dr. Christian" radio show, which evolved into a six-film series. The second, best of the group, has Hersholt confronted by an epidemic of spinal meningitis while attempting to eradicate a slum area. Dorothy Lovett is his committed nurse, as she was in most of the entries, with Robert Baldwin, Vera Lewis and Maude Eburne also cast. However, the outstanding portrayal is by Tom Neal, as a cynical tough guy, an image he projected throughout his career as well as in real life.

GRANDPA GOES TO TOWN (Republic 1940)

Directed by Gus Meins, who also produced this sixth entry in the Higgins Family series. The real-life family consisting of James, Lucile and Russell Gleason star, with Lois Ranson and Tommy Ryan as the younger children. Stealing the film, however, is Harry Davenport in an uninhibited performance as Lucile's father. The family buys the rundown Palace Hotel in a ghost town which booms when Russell mistakenly believes a scene from a movie filming nearby is actual and spreads news of a

gold strike. Celebrities in the cast include boxer-turned-comic Maxie Rosenbloom, South American heavyweight champion Arturo Godoy and wife Ledda, Noah Beery, Walter Miller, Douglas Meins (son of the director) and veteran double-talker Cliff Nazarro. The movie spoofing is broad, extending to Miller's character, director Sherman (referring to Republic workhorse George Sherman).

SAILOR'S LADY (20th Century-Fox 1940)

Directed by Allan Dwan. An incredible cast makes this nautical comedy a film buff's delight. The story by Lt. Commander Frank "Spig" Wead, a friend and collaborator of John Ford, is episodic and serves as a peg for the comedy and musical interludes. Sailor Jon Hall's romance with Nancy Kelly is complicated by her attempts to adopt orphaned baby Bruce Hampton (playing a girl). Dana Andrews, who's involved with Katharine (Kay) Aldridge, wants to break up Hall and Kelly's relationship, while Larry (Buster) Crabbe as a religious sailor also loves Kelly. Wally Vernon and Joan Davis are the requisite comedy couple, performing an Apache dance. There also are bits by Don "Red" Barry, Kane Richmond, George O'Hanlon, Peggy Ryan, Ward Bond, Barbara Pepper, John Kellogg, Marie Blake, Bernadene Hayes, Walter Miller, Irving Bacon, and many etcs. Titled *Sweetheart of Turret One* during production, this is truly, as a popular saying at the club went, a "What a cast" picture.

SAPS AT SEA (United Artists 1940) Directed by Gordon Douglas. As Stan Laurel and Oliver Hardy's last for producer Hal Roach, this represented the end of a comedy era. Many feel it to be their final really good film and, at 57 minutes, it's all Laurel and Hardy. The typically nonsensical plot has the boys cast adrift with a criminal when Ollie has a breakdown due to stress on the job at a horn company. Comedy actors Harry Langdon and Charles Rogers, together with Felix Adler and Gil Pratt, fashioned the gags into a plot. James Finlayson and cross-eyed Ben Turpin (last film) head the supporting cast, but Richard Cramer steals honors as the crook who introduces his gun as if it were a son. Art Lloyd's crisp photography is also an asset. Film's production titles, *Jitterbugs* (the name of one of the duo's later films) and *Two's Company*, gave way to the short TV version, *Horn Hero*.

DOCTORS DON'T TELL (Republic 1941) Directed by Jacques Tourneur. Familiar but very well done drama of interns John Beal and Edward Norris, friends and rivals for attractive Florence Rice (Beal's favorite leading lady). Beal is the nice guy; Norris an opportunist not above dealing with criminals for some quick money. Ward Bond and Douglas Fowley give their usual winning

DOCTORS DON'T TELL *(Republic 1941) Good friends are John Beal, Florence Rice (a favorite leading lady of his) and Edward Norris.*

performances, while singer Bill Shirley has a rare dramatic part. Grady Sutton wins some laughs as a medical student who can't stand the sight of blood and so becomes a druggist. An early effort from a *noir* director—with songs.

MR. CELEBRITY a.k.a. TURF BOY (PRC 1941) Directed by William Beaudine. This is a routine story of an orphan, Robert "Buzzy" Henry, and his veterinarian uncle, James Seay, traveling the racetrack circuit just ahead of the boy's wealthy grandparents (William Halligan and Laura Treadwell) who want custody. Mainly produced for nostalgia buffs, in that it has a veteran silent film director and stars Francis X. Bushman and Clara Kimball Young, as well as boxer James J. Jeffries, as themselves. Bushman insists that he never used a double, even for the chariot race in *Ben Hur* (1925), Young tells of her film career in 1912 Flatbush and of Valentino having supported her (in *Eyes of Youth*, 1919), while Jeffries talks about boxing in the 1890s. Young Henry later became a top movie stuntman, while leading lady Doris Day did not become the later actress-singer.

SAILOR'S LADY *(20th Century-Fox 1940) Sailors and their ladies are Dana Andrews, Kay Aldridge, Jon Hall, Nancy Kelly, Wally Vernon and Joan Davis.*

MR. CELEBRITY *(PRC 1941) Oldtimers at a custody hearing—Francis X. Bushman, Larry Gray (partially hidden), Clara Kimball Young, Johnny Berkes and James Jeffries.*

TWO IN A TAXI (Columbia 1941) Directed by Robert Florey. Unpretentiously simple is the premise: cabby Russell Hayden wants to buy a gas station and marry sweetheart Anita Louise, while pal Noah Beery, Jr., functions in his usual role of best friend. Placing this out of the ordinary are the surprisingly radical speeches of intellectual cab driver Henry Brandon. The film was released just five months before Pearl Harbor, when such sentiments would've been more noticeable, and undoubtedly reflect the beliefs of scripter Malvin Wald, rather than his collaborators, Howard J. Green and Morton Thompson. [Presented at The CoOp, October 20, 1979, as a tribute to Robert Florey, 1900-1979.]

DUKE OF THE NAVY (PRC 1942) Directed by William Beaudine. Starring for PRC in the early Forties, Ralph Byrd seizes his best comedy opportunity here, playing a breezy sailor, named Bill (Breezy) Duke, who, in the company of his dumb pal Stubby Kruger (a real-life swimming champion), encounters confidence men and buried treasure. Pleasant outdoor locales replace the often cramped sets of many of the company releases. Veda Ann Borg seems miscast as a society type, even a phony one, but she's obviously having so good a time it hardly matters. Portly Herbert Corthell has a priceless line as the con artist; addressing valet Val Stanton, he dismisses a card sharp scheme because it was used in *The Lady Eve.* "You may have seen the picture," he blithely remarks.

MY HEART BELONGS TO DADDY (Paramount 1942) Directed by Robert Siodmak. An original screenplay by F. Hugh Herbert concerns a pregnant, widowed bubble dancer, Martha O'Driscoll, who moves into the home of widowed astrophysicist Richard Carlson. He lives with his mother-in-law Florence Bates and sisters-in-law Frances Gifford and Velma Berg. Provocative aspects are given a comic touch, with an outstanding performance by Cecil Kellaway as a cab driver and man of many talents. In fact, his character seems to be the good side of the warlock he played in *I Married a Witch* (also 1942), his accomplishments almost verging on magic. A very entertaining comedy with deft touches. Although not a musical, the film has lots of songs on the soundtrack, mainly borrowed from the studio's big and bright *The Fleet's In* (1942).

ONE THRILLING NIGHT (Monogram 1942) Directed by William Beaudine. Still funny World War II comedy with John Beal and Wanda McKay as small-town newlyweds spending a one-night honeymoon in New York City before his army induction next morning. Intruders led by criminal Tom Neal and his cohorts constantly invade their privacy, searching for Pierce Lyden's loot. For once, Warren Hymer isn't a dumb crook, but rather the none-too-bright house detective, yet J. Farrell MacDonald is seen familiarly as a police sergeant and Barbara Pepper plays a moll. Filmed in six days under the title *Do Not Disturb*, it is called *Horace Takes Over* in 16mm. Musical director Frank Sanucci

MY HEART BELONGS TO DADDY *(Paramount 1942) New mother Martha O'Driscoll's heart really belongs to Richard Carlson (goateed). Mabel Paige and Cecil Kellaway assist.*

incorporates his "Alibi" theme from the "Range Busters" Westerns. [At a 1989 screening at The Wiskowski Society, John Beal said that this was one of his favorite films, because it gave him a rare opportunity to indulge in slapstick. He also explained why his character kept placing the "Do Not Disturb" sign *inside* the room—"Because he's stupid."]

THERE'S ONE BORN EVERY MINUTE (Universal 1942)

Directed by Harold Young. Filmed as *Man or Mouse*, which also was the title of Robert B. Hunt's original story that he and Brenda Weisberg adapted. Okay, this is important as offering the film debut of nine-year-old Elizabeth Taylor, who displays star quality even then, especially when looking at the camera saucily during a huge closeup. (Obviously, she knew even then!) Apart from Taylor, the comedy is a good vehicle for Hugh Herbert as a daffy pudding manufacturer pressed to run for mayor of Witumpka Falls. Carl "Alfalfa" Switzer

portrays Taylor's brother and there isn't a Liz love in sight. Others in this merry mixture: Peggy Moran, Tom Brown, Guy Kibbee, Edgar Kennedy, William Henry (a.k.a. Scott Jorden)

GHOSTS ON THE LOOSE (Monogram 1943)

Directed by William Beaudine. Distinguishing this funny East Side Kids comedy from many others is the presence of Bela Lugosi and Ava Gardner, an odd combination indeed. They actually have nothing to do with each other in the Sam Katzman-Jack Dietz production, as Ava is Huntz Hall's sister and the bride of Rick Vallin, while Bela is the leader of a band of Nazi spies. Led by Leo Gorcey, the gang stumbles upon the bad guys by mistaking their hideout for the home of the newlyweds. No ghosts loose here, although the saga was also called *Ghosts in the Night*.

ONE THRILLING NIGHT *(Monogram 1942) Newlyweds John Beal and Wanda McKay just can't seem to start their honeymoon properly.*

THERE'S ONE BORN EVERY MINUTE *(Universal 1942) At a reception for mayoral candidate Hugh Herbert, Peggy Moran and Tom Brown cause attention. Elizabeth Taylor made her debut, as a child, in this.*

WHEN THE LIGHTS GO ON AGAIN *(PRC 1944) On a late date, Jimmy Lydon tells sweetheart Barbara Beldon that he isn't returning to college but will wait for the draft.*

CLUB HAVANA *(PRC 1945) In the club's powder room, Margaret Lindsay acts out one of the many subplots.*

SOMEONE TO REMEMBER (Republic 1943)

Directed by Robert Siodmak. Well-liked drama with comedienne Mabel Paige in a fine performance as a lonely old woman whose life is suddenly revitalized upon sharing her building with a group of college boys. Among the students are Peter Lawford and John Craven, the latter becoming Paige's favorite because she believes he's her grandson. From the pen of Ben Ames Williams, who also wrote the more vigorous *Leave Her to Heaven*, this sentimental charmer was known in production as *The Prodigal's Mother*. Warners remade it as *Johnny Trouble* (1957) starring Stuart Whitman and, in her last role, the grand Ethel Barrymore.

OH, WHAT A NIGHT! (Monogram 1944)

Directed by William Beaudine, just by coincidence. Nice comedy about jewel thieves who fall out among themselves. Edmund Lowe and Pierre Watkin are after dowager Marjorie Rambeau's Kimberley King. Lowe falls for Watkin's unsuspecting niece Jean Parker and finds that he has to keep a promise to Detective Alan Dinehart and make certain that the diamond remains unstolen. Apart from Lowe's always deft playing and Parker's beauty, a number of popular songs on the soundtrack make this a particular delight.

WHEN THE LIGHTS GO ON AGAIN (PRC 1944)

Directed by William K. Howard. Based on a story by actor Frank Craven, this proves to be PRC's most touching film, possibly its only touching film. James Lydon is a shell-shocked war vet, returning home to an uncertain future. Grant Mitchell is outstanding as his distant father, who has trouble expressing his love for his son, and George Cleveland is equally fine as Mitchell's wise old dad. Big things were predicted for Barbara Belden, quite good as Lydon's patient sweetheart, but this proved to be her only shot at stardom. Regis Toomey, Dorothy Peterson and Harry Shannon have other leads. Use of fog and flashbacks create a surrealistic atmosphere, which is effective but doesn't dominate the proceedings. The song "When the Lights Go on Again All Over the World" (Eddie Seiler-Sol Marcus-Bennie Benjemen) expressed World War II sentiment.

CLUB HAVANA (PRC 1945)

Directed by Edgar G. Ulmer. B picture version of *Grand Hotel*, set in a nightclub. Tom Neal stars as an intern who tries to help everyone, including Margaret Lindsay, a divorcée having problems with lover Don Douglas. Interwoven characters include pianist Eric Sinclair, powder room maid Gertrude Michael, gigolo Paul Cavanagh, wealthy Renie Riano, Neal's girl Dorothy Morris, gangster Marc Lawrence, telephone operator Sonia Sorel, estranged couple Ernest Truex and Helene Heigh, headwaiter Pedro de Cordoba. The setting enables the use of two popular Latin numbers, "Tico Tico" (Zequinha Abreu) and "Besame Mucho" (Consuela Velazques), performed by Isabelita (later Lita Baron, Mrs. Rory Calhoun) and Carlos Molina and his Music-Makers of the Americas. Iris and Pierre do the samba, while Kristine Miller and John Dehner have early bit parts. All in 62 minutes.

THE MAN WHO WALKED ALONE (PRC 1945)

Produced, written and directed by Christy Cabanne. The title might indicate a serious drama about a returning World War II veteran, but the Cabanne picture is a bright comedy variation. David (commonly known as Dave) O'Brien, playing a wounded war hero, seeks out Plainfield, the hometown of a dead buddy. He meets socialite Kay Aldridge, escaping marriage to stuffy Smith Ballew, and a romance begins, one punctuated by fights, misunderstandings and sessions in jail. Walter Catlett and Guinn (Big Boy) Williams have good costarring parts, while such old-timers as Jack Mulhall, Lloyd Ingraham (director-actor) and Elmo Lincoln, the first Tarzan, have small parts. The gag of giving the hero a feminine name, Marion, and the heroine a masculine one, Willie, was reused in Raoul Walsh's *Battle Cry* (1955) and seems irrelevant in the days of actors called Mandy and actresses named Glenn. *Man* won a very rare PRC Oscar nomination for Karl Hajos, Best Scoring of a Dramatic or Comedy Picture.

HER SISTER'S SECRET (PRC 1946)

Directed by Edgar G. Ulmer. High quality romantic drama set in New Orleans at Mardi Gras starring a trio of Warner Bros. contractees and Regis Toomey, who had leads at Warners in the early Thirties. Nancy Coleman has a baby by soldier Phillip Reed and, unsure that he'll ever return to her, allows sister Margaret Lindsay to raise the child as her own. Henry Stephenson and Fritz Feld get good roles in the Anne Green screenplay, based on the Gina Kaus novel *Dark Angel*. (The 1935 Goldwyn film *The Dark Angel* is no relation to the PRC feature.) Good photography by Frank (Franz) Planer.

PARTNERS IN TIME (RKO 1946) Directed by William Nigh. From 1931 until 1955, the "Lum and Abner" show held forth on radio, spanning four different networks and many more sponsors. Stars Chester Lauck and Norris Goff played all of the male roles, the stories revolving around their comical adventures in the Jot 'em Down Store of Pine Ridge, Arkansas. It was so popular that Water, Arkansas, in 1936 changed its name to Pine Ridge. The first of six RKO features with the characters came in 1940; this was the last and best. While portraying their elderly counterparts, Lauck (Lum) and Goff (Abner) are seen for the first time as the young men they

PARTNERS IN TIME *(RKO Radio 1946) Lum and Abner without makeup—Chester Lauck and Norris Goff of the radio, in the last of a six picture series.*

really were. This occurs in the lengthy flashback to 1904, when Goff arrives in town. He and Lauck become friends and rivals for the same woman, played by Pamela Blake. Lum and Abner relate the story to a contemporary couple, Teala Loring and John James, who have had a fight. Danny Duncan and Grady Sutton each play two roles, while Dick Elliott reprises the hearty and overbearing Squire Skimp.

HER SISTER'S SECRET *(PRC 1946) The Mardi Gras sequence of a drama peopled by Warner Bros. expatriates.*

THE BURNING CROSS (Screen Guild 1947)

Directed by Walter Colmes, who produced from an original screenplay by Aubrey Wisberg. Worthy exploitation-type drama—controversial when released—which exposes the inner workings of the Ku Klux Klan, not being afraid to identify the organization by name. Hank Daniels, former MGM contractee, plays a war veteran embittered by the lack of work and the revelation that his sweetheart Virginia Patton is now engaged to an Italian-American, John Fostini. Falling for the KKK line, he joins the Klan before realizing what it really represents. Excellent actors Joel Fluellen and Maidie Norman portray a threatened black couple. Fostini and Ross Elliott are strikers, being tarred and feathered, an uncommon screen occurrence. Patton has a rare starring part in this feature, which places content before cast. [At The CoOp in 1980 on a Worst Film Festival, with the disclaimer that it was really too good to be included (and deserved showing at any rate).]

REACHING FROM HEAVEN (*The Lutheran Church 1947*) *Hugh Beaumont and Cheryl Walker as construction superintendent and company accountant in a moving religious feature.*

REACHING FROM HEAVEN (Visual Education Service of The Lutheran Church 1947)

Directed by Frank Strayer. Hugh Beaumont and Cheryl Walker took time out from starring in the Michael Shayne series for PRC to make this religious feature. John Qualen, as a Swedish immigrant, gets top honors, however. One of a large number of little known features made for church audiences, this has been available for years through 16mm rental outlets. Wealthy Walker injures displaced Qualen in an auto accident and takes a job in a contracting company, in repentance, to pay the victim's bills. Beaumont happens to work there and attempts to instill religious beliefs in the woman, while falling in love with her. Nicely done, without becoming overly intimidating,

the Roland Reed Production attempts to show that helping others increases a person's true worth. Add this title to the credits of its well-known cast: Regis Toomey, Margaret Hamilton, Nana Bryant, Addison Richards, Charles Evans, Mae Clarke, George Chandler, Ann Doran, Jack Lambert, George Eldredge and Gene Roth.

SECOND CHANCE (Protestant Films 1950)

Directed by William Beaudine, screenplay by Robert Presnell, Sr. Another religious feature, but one stolen by its star, Ruth Warrick, giving what may be her finest performance, maturing from young bride to disillusioned older woman over the course of the story. Reviewing her life, she sees how she became materialistic as husband John Hubbard's fortunes increased and how they suffered the loss of one son in World War II and the estrangement of the other, due to his impulsive marriage. Hugh Beaumont is the family minister, whose requests for Hubbard and Warrick's services increase over time. In real life, Beaumont *was* a minister and he easily took to the sermonizing inherent in these films, whereas some of his fellow actors looked embarrassed. Title, used for several other films, refers to Warrick's lease on life after learning that she doesn't have a serious illness.

BAIT (Columbia 1954)

Produced and directed by Hugo Haas. The Czech-born filmmaker Haas always moralized in his films, but—unlike the above religious features—he showed as much sin as he could. He usually cast himself in the mold of an Emil Jannings in *The Blue Angel* (1930), as a cuckolded older husband. Generally, Haas wrote his own scripts, but that for *Bait* is attributed to veteran Samuel W. Taylor. Consistent, however, is his casting of a blonde bombshell in the lead, either Beverly Michaels or Cleo Moore. The latter has the honors here, playing Haas' sexy wife; she bathes in a small tub and shows more back than normally allowable for the time. Haas decides to use Moore as a means of getting rid of John Agar, his young and handsome partner in a gold mine. A prologue by Sir Cedric Hardwicke in an ethereal locale sets the stage for what should be considered the best of Haas' personal films.

JAIL BUSTERS (Allied Artists 1955)

Directed by William Beaudine. Production title, *Doing Time*. By now, the Bowery Boys comedies were Allied Artists releases rather than Monogram, the former company having succeeded the latter in name and scaled-up production values. The Boys were down to just four, Leo Gorcey (Slip), Huntz Hall (Sach), Bennie Bartlett (Butch) and David Condon a.k.a. Gorcey (Chuck), with Bernard Gorcey (Louie) as the sweet shop proprietor. Yet, this happens to be one of the funniest of the later entries, as the Boys deliberately go to prison as undercover reporters to investigate corruption. Barton MacLane as a tough guard gets laughs and heads the all-male supporting cast of such favorites as Lyle Talbot, Fritz Feld, Anthony Caruso, Percy Helton of the raspy voice and Ray Walker. The end was near, as Leo and father Bernard and Bartlett would soon depart the series.

THE CARELESS YEARS (United Artists 1957) Directed by Arthur Hiller. Effective youth drama about teens Dean Stockwell and Natalie Trundy wanting to marry. Her parents, Barbara Billingsley and John Stephenson, and his, John Larch and Virginia Christine, say that they're too young and should wait, so the two try to elope. Stockwell was just 20 and Trundy, in her film debut, reportedly only 14 when production began. Possessed of a quiet beauty and an intelligent personality, Trundy did too few films but later made most of the *Planet of the Apes* features for producer husband Arthur P. Jacobs. Produced by Edward Lewis for Kirk Douglas' Bryna Productions, *The Careless Years* features two songs sung by Sue Raney, "Butterfingers Baby" and the poignant title tune (both by Joe Lubin).

BAIT *(Columbia 1954) One of Hugo Haas' morality stories: John Agar, Cleo Moore and Haas mine for gold and find greed and lust.*

DIARY OF A HIGH SCHOOL BRIDE (American International 1959) Produced, directed and co-written by Burt Topper, collaborating with Mark and Jan Lowell from an original story by the Lowells. While this can't be seriously considered one of the best AIP entries, it is a fascinating mixture of most of the studio's major genres—exploitation, musical and horror and the inevitable teenage film. When 17-year-old Anita Sands weds Ronald Foster, 24, the trouble begins, largely in the person of her disturbed ex-beau Chris Robinson. A fight in a movie studio provides some horror touches. As for the music, Tony Casanova does "When I Say Bye Bye" and the title song, both of which he apparently wrote. (The credits fail to mention a composer, perhaps for good reason.)

JAIL BUSTERS *(Allied Artists 1955) Leo Gorcey and Huntz Hall in one of the best of the later Bowery Boys comedies.*

THE STOOLIE (Avco Embassy 1972/Continental 1974) Directed by John G. Avildsen and George Silano, with Avildsen and Charles Clifton as cinematographers. In 1989, Jackie Mason, successful stand-up comic-turned-failed political campaigner, announced after bombing in *Caddyshack 2*, "I will never make a movie again. Making movies is murder; it's not for me." Not that anybody was begging him. He referred to *The Stoolie* as a failed vehicle to make himself a star, one in which he used his own money as executive producer. In this seriocomedy, he's a small-time crook who works with detective Dan Frazer in trapping fellow thieves with bait money. When he decides to take some of the cash and seek the good

THE STOOLIE *(Avco Embassy/Continental 1972) Both comic and dramatic, Jackie Mason scores in an unseen effort.*

73

life in Miami Beach, Mason promptly falls in love with secretary Marcia Jean Kurtz and finds that Frazer is on his trail. Despite production difficulties and the fact that hardly anyone has seen the film, Mason delivers a solid performance, combining poignancy with his usual, strangely endearing comic image in this item shot in Weehawken, New Jersey, and Miami Beach under the titles *Roger the Stoolie* and *Roger of Miami Beach*.

ROOMMATES (Platinum Pictures 1981) Directed by Chuck Vincent. A sex film with quality, if such is possible, this New York-made pic is one of the best of its kind. Winner of seven Erotic Film Awards, *Roommates* is considered a landmark among adult movies. Samantha Fox, Kelly Nichols and Veronica Hart are the three roomies who find encounters of the closest kind, with varying degrees of satisfaction. The acting and production values are unusually good. Fox, it should be mentioned, is not the pop singing star of the later Eighties. [As film reviewer for *Boxoffice*, I was called upon to see many pornos. One was as good, or bad, as another, giving truth to the old adage, "If you've seen one...." This, however, has real merit.]

STRANGER THAN PARADISE (Samuel Goldwyn 1984) Written and directed by Jim Jarmusch. After viewing this very low budget black-and-white comedy, one might wonder what it is all about. Lengthy, static scenes punctuated by long black fades lead into more of the same, with two unattractive look-alike New York hustlers, and a young woman of somewhat distant charm, the Hungarian cousin of one of them, as the leading players (John Lurie, Richard Edson and Eszter Balint). In the first section, they're living together somewhat uneasily in a smallish Manhattan apartment; in the second, they're visiting with her elderly aunt in Cleveland—Cecillia Stark, an unintentionally funny lady in her only film (she died soon after). And in the third, the unlikely trio heads for Florida—Paradise—where Balint stumbles upon some lost loot. Lurie then mistakenly believes that she's heading back to Hungary and boards a plane bound for the homeland he's long forsaken. The first third of the film was originally made as a short. Expanded into a feature, it won Jarmusch a Cannes Film Festival Award for best first feature by a director. *Paradise* earned much notoriety for the filmmaker, who went on to higher budgeted features in the same offbeat vein. This is the kind of film on which most of the crew doubled on assignments, to keep down the very minimal costs. Jarmusch also edited with Melody London, Lurie composed the music and producer-production manager Sara Driver played a small part (Girl with Hat). Cinematographer Tom DiCillo also managed to fit in a small part (Airline Agent) between his duties on the starkly-shot feature.

(Upper left) ROOMMATES *(Platinum Pictures 1981) A quality sexer, proving that all things are possible. Samantha Fox (top), Kelly Nichols and Veronica Hart are leading practitioners of the genre.*

(Left) STRANGER THAN PARADISE *(Samuel Goldwyn Company 1984) Eating goulash in a definitely offbeat comedy are John Lurie and Richard Edson, while Cecillia Stark insists upon speaking Hungarian.*

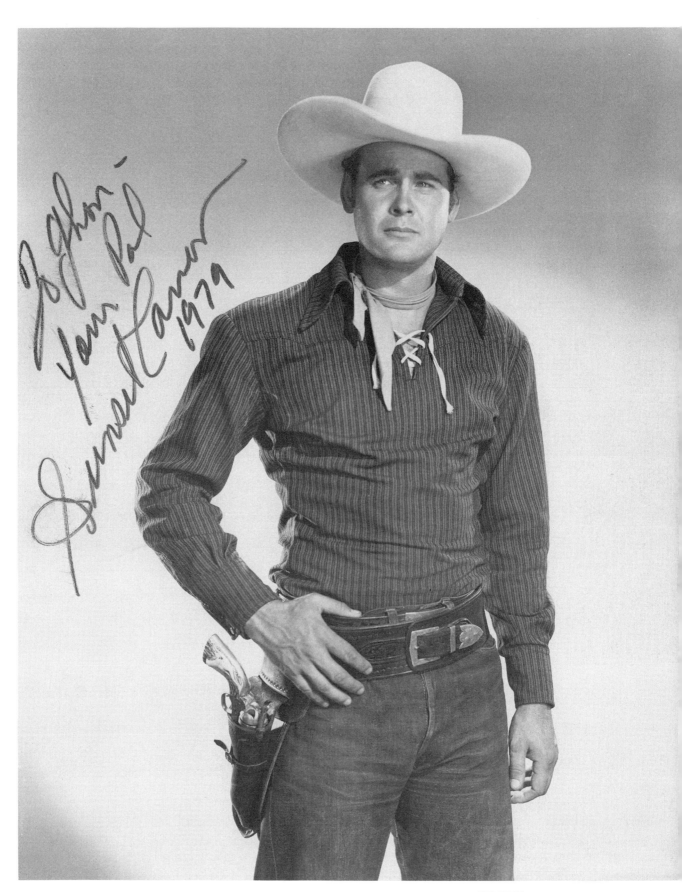

SUNSET CARSON

JENNIFER HOLT

(Below, left)
BRODERICK CRAWFORD *in* The
Last Posse *(Columbia 1953)*

TIM HOLT

GEORGE O'BRIEN

KERMIT MAYNARD

(Below, left)
TOM KEENE

LOIS WILSON *in* Rider Of Death
Valley *(Universal 1932)*

THE SUNRISE TRAIL (Tiffany 1931) Directed by J.P. McCarthy. Produced by Trem Carr, who was later prolific at Monogram, this appears to be inspired by the gangster movies of the day. Some drawn out scenes show that here characterization comes before action, as young drifter Bob Steele joins Eddie Dunn's rustling gang. Dunn, later seen in films as dumb detectives or policemen, vies with Steele for hostess Blanche Mehaffey (in blonde wig) before our hero reveals himself to be an undercover agent. Particularly good is Jack Clifford as a likeable badman; he was once a boxer and the dance partner of ex-wife Evelyn Nesbit Thaw (she was portrayed in *Ragtime*, 1981).

WILD HORSE a.k.a. SILVER DEVIL (Allied 1931) Directed by Richard Thorpe and Sidney Algier. Breezy Hoot Gibson vehicle with comedy and action, plus two comic reliefs (apart from Hoot himself): Stepin Fetchit, who's frequently hilarious, and Skeeter Bill Robbyns, who's ultimately dead. Silent feature players in evidence include Edmund Cobb, Neal Hart and Alberta Vaughn.

END OF THE TRAIL (Columbia 1932) Directed by D. Ross Lederman. Considered to be Tim McCoy's masterpiece, as he portrays a disgraced Army officer who pleads the Indian's cause. Filmed in Lander, Wyoming, with a real Arapahoe tribe, the Stuart Anthony story gets a bit heavy as McCoy loses foster son Wally Albright and comic sidekick Wade Boteler to troopers' bullets. Necessary comedy comes from Boteler and particularly Luana Walters as an Indian maiden who wants to be more to McCoy than a sister. A potentially tragic ending gave way to a more acceptable conclusion, although film historian William K. Everson prefers the former and has shown the film that way. Wheeler Oakman is this Western's only real villain.

THE FOURTH HORSEMAN (Universal 1932) Directed by Hamilton MacFadden. Made under the title *Pony Boy* in Southern California's mountain town of Bishop, this excellent Tom Mix vehicle features Margaret Lindsay in her first leading role, at 19. When bad guy Fred Kohler's gang surrounds the town and begins shooting it up, Tom becomes the fourth—and only surviving—horseman to ride for help. Others are Raymond Hatton and, seen only in long shots, Edmund Cobb and Buddy Roosevelt. Tops in action, *The Fourth Horseman* was remade as Bob Baker's *Ghost Town Riders* (1938).

THE FOURTH HORSEMAN *(Universal 1932) Badmen attempt to ambush the horsemen of the title in a canyon. A Tom Mix Production, starring Mix.*

END OF THE TRAIL *(Columbia 1932) Cavalry officer Wheeler Oakman accepts Tim McCoy's saber as a gesture of military procedure; considered to be McCoy's finest film.*

HELLO TROUBLE *(Columbia 1932) The Silver Circle Ranch isn't for sale, Alan Roscoe learns from half owner Buck Jones. Representing the other half, Lina Basquette is unaware that silver ore enriches its range.*

RIDER OF DEATH VALLEY *(Universal 1932) Director Al Rogell poses with star Tom Mix. This was signed by Rogell only weeks before his death at 86 in 1988.*

FROM BROADWAY TO CHEYENNE a.k.a. Broadway to Cheyenne (Monogram 1932) Directed by Harry Fraser. Half gangster movie and half Western, it has New York police detective Rex Bell chasing Bronx beer baron Robert Ellis all the way to Cheyenne. There's lots of action and horseplay as gangster Alan Bridge machine guns cattle and Bell penetrates Mathew Betz's Soft Drink Emporium—actually a Western speakeasy. The Wellyn Totman-Fraser screenplay has Bell echoing Edward G. Robinson in *Little Caesar* (1930), to Ellis: "You can dish it out but you can't take it." Tops in action. In the cast are Marceline Day, Gwen Lee, George Hayes and Huntley Gordon.

HELLO TROUBLE (Columbia 1932) Originally *Born to Trouble*. Directed and written by Lambert Hillyer. Ex-Texas Ranger Buck Jones searches for a rancher's killer, battles Ward Bond (with speeded-up action), faces badman Wallace MacDonald and romances darkly beautiful Lina Basquette. Canyon of the Caves scenes were filmed at Griffith Park's popular Bronson Canyon. Russell Simpson, Walter Brennan and silent actor-director-writer King Baggott are featured in this winner, the first film shown at The CoOp and a perennial thereafter.

MYSTERY RANCH (Fox 1932) Directed by David Howard. "I'll see you in Hell," says villainous Charles Middleton as he leaps to his death to avoid capture by steadfast George O'Brien. That points up the morality of the average Western, as well as the ultimate fate of the average badman. All along, Middleton had been trying to force Cecilia Parker to surrender her ranch, and her hand, to him. Joseph August's photography emphasizes the dark elements of Al Cohn's script, adapted from the novel *The Killer* by Stewart Edward White.

RIDER OF DEATH VALLEY (Universal 1932) Originally *Destry of Death Valley*; TV title: *Riders of the Desert* (not to be confused with a 1932 Bob Steele Western of that name). Directed by Albert Rogell. This second sound feature of Tom Mix, produced by its star, is an admirable sagebrush version of von Stroheim's *Greed* (1924), filmed in Arizona's Death Valley. To protect little Edith Fellows' claim to a gold mine, Tom faces death in the endless sands. Lois Wilson and Fred Kohler also star, with a von Stroheim favorite—Mae Busch—featured.

SON OF OKLAHOMA (World Wide 1932) Directed by Robert North Bradbury. Bob Steele, son of the director, stars as a youth long separated from parents Robert Homans, a lawman, and Josie Sedgwick, a saloon keeper. Okay oater is made significant by the fact that a one-reel version of this was given a Yiddish sound track, distributed as *The Cowboy*, and thought to be an authentic Western shot in Palestine (!).

BREED OF THE BORDER (Monogram 1933)

Directed by Robert North Bradbury. Bob Steele again, in a Harry O. Jones script mixing traditional and modern themes. Bob drives a racing car and duels with Fred Cavens (an expert fencer who taught many stars to use a sword). Monogram was allowing offbeat elements into its Steele and Rex Bell series, this being an excellent example. Marion (Peanuts) Byron, George (now bearded by not yet Gabby) Hayes and Ernie (S.) Adams lend admirable support.

SCARLET RIVER (RKO 1933)

Directed by Otto Brower. Beginning as a spoof of Western movie-making and ending as a typical saving-the-heroine's-ranch-from-the-wicked-foreman plot, this emerges as best of the early Tom Keene series. Supplementing the top cast—Dorothy Wilson, Betty Furness, Lon Chaney, Jr., Edgar Kennedy, Roscoe Ates, Yakima Canutt, Hooper Atchley—are some RKO guest stars— Joel McCrea, Myrna Loy, Bruce Cabot, Julie Haydon, Rochelle Hudson.

THE THRILL HUNTER (Columbia 1933)

Directed by George B. Seitz. Buck Jones, considered to be the best actor starring in B Westerns at the time, often performed with tongue in cheek. Using some ingredients from his Fox silent *Skid Proof* (1923), Buck plays a braggart who becomes a stunt man in cars and planes and then a movie star. Dorothy Revier is his leading lady in this comedy that was filmed under the title *The Lovable Liar*.

TO THE LAST MAN (Paramount 1933)

TV title: *Law of Vengeance*. Directed by Henry Hathaway. A 1921 Zane Grey story inspired Jack Cunningham's screenplay centering on the Colby-Hayden feud, spreading from Kentucky to Nevada. Best of the many Paramount-Grey adventures, it features a nude swimming scene by heroine Esther Ralston. Actually she wore a bathing suit and a long shot of an artist's model running out of the water was used as hero Randolph Scott dealt with villainous Jack LaRue. Titles introduce the actors by name as they appear; the stellar cast includes Scott, Noah Beery, Buster Crabbe, LaRue, Gail Patrick, Barton MacLane, Fuzzy Knight, John Peter Richmond (Carradine), Jay Ward (later the TV animator for "Rocky and Bullwinkle"), and even Shirley Temple. Also made as a 1923 silent.

BREED OF THE BORDER (*Monogram 1933*) *In the leads are Bob Steele, Marion Byron, a younger George Hayes and John Elliott; Hayes wasn't as yet the beloved Gabby.*

COWBOY HOLIDAY (*Beacon 1934*) *A posed shot with Janet Chandler and (Guinn) Big Boy Williams, billed without his first name; a very funny oater.*

COWBOY HOLIDAY (Beacon 1934)

Directed and written by Robert Hill. Wild and woolly Western—and the funniest oater ever shown at The CoOp. Lots of running around in drag as Guinn "Big Boy" Williams tracks a Mexican bandit. Leading lady Janet Chandler remembers the camaraderie of cast and crew on location in California's High Sierras—it certainly shows in the picture.

FIGHTING HERO (Reliable 1934)

Directed by Harry S. Webb. More fun, as Tom Tyler draws intentional laughs with his ardent pursuing of señorita Renee Borden. The plot has him posing as a bandit to capture express company robbers.

THE THRILL HUNTER
(Columbia 1933) At-
tacking Western star
Buck Jones are Hank
Bell with slat, Roy
Bucko, Frank Ellis grab-
bing, Glenn Strange
restraining.

THE TRAIL BEYOND *(Monogram 1934) On location are John Wayne, Verna Hillie and Noah Beery Jr. in the best of Wayne's Lone Star entries.*

IN OLD SANTA FE (Mascot 1934) Directed by David Howard and Joseph Kane. A Ken Maynard special, introducing singing cowboys Gene Autry and Smiley Burnette. Horse racing at a dude ranch forms the plot, after Ken rides into view warbling "As Long As I've Got My Dog," dubbed by Bob Nolan of The Sons of the Pioneers. Super cast, too: H.B. Warner, Evalyn Knapp, George Hayes, Kenneth Thomson, Wheeler Oakman and George Chesebro.

THUNDER OVER TEXAS (Beacon 1934) Directed by John Warner (Edgar G. Ulmer), based on a story by his wife Sherle Castle. Very oddball Western has comics Benny Corbett, Victor Potel and Tiny Skelton imitating radio personalities, while Guinn "Big Boy" Williams protects tiny Helen Westcott's interests. First film for the six-year-old actress, much later Gregory Peck's wife in the classic *The Gunfighter* (1950). For years, leading lady Marion Shilling was unaware that the director was actually the auteurist Ulmer.

THE TRAIL BEYOND (Monogram 1934) Directed by Robert North Bradbury. Based on James Oliver Curwood's novel *The Wolf Hunters*, this top-notch John Wayne-Lone Star Western was remade—somewhat—by the studio 15 years later as the Kirby Grant Mountie pic *The Wolf Hunters*. It also was the basis for the silent *The Wolf Hunters* (Rayart 1926). Collegians Wayne and half-breed Noah Beery, Jr., manage to escape card sharps on a train (the leap into the water is stock from *Monte Carlo Nights*, released just five months earlier), arrive in the North Woods and search for the map to a gold mine. Highlight is a missed stunt by Yakima Canutt, Wayne's double, who attempts a horse-to-wagon transfer, falls, remounts and succeeds. Also starring are Noah Beery

(Sr.) and leading lady Verna Hillie, who also graced Wayne's previous release *The Star Packer* and here participated in a drinking contest on location. She thought she was keeping up quite well, until she attempted to rise, and couldn't. Filmed at June Lake, Tioga Pass, near Bishop, California.

BETWEEN MEN (Supreme 1935) Directed by Robert North Bradbury. Strong revenge tale with a powerful theme. The Charles Francis Royal story has William Farnum turning to lawlessness when he believes son Harry Downing has been killed. The boy grows into Johnny Mack Brown, who has the eventual showdown with Farnum. The father sacrifices himself to Earl Dwire's gang, for the sake of Johnny and sweetheart Beth Marion.

THE EAGLE'S BROOD (Paramount 1935) Directed by Howard Bretherton. Based on Clarence E. Mulford's 1931 story "Hopalong Cassidy and the Eagle's Brood," the second Hoppy Western is the first top-notch one. William Boyd and Jimmy Ellison, as pal Johnny Nelson, search for George Mari, orphaned by outlaws, the grandson of old bandit El Toro (William Farnum again). George Hayes, before he became sidekick Windy, and Paul Fix are members of bad guy Addison Richards' gang; leading lady Joan Woodbury is billed as Nana Martinez, to capitalize on her talents as a Spanish-type dancer.

THE EAGLE'S BROOD *(Paramount 1935) In the second of the Hopalong Cassidy series is an encounter between two DeMille performers, past and future: William Boyd and Joan Woodbury (billed as Nana Martinez).*

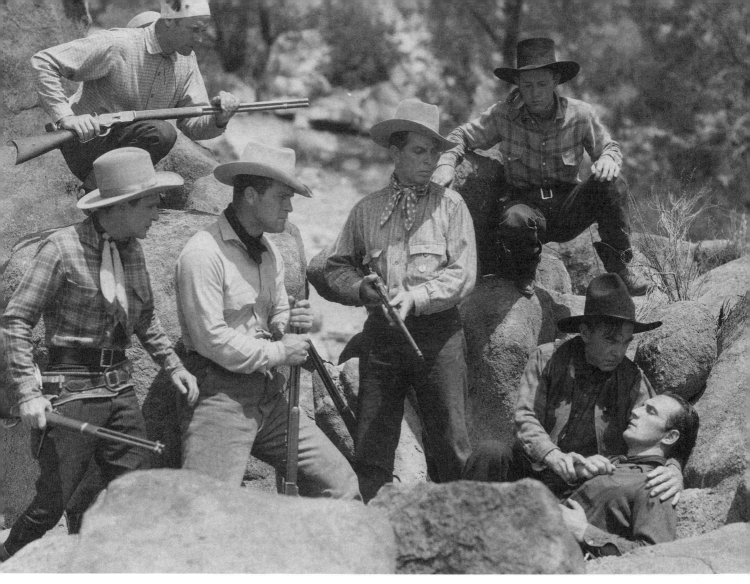

POWDER SMOKE RANGE *(RKO Radio 1935)* Wally Wales *(aka Hal Taliaferro, on rock)*, Bob Steele, Guinn Williams, Hoot Gibson and Buzz Barton watch Harry Carey comfort a dying Tom Tyler in the first Three Mesquiteers Western.

THE BOLD CABALLERO *(Republic 1936) As Zorro's alter ego, Robert Livingston confers with Heather Angel.*

POWDER SMOKE RANGE (RKO Radio 1935)
Directed by Wallace Fox. Initial film with William Colt MacDonald's "Three Mesquiteers" characters. Harry Carey (as Tucson Smith), Hoot Gibson (Stony Brooke) and Guinn Williams (Lullaby Joslin) save Bob Steele's ranch from crooked Mayor Sam Hardy. Outstanding is Tom Tyler as the chief gunman, while Hardy—often in comic roles—earned criticism for his villainy. Boots Mallory is female lead to an all-star cowboy cast: Franklyn Farnum, William Desmond, William Farnum, Buzz Barton, Wally Wales (later Hal Taliaferro), Art Mix, Buffalo Bill, Jr. (Jay Wilsey), and Buddy Roosevelt.

WHEN A MAN'S A MAN (Fox 1935) Directed by Edward F. Cline. Some feel this Sol Lesser-John Zanft production is one of the best Westerns ever made. George O'Brien's personality extends to not taking villain Harry Woods seriously and all ends pleasantly as he saves rancher Dorothy Wilson's water supply and overcomes Paul Kelly's bid for her affections. Filmed in St. George, Utah, this remake of the 1924 Associated First National silent, based on Harold Bell Wright's novel, is called *Saga of the West* on TV.

THE LAST OUTLAW (RKO Radio 1936) Silent stars still functioning: Hoot Gibson, Henry B. Walthall (shortly before his death) and Harry Carey in a John Ford story.

BORN TO THE WEST (Paramount 1937) Although John Wayne stars, Johnny Mack Brown and Marsha Hunt don't appear to notice his absence.

THE BOLD CABALLERO (Republic 1936) Directed by Wells Root. Several firsts: Republic's first association with the Zorro character, its initial color film—although only B&W prints are available on the Magna-Color/

Natural Color presentation— and a writer's first credit as director. Based on Root's original screenplay *The Return of Zorro* and the character created by Johnston McCulley in *The Curse of Capistrano*. Robert Livingston stars as Don Diego/Zorro, escaping a charge of killing Governor Robert Warwick and instructing evil Commandante Sig Rumann in the fine art of wooing Heather Angel, Warwick's daughter. At one point, Livingston disguises himself as Angel's duenna, adding to Diego's foppish reputation.

EMPTY SADDLES (Universal 1936) Directed by Lesley Selander, produced by star Buck Jones. Distinguishing a typical cattlemen-sheepmen conflict is the presence of legendary Louise Brooks, her famed bangs gone in favor of a more conventional cut. Buck encounters a ghost, but Louise proves more spirited.

THE LAST OUTLAW (RKO 1936) Directed by Christy Cabanne. John Ford made a short silent version of this for Universal in 1919 and also provided the script, with E. Murray Campbell, for this remake adapted by John Twist. Emphasis is on comedy as old outlaw Harry Carey is released from prison only to find that the Old West no longer exists. Best scene has Hoot Gibson taking him to see a singing cowboy movie and Carey reacting to star Fred Scott. Cast includes Henry B. Walthall, Margaret Callahan, Tom Tyler, Russell Hopton. Bits by Alan Curtis, Harry Woods, Barbara Pepper, Jack Mulhall, Ralph Byrd, Dennis O'Keefe.

THE LONELY TRAIL (Republic 1936) Directed by Joseph Kane. Best of John Wayne's 1935-36 Republic series, as he makes post-Civil War Texas safe from Cy Kendall and his carpetbaggers. In the cast are Ann Rutherford, Snowflake (Fred Toones), Denny Meadows (Dennis Moore), Yakima Canutt. Remade as The Three Mesquiteers' *West of Cimarron* (1941).

RED RIVER VALLEY (Republic 1936) Directed by B. Reeves Eason. Lots of action, plus comedy and songs, both in and out of the water as Gene Autry and Smiley Burnette work to save an irrigation project. Frances Grant and Charles King are in support. Remade by Roy Rogers in 1941. *Man of the Frontier* is the TV title of this one.

RIP ROARIN' BUCKAROO (Victory 1936) Directed by Robert Hill. Very entertaining Tom Tyler entry, as a boxer heads West to catch crooked promoters. Among Tyler's best for sheer energy, it also has Beth Marion, Charles King, ethnic Sammy Cohen and nice locales.

SONG OF THE TRAIL (Ambassador 1936)

Directed by Russell Hopton, the actor. Often seen as a mountie, Kermit Maynard—Ken's likeable younger brother—here plays a rodeo rider involved in a fight over a mine. Kermit's trick riding is in evidence—he also doubled some of Ken's stunts—and the star is aided and abetted by George Hayes, Fuzzy Knight, Wheeler Oakman and two leading ladies: bad Evelyn Brent and good Antoinette Lees (later Andrea Leeds of *Stage Door* fame). Based on James Oliver Curwood's story "Playing With Fire."

BORN TO THE WEST (Paramount 1937)

Directed by Charles Barton. The year in which Western pictures peaked surely must be 1937. The Mesquiteer and Hoppy entries were of a very high calibre in '37, in terms of production values and plots. Equally entertaining is this John Wayne-Johnny Mack Brown adventure, credited to Zane Grey and a remake of the 1926 Jack Holt silent. Duke is an irresponsible sort who loses cousin Johnny's cattle money to crooked gamblers. The cast includes Marsha Hunt, Monte Blue, Sid Saylor (Wayne's sidekick) and James Craig, but does *not* feature Alan Ladd, erroneously credited. Reissued as *Hell Town*.

HEART OF THE ROCKIES (Republic 1937)

Directed by Joe Kane. Excellent scenics and action as Robert Livingston, Ray Corrigan and Max Terhune—The Three Mesquiteers—penetrate a game preserve and do battle with a thieving mountain family. To save under-age Lynn Roberts from marriage to unwanted Yakima Canutt, Livingston engages the great stuntman in a vicious, vigorous fight. Sammy McKim, J.P. McGowan, Hal Taliaferro, even Herman's Mountaineers figure in the action.

HIT THE SADDLE (Republic 1937)

Directed by Mack Wright. Very possibly the best Three Mesquiteers Western as the trio—Bob Livingston (Stony), Ray Corrigan (Tucson), Max Terhune (Lullaby)—protect the interests of wild horses on a government range. J. P. McGowan and Yakima Canutt provide opposition. At the end, Corrigan has to buy off sexy señorita Rita Cansino to save hot-headed Livingston from her wiles. She announces that she's going to Hollywood to become a movie star (!). She really did, as Rita Hayworth.

THE MYSTERY OF THE HOODED HORSEMEN (Grand National 1937)

Directed by Ray Taylor. The Horsemen, headed by Charles King, covet Joseph Girard and Lafe McKee's gold. Tex Ritter to the rescue, romancing Iris Meredith in the process. Valuable not so much for its traditional sagebrush ingredients, but for the way in which Tex sings the traditional songs, "A'Ridin' Old Paint" and "I'm a Texas Cowboy" (which he was).

HEART OF THE ROCKIES (*Republic 1937*) *Suspected cattle rustler Maston Williams is captured by Mesquiteers Robert Livingston, Ray Corrigan and Max Terhune; all are actually their stunt doubles.*

THE MYSTERY OF THE HOODED HORSEMEN *(Grand National 1937) Ready for the marauders are Tex Ritter, Joseph Girard and Horace Murphy, the latter obviously the comedy relief.*

TEXAS TRAIL *(Paramount 1937) Rustlers attempt to take the Bar 20 cattle during a canyon raid.*

RIDERS OF THE WHISTLING SKULL (Republic 1937) Directed by Mack V. Wright. Greatly atmospheric Three Mesquiteers (Livingston-Corrigan-Terhune) epic, featuring a search for a lost Indian city. In the city are Mary Russell, Fern Emmett and Yakima Canutt. Remade as a Charlie Chan mystery, *The Feathered Serpent* (Monogram 1949), with Roland Winters and Robert Livingston. Filmed in The Painted Desert near Salton Sea, this was the favorite Western of Joe Judice, founder of Joe's Place.

TEXAS TRAIL (Paramount 1937) Directed by David Selman. Fine Hoppy Western, with William Boyd and pals George (Windy, latter Gabby) Hayes and Russell Hayden heading a Bar 20 drive of mounts for the Spanish-American War. Action in and around a canyon make it tops. A recurring musical theme is used effectively, and Judith Allen and Billy King augment the proceedings. Credited to Clarence Mulford's 1922 novel *Tex*.

THUNDER TRAIL (Paramount 1937) Directed by Charles Barton. The oft-told tale of brothers separated as youths, growing up on opposite sides of the law and finally encountering each other as would-be enemies. Funny twist has all-American Gene Reynolds growing into Spanish Gilbert Roland, because of the influence of foster father J. Carrol Naish, a Mexican; actually Roland was Mexican and Naish an Irishman. Good cast includes Charles Bickford, Marsha Hunt, Monte Blue and James Craig. Based on Zane Grey's 1929 tale *Arizona Ames*, it went through such production titles as Grey's original monicker, *Buckaroo, Riders of the Panamint* and *Gun Smoke*, and lifted its score from Cecil B. De Mille's *The Plainsman* (1936). It later was reissued as *Thunder Pass*.

THE TRIGGER TRIO (Republic 1937) Directed by William Witney. Another superior Three Mesquiteers effort, even with Ralph Byrd substituting for the injured Robert Livingston, hurt in a real-life swimming accident. As Larry Smith, Tucson's brother, he joins Ray Corrigan and Max Terhune in combatting an epidemic of hoof and mouth disease. Outstanding support from Hal Taliaferro, with Sandra Corday, Robert Warwick, Sammy McKim, Cornelius Keefe (a.k.a. Jack Hill).

THUNDER TRAIL *(Paramount 1937) During a fight, James Craig and Gilbert Roland learn that they're brothers. Odd processing of the still has it appear that Roland sports three arms.*

HIT THE SADDLE (Republic 1937)
The Three Mesquiteers—Livingston,
Terhune and Corrigan—with
Sammy McKim and Rita Cansino
(Hayworth, that is).

YODELIN' KID FROM PINE RIDGE (Republic 1937) Directed by Joe Kane. A Gene Autry starrer notable for unusual elements, as well as for being the last stand of silent star Betty Bronson. Set in the Turpentine Forest of Georgia, it paints the local inhabitants as suspected rustlers. Charles Middleton, usually a villain, is Gene's beleaguered father, with Art Mix as a fake Autry. Mix in songs by Autry and costar Smiley Burnette and rodeo scenes for good results.

BORDER WOLVES (Universal 1938) Directed by Joseph H. Lewis. Singing Bob Baker rides the Hoot Owl Trail, along which outlaws find a haven after performing lawless deeds. The director and cinematographer Harry Neumann use creative camera work to make this a visual treat, with Constance Moore, Fuzzy Knight and Dickie Jones joining Singing Bob in the Sonora-filmed feature. Baker starred from 1937-39, then played increasingly smaller parts until the mid-Forties.

BORDER WOLVES *(Universal 1938) Time for a musical interlude with Constance Moore (who sang well) and Dickie Jones listening to Bob Baker.*

IN OLD MEXICO (Paramount 1938) Directed by Edward D. Venturini. In this sequel to *Borderland* (1937), William Boyd as Hoppy has the film stolen from him by Jan Clayton as a wacky señorita and Paul Sutton as outlaw The Fox. Clayton, wed to costar Russell Hayden for awhile, later starred on TV's "Lassie" and was here making her film debut as Jane Clayton in a gem-like comedy portrayal. Sutton's rich voice was used as radio's "Sergeant Preston of the Yukon." George Hayes is also along for the ride through the yarn's New Mexico setting.

RAWHIDE (20th Century-Fox 1938) Directed by Ray Taylor. Except for the off-beat presence of baseball great Lou Gehrig, critics tend to dismiss this Smith Ballew starrer. Really, the Sol Lesser production is quite entertaining and Gehrig impresses in an oddball assignment. He naturally plays himself, teaming up with lawyer Ballew to save the ranch of Lou's screen sister, Evalyn Knapp. As usual, Ballew has a few songs.

THE TERROR OF TINY TOWN (Columbia 1938) Directed by Sam Newfield. Typical land-grabbing plot with the novelty of an all-midget cast—except for normal-sized Alden (Stephen) Chase and some children used as extras. Lead is Billy Curtis, much later pitted against Clint Eastwood in *High Plains Drifter* (1973), here combatting badman Little Billy. Often considered one of the worst films ever, it's fun on any level, and it has songs by L. Wolfe Gilbert and Lew Porter.

RAWHIDE *(20th Century-Fox 1938) Ready for the bad guys in the Sol Lesser production are star Smith Ballew and Lou Gehrig, the baseball great.*

THE ADVENTURES OF THE MASKED PHAN-TOM (Equity 1939) Directed by Charles Abbott. All right, this is really curious but very funny. Monte (Alamo) Rawlins stars for the only time, as the title character pursuing gold mine bandits with the aid of musical and comic sidekicks Larry Mason (better known as Art Davis) and Sonny LaMont, plus dog Boots and horse Thunder. Betty Burgess is the pretty but equally obscure heroine. A treat if you're in a silly mood.

DAYS OF JESSE JAMES (Republic 1939) Directed by Joseph Kane. This was the third and last Republic Western to showcase Donald Barry. As outlaw Jesse, he steals the film from star Roy Rogers as the intrepid detective on Barry's trail. Barry's next feature, *Ghost Valley Raiders* (1940), launched him as a star—soon to be Don "Red" Barry. Meanwhile, *Days* has fast action and a top supporting cast: George "Gabby" Hayes, Pauline Moore, Harry Woods, Scotty Beckett, Monte Blue.

RACKETEERS OF THE RANGE (RKO 1939) Directed by D. Ross Lederman. Modern sagebrush outing with a twist—rustlers use trucks, not only as transport for stolen cattle but also as slaughterhouses. Figuring in the fast-moving action are Marjorie Reynolds, comic Chill Wills and Ray Whitley (who also wrote the songs), making this one of star George O'Brien's best.

ROUGH RIDERS' ROUND-UP (Republic 1939) Directed and produced by Joe Kane. Republic often recycled their plots and this originally saw service as *The Leathernecks Have Landed* (1936). As a Roy Rogers vehicle, it makes for a very fast-moving hour: Rough Riders returning from the Spanish-American War join the border patrol in pursuit of gold bandits. Leading lady Mary Hart was better known as Lynne Roberts, while the cast also includes Raymond Hatton, Dorothy Sebastian, Duncan Renaldo and future Western star George Montgomery. Quickly revamped as the plot for *The Girl From Havana* (1940).

THREE TEXAS STEERS (Republic 1939) Directed by George Sherman. Thumbs down, voted The CoOp members on this John Wayne-Ray Corrigan-Max Terhune entry in Three Mesquiteers series. Our heroes aid Carole Landis' circus; Dave Sharpe, Ralph Graves and Roscoe Ates figuring in the plot. With emphasis on comedy, this is the weakest of the eight generally excellent Wayne-Mesquiteer films. All of the others really belong in this book.

THE ADVENTURES OF THE MASKED PHANTOM *(Equity 1939) A goofy treat, starring Betty Burgess and Monte (Alamo) Rawlins.*

RACKETEERS OF THE RANGE *(RKO Radio 1939) In one of his last starrers, George O'Brien prepares to rope a guard for the rustlers.*

OVERLAND STAGE RAIDERS
(Republic 1938) A Three Mes-
quiteers pose: John Wayne, Louise
Brooks (in her last film), Ray
Corrigan and Max Terhune
(seated). See Three Texas Steers
(1939).

LAW AND ORDER (Universal 1940) Directed by Ray Taylor. Universal got lots of mileage out of the reworking of the Earp-Clanton shootout in Tombstone, Arizona. In this, one of the best of the Johnny Mack Brown series, the star is aided by Fuzzy Knight and gambler James Craig in ridding the town of Rhyolite of the lawless Daggetts (Harry Cording, Ted Adams, Ethan Laidlaw). Nell O'Day and Jimmy Dodd also get into the fight. Other versions: 1932, Walter Huston; 1953, Ronald Reagan; and the serial *Wild West Days*, 1937, also with Johnny Mack. Based on W. R. Burnett's novel *Saint Johnson*, it was filmed under the title *Man From Cheyenne*, and on TV, it's called simply *The Law*.

THE MAN FROM TUMBLEWEEDS (Columbia 1940) Directed by Joseph H. Lewis. As Wild Bill Saunders, Bill Elliott emulates his idol William S. Hart, even borrowing the title of Hart's last starrer (*Tumbleweeds*, 1925). The plot, however, anticipates *The Dirty Dozen* as Bill has convicts paroled to his custody to clean up the lawless town. Raphael (Ray) Bennett, Iris Meredith and Dub Taylor serve as villain, heroine and sidekick, with Bruce Bennett in briefly as the warden. Only a somewhat mild ending prevents this from being called Elliott's best Western ever, otherwise it's tip-top even without a music score (or songs).

MELODY RANCH (Republic 1940) Directed by Joseph Santley. Above average Gene Autry special, which originally runs 84 minutes. The 54 minute TV version, however, retains most of the action and songs as Gene, a radio star, returns to hometown Torpedo, Texas, to find brothers Barton MacLane, Joe Sawyer and Horace McMahon running things. Above average cast, too: Ann Miller, Jimmy Durante, George "Gabby" Hayes, Jerome Cowan, Vera Vague (Barbara Jo Allen), Mary Lee, Billy Benedict, Veda Ann Borg, Bob Wills and His Texas Playboys. Note: John Wayne has been credited as doing a stunt on the Toonerville-type trolley at the climax, but this is absurd.

WAGONS WESTWARD (Republic 1940) Directed by Lew Landers. Republic used this plot far too often—an honest man impersonating his bad twin to clean up a gang (for the most part, it was done as a gangster movie). Here, Chester Morris—admittedly not an ordinary Western type—takes the dual roles, romancing Anita Louise and Ona Munson as the good and bad heroines in the process. Although the results are quite good, this version is not well liked because the beloved Buck Jones is cast as a crooked sheriff. Buck, however, is quite good, too, as are George "Gabby" Hayes, Guinn "Big Boy" Williams and Douglas Fowley.

THE MAN FROM TUMBLEWEEDS *(Columbia 1940) Heroine, hero, villain: Iris Meredith (formerly Iris Shunn, Iris March), Bill (Gordon) Elliott, Francis Walker.*

MELODY RANCH *(Republic 1940) Riding from Melody Ranch, Billy Benedict and Gene Autry are attacked. A super Western.*

WAGONS WESTWARD *(Republic 1940) Buck Jones in a rare—and unappreciated—villain's role, with Ona Munson and Anita Louise.*

A MISSOURI OUTLAW *(Republic 1941) Tough Don "Red" Barry in a revenge tale with Frank LaRue.*

CYCLONE ON HORSEBACK (RKO 1941) Directed
by Edward Killy. At least one of the lengthy Tim Holt series for one studio should be included and *Cyclone* easily qualifies. Lots of action as telephone lines are strung and deadlines are met, despite a dynamite-laden plot. Harry Worth leads the bad guys against the good, which number Marjorie Reynolds, Dennis Moore, Ray Whitley and Lee (Lasses) White.

A MISSOURI OUTLAW (Republic 1941) Directed
by George Sherman. Strong revenge tale as Don "Red" Barry goes after the members of the protective association who caused the death of his father, Sheriff Noah Beery. Offering distaff beauty is Lynn (formerly Marilyn) Merrick.

TONTO BASIN OUTLAWS (Monogram 1941)
Directed by S. Roy Luby. The Range Busters were Monogram's answer to Republic's The Three Mesquiteers, especially with two former Mesquiteers as stars: Ray (Crash) Corrigan and Max (Alibi) Terhune. Add John (Dusty) King's singing and Terhune's wisecracking dummy Elmer and you have another series. The light-hearted attitude is more evident in Crash's relationship with villain Tristram Coffin, a former fraternity brother. Now we have to be convinced that Crash ever attended college. Jan Wiley is an undercover reporter as the trio investigates Wyoming cattle rustlers on behalf of The Rough Riders.

DAWN ON THE GREAT DIVIDE (Monogram 1942) Directed by Howard Bretherton. Written by Adele Buffington under a masculine pseudonym, Jess Bowers, *Dawn* is more a sentimental tribute than a top drawer feature. It not only contains Buck Jones' last

BELLS OF ROSARITA *(Republic 1945) A typical pose for Dale Evans and Roy Rogers, in an all-star feature.*

performance, seen posthumously, but also ends the Jones-Tim McCoy-Raymond Hatton marshals series with Rex Bell taking over for McCoy. Riding the wagon train to destiny is a particularly strong cast—Mona Barrie, Robert Lowery, Betty Blythe, Jan Wiley, Harry Woods, Roy Barcroft, among others.

BEYOND THE LAST FRONTIER (Republic 1943) Directed by Howard Bretherton. Eddie Dew stars
as John Paul Revere (later, and better, played by Bob Livingston), undercover Texas Ranger infiltrating a gang running contraband. Easily stealing the film is fourth-billed Bob Mitchum as gang member Trigger Dolan, who poses as a Ranger and makes this a better than average Western. Onlooking are Smiley Burnette and Lorraine Miller.

FRONTIER LAW (Universal 1943) Directed and
written by Elmer Clifton. Nice one-shot (that is, non-series) about a Wyoming cattle and sheep conflict. Ex-gunman Russell Hayden carries no guns but can't stay out of the action, while bear trapper Fuzzy Knight keeps falling into his own snares. Hayden was thought to be better as a sidekick, romantic type, rather than hero, a sentiment not echoed from this corner. Dennis Moore, fine as a hero in cheap productions, was even better as a badman. Jennifer Holt, Jack Ingram and Johnny Bond and His Red River Valley Boys mix in. The production title of this was *Gunfighters.*

SILVER SPURS (Republic 1943) Directed by Joseph
Kane. Not quite Roy Rogers' answer to Gene Autry's *Melody Ranch,* but good nevertheless. An equally fine cast—John Carradine, Phyllis Brooks, Smiley Burnette, Jerome Cowan, Joyce Compton, Hal Taliaferro, Bob Nolan and The Sons of the Pioneers—and action help. By now acclaimed King of The Cowboys, Roy here is framed for murder, and is out to clear his name and bring the badmen to justice.

FIREBRANDS OF ARIZONA (Republic 1944) Directed by Lesley Selander. Really wild 'n' woolly, a spoof of the genre with nothing to be taken seriously. Smiley Burnette, top-billed over hero Sunset Carson, plays his usual Frog Millhouse character as well as notorious outlaw Beefsteak Discoe. Earle Hodgins, Peggy Stewart and Roy Barcroft join in the one-of-a-kind action.

LUMBERJACK (United Artists 1944) Directed by Lesley Selander. Non-stop action in timber country makes this the last really top-notch Hoppy feature. By now, Paramount had relinquished distribution; soon, star William Boyd would take over production chores. Andy Clyde and Jimmy Rogers (son of Will) are Hoppy's sidekicks in this entry with a cast that also includes Ellen Hall, Douglass Dumbrille, Herbert Rawlinson, Francis McDonald, Ethel Wales and Hal Taliaferro.

BELLS OF ROSARITA (Republic 1945) Directed by Frank McDonald. At this point, Republic's scriptwriters were hampered by Roy Rogers' being cast as himself, a movie star. *Bells* capitalizes on such by also casting every other B Western star on the lot for an entertaining outing. Helping Roy, Bob Nolan and The Sons of the Pioneers save Dale Evans' circus are Wild Bill Elliott, Allan Lane, Donald Barry, Robert Livingston and newcomer Sunset Carson. Adding to the all-star atmosphere are Adele Mara, Grant Withers, Roy Barcroft and Addison Richards.

THE DALTONS RIDE AGAIN (Universal 1945) Directed by Ray Taylor. Fast-moving sequel to *When the Daltons Rode* (1940) mainly in name, and well photographed—including a prairie fire—by Charles Van Enger. Told in flashback as surviving brother Alan Curtis relates the events surrounding the aborted robbery of

THE DALTONS RIDE AGAIN *(Universal 1945) As the Dalton boys, Alan Curtis (Emmett), Lon Chaney Jr. (Grat), Kent Taylor (Bob), Noah Beery Jr. (Ben).*

GANGSTER'S DEN *(PRC 1945) The emphasis is on comedy in this one: Buster Crabbe, Al St. John and kitchen help Emmett Lynn.*

BEAUTY AND THE BANDIT *(Monogram 1946) Expert rider Ramsay Ames pretends that she needs lessons from Gilbert Roland as The Cisco Kid; he's happy to oblige.*

the Coffeyville, Kansas, bank by Kent Taylor, Lon Chaney, Jr., and Noah Beery, Jr. An outstanding cast makes it even better than average: Martha O'Driscoll, Thomas Gomez, John Litel, Milburn Stone, Douglass Dumbrille, Jess Barker.

FLAME OF THE WEST (Monogram 1945) Directed

by Lambert Hillyer. Highly unusual Johnny Mack Brown feature, intelligently written by Adele Buffington, has its star actually playing a character part in deference to veteran screen villain Douglass Dumbrille, here emerging as the hero. When Dumbrille is killed trying to clean up the town, Johnny—a mild mannered doctor—takes up his guns to finish the job. Songs by Pee Wee King and His Golden West Cowboys and Joan Woodbury enhance the story, which also has in its cast Raymond Hatton, Lynne Carver, Harry Woods and John Merton. Just fine. Production title was *Flaming Frontier*.

GANGSTER'S DEN (PRC 1945) Directed by Sam

Newfield. Funny Buster Crabbe outing revolves around Al (Fuzzy) St. John's attempts to run a saloon, with interference from cook Emmett Lynn. Fuzzy hires drunk Charles King to be his bodyguard. King, a top Western villain, succeeds with his dumb comedy part. Kermit Maynard also is on board, along with Sydney Logan (the heroine). [Shown in 1968 at The CoOp's Charles King Festival, when some of the musical buffs mistook him for the star of MGM's *The Broadway Melody* (1929)— same name, no relation—and wondered why he did so many Westerns.]

SANTA FE SADDLEMATES (Republic 1945)

Directed by Thomas Carr. Sunset Carson was tall in the saddle and a good action star if not actor. Linda Stirling was as beautiful a heroine as possible. Together, they make this fast-paced tale of diamond smuggling a treat. In the cast: Olin Howlin (Howland), Roy Barcroft and Johnny Carpenter, future star of some incredibly cheap oaters.

BEAUTY AND THE BANDIT (Monogram

1946) Directed by William Nigh. As The Cisco Kid and a French lady masquerading for a time as a man, Gilbert Roland and Ramsay Ames make beautiful music together. Roland wasn't afraid to introduce romance to his Westerns and Ames reciprocates, not that the action is overlooked. In a sexy scene, she washes his shirt and then drapes it over her front and shoulders to simulate an embrace from the not entirely indifferent Cisco.

STAGECOACH TO DENVER *(Republic 1946) Allan Lane (before being called Rocky) in action as Red Ryder.*

LAWLESS BREED (Universal 1946) Directed by Wallace W. Fox. Fine Kirby Grant songs-and-action feature, the Bob Williams screenplay having the same plot as the classic British short *The Stranger Left No Card* (1953). That is, the creation of a fictitious man in order to commit a crime; in this instance, bank president Dick Curtis impersonates a nonexistent sea captain brother to get away with his theft. Fuzzy Knight, who was in every Universal B Western from 1937-46, Jane Adams, Charles King and Claudia Drake also appear. On TV, this one's called *Lawless Clan*. Remade as *The Vanishing Westerner* (Republic 1950) with Monte Hale, Arthur Space in the dual role and Curtis in a bit (see 1950 entry).

OUT CALIFORNIA WAY (Republic 1946) Directed by Lesley Selander. Early Monte Hale starrer, in Trucolor, has a tuneful moviemaking background as our hero attempts to break into films. Guest stars are Roy Rogers, Allan Lane, Dale Evans, and Donald Barry, plus Adrian Booth, Bobby Blake (post "Our Gang"), John Dehner, St. Luke's Choristers, and Foy Willing and The Riders of the Purple Sage. Hale's later vehicles were in black and white, not nearly as elaborate, and tuneless.

SHERIFF OF REDWOOD VALLEY (Republic 1946) Directed by R. G. Springsteen. Top Red Ryder sagebrush saga, starring Bill Elliott plus Bobby Blake as Little Beaver, with Alice Fleming as The Duchess. Bob Steele, beginning his character parts as his starring days ended, plays The Reno Kid, an escaped convict, complete with wife and son (Peggy Stewart and John Wayne Wright). Proving Steele innocent of all charges occupies the time of acting Sheriff Elliott.

STAGECOACH TO DENVER (Republic 1946) Directed by R. G. Springsteen. Now cast as Red Ryder, Allan Lane is overshadowed by the playing of Peggy Stewart as a member of Roy Barcroft's gang in a scheme to take over Marin Sais' property. In the later Jim Bannon/Red Ryder Westerns for Eagle Lion, Sais played his aunt The Duchess, a part taken here by Martha Wentworth. Continuing as Little Beaver is Bobby Blake, while Emmett Lynn is comical Coon-Skin.

STAGE TO MESA CITY (Eagle Lion 1947) Directed by Ray Taylor. One of the last series Westerns to be released by E-L, formerly PRC, has Marshals Lash LaRue and Al "Fuzzy" St. John saving a stage line from bandits. The always comely Jennifer Holt co-stars, along with George Chesebro, Terry Frost, Marshall Reed and Russell Arms, a few years away from singing fame on TV's "Your Hit Parade."

OUT CALIFORNIA WAY *(Republic 1946) Looking on are Tom London (kneeling), Globe Pictures director Nolan Leary, casting director Tom Quinn and gateman Frank O'Connor as Monte Hale comforts Bobby Blake, who's had a horse fall.*

STAGE TO MESA CITY *(Eagle-Lion/PRC 1947) Lash LaRue and Al St. John, U.S. Marshals, fire at the gang headed by crooked lawyer Marshall Reed.*

VIGILANTES OF BOOMTOWN (Republic 1947) Directed by R. G. Springsteen. The Red Ryders often had historical backgrounds, this Earle Snell screenplay centering around the James J. Corbett-Bob Fitzsimmons heavyweight fight in Carson City, Nevada, in 1897. Allan Lane as Red helps protect the box office receipts. Bobby Blake, Peggy Stewart, Martha Wentworth, Roscoe Karns, Roy Barcroft, George Turner (Corbett), John Dehner (Fitzsimmons); narrated by LeRoy Mason in one of his last assignments. Subject also used in *City of Badmen* (20th-Fox, 1953).

THE DUDE GOES WEST *(Allied Artists 1948) In Indian garb, Eddie Albert and Gale Storm star in a comedy and action romp.*

EYES OF TEXAS (Republic 1948) Directed by William Witney. Rather sadistic Roy Rogers feature with Nana Bryant as a lady lawyer who turns out to be the vicious head of a gang of land grabbers. Roy gets horsewhipped in beautiful Trucolor by nasty Roy Barcroft, and is helped by Andy Devine, Lynne Roberts, Bob Nolan and The Sons of the Pioneers.
[When The CoOp had a Nana Bryant Festival for her daughter-in-law, the latter disliked Bryant's character so much that she hated the film.]

EYES OF TEXAS *(Republic 1948) Roy Barcroft kills Danny Morton as lawyer Nana Bryant watches; Morton wanted her ranch. A quite sadistic Roy Rogers feature.*

CHECK YOUR GUNS *(Eagle-Lion 1948) Nancy Gates, formerly of RKO, joins Eddie Dean for his very best Western.*

CHECK YOUR GUNS (Eagle Lion 1948) Directed by Ray Taylor. Just about the best Eddie Dean starrer, as he plays the sheriff who cleans up lawless Red Gap, taking time out to sing with Andy Parker and The Plainsmen, banter with bumbling Deputy Roscoe Ates and pay attention to pretty Nancy Gates.

THE DUDE GOES WEST (Allied Artists 1948) Directed by Kurt Neumann. An action-packed Western spoof which succeeds as both an oater and a satire, with Eddie Albert recounting how he left Brooklyn in 1876 to become a gunsmith in lawless Nevada. Along the way, he manages to sing pleasantly (a musical talent films rarely exploited), romance Gale Storm who mistrusts men, become a Piute blood brother, and encounter hordes of villains. The film also succeeds in killing off the entire costarring cast, and a formidable one it is: Gilbert Roland, Barton MacLane, Binnie Barnes, James Gleason, Tom Tyler.

THE GAY RANCHERO (Republic 1948) Directed by William Witney. Another Roy Rogers entry on the bloody side, this one with a Mexican accent. Tito Guizar costars and warbles memorably "You Belong to My Heart" (Agustin Lara-Ray Gilbert) and "Granada" (Lara). One of the writers of the title tune was Abe Tuvim, whose daughter gained fame as Judy Holliday. In the *Ranchero* cast: Andy Devine, Jane Frazee, Estelita Rodriguez and, of course, Bob Nolan and The Sons of the Pioneers.

THE HAWK OF POWDER RIVER (Eagle Lion 1948) Directed by Ray Taylor. Title role in this Eddie Dean oater is played by Jennifer Holt, female head of a marauding gang. Interesting twist has her being killed as she's surrendering her gun, a lapse of judgment if not Joe Gluck's editing. June Carlson thus becomes the surviving female lead, with other parts taken by Roscoe Ates, Terry Frost, Charles King, Marshall Reed and Andy Parker and The Plainsmen. That same year, Holt played a similar role in Jimmy Wakely's *Range Renegades* at Monogram.

PANHANDLE (Allied Artists 1948) Directed by Lesley Selander. Fast, tough Rod Cameron Sepiatone Western has him playing a former Texas marshal, now a gunfighter, out to prove that casino owner Reed Hadley had Cameron's newsman brother John Champion killed. Anne Gwynne and Cathy Downs are the leading ladies. Film became a turning point for bit actor Blake Edwards, who plays Hadley's hired gun. It marked his debut on the other side of the cameras, since he and Champion co-produced and co-wrote the story. Adding directing to his talents, Edwards later concentrated on comedies. *Panhandle* originally—and unthinkably—was to have ended with Cameron being killed. It was remade by Selander and Champion as *The Texican* (Columbia 1966) with Audie Murphy and Broderick Crawford.

THE STRAWBERRY ROAN (Columbia 1948) Directed by John English. Produced by and starring Gene Autry, making his Cinecolor debut, this is a top outing. He's the foreman for rancher Jack Holt, whose son Dick Jones is injured by a wild horse, Champion. Gene forsakes his own paint to ride and protect the steed, becoming a wanted man in the process. There is no clear-cut villain, even Eddie Parker and Jack Ingram being merely men after the reward for Gene's capture. Champion, Jr., has the role of Champion, the star's longtime mount, with Gloria Henry, Pat Buttram and Rufe Davis also on hand. Autry's other color starrer, *The Big Sombrero* (1949), is of lesser quality.

THE GAY RANCHERO *(Republic 1948) Using modern technology, Roy Rogers and Tito Guizar—playing a bull-fighter—combat gold hijackers.*

PANHANDLE *(Allied Artists 1948) Cathy Downs and Rod Cameron load up supplies in one of Rod's best vehicles.*

THUNDERHOOF (Columbia 1948) Directed by Phil Karlson. Undoubtedly the best three-character Western ever, taking place on the desert as Preston Foster and William Bishop vie over Mary Stuart, Foster's wife, and the title stallion they seek. Originally in Sepiatone.

BRIMSTONE (Republic 1949) Directed by Joseph Kane. Released the same year as Republic's *Hellfire*, which might have made a good double bill, *Brimstone*, in Trucolor, actually refers to the character of cattleman-bandit Walter Brennan. He tends to dominate, despite an impressive cast of over six-footers, led by Rod Cameron. Brennan and his boys Jim Davis, James Brown and Jack Lambert turn to robbing banks—trains and stagecoaches aren't immune either—and contend with lawman Cameron, posing as The Ghost. Sheriff Forrest Tucker is dishonest, Marshal Jack Holt and Deputy Guinn (Big Boy) Williams upstanding, and Adrian Booth the sweetheart of Brown, rather than the star. In the blazing climax, Brennan gets to utter the immortal line, "I'll nail your hide to my barn door," before expiring.

CHALLENGE OF THE RANGE (Columbia 1949) Directed by Ray Nazarro. Lively Durango Kid/Charles Starrett action piece concerning a range war prompted by a land grabbing scheme. Billy Halop, former Dead

CHALLENGE OF THE RANGE *(Columbia 1949) Charles Starrett, without his Durango Kid guise, astride Raider and Smiley Burnette on Ring-Eye (formerly Black Eyed Nellie).*

MASSACRE RIVER *(Allied Artists 1949) Indians attack, but the characterizations outweigh the action content in this instance.*

End Kid, is cast interestingly as the hot-head son of Steve Darrell, a rancher suspected of being behind the raids. Paula Raymond plays another rancher's daughter, in love with Halop. What, you ask, is a city tough doing out West? True, this was Halop's only oater, but as a boy he starred on radio as Bobby Benson, a Western lad, and portrayed the character at rodeos. Smiley Burnette provides comedy, Jock Mahoney doubles for Starrett, and stock from an earlier Durango, *Galloping Thunder* (1946), is employed.

MASSACRE RIVER (Allied Artists 1949)

Directed by John Rawlins. Based on the novel by Harold Bell Wright and shot in Arizona, this epic's cavalry background takes second place to the human element. Despite its title, the film has a lack of action as it becomes instead the tale of a man whose love for a bad woman is his downfall. Guy Madison and Rory Calhoun, both to star in dozens of Westerns, head the cast, with the distaff side represented by Cathy Downs and Carole Mathews, the latter particularly strong as the saloon owner.

POWDER RIVER RUSTLERS (Republic 1949)

Directed by Philip Ford. Railroad marshal Allan "Rocky" Lane, at El Dorado on the Powder River, sees that the local citizenry isn't defrauded. A goodie, with Lane in top form, John MacBurnie's sturdy photography and able support from Eddy Waller as Nugget, Roy Barcroft and Francis McDonald. Unknown Gerry Ganzer is the leading lady, her career extending until at least 1952.

RIM OF THE CANYON (Columbia 1949)

Directed by John English. Produced by Gene Autry, who plays himself and his father in a prologue. Escaped convicts descend upon a ghost town to get the money buried there years before. A strong cast—Nan Leslie, Thurston Hall, Clem Bevans, Walter Sande, Jock O'Mahoney (later Mahoney), Francis McDonald, Alan Hale, Jr., Denver Pyle—a good plot and title, to boot. However, the screenplay by John K. Butler was based on the more intriguingly named "Phantom .45's Talk Loud" by Joseph Chadwick, as published in *Western Aces* magazine.

RIMFIRE (Lippert/Screen Guild 1949)

Directed by the veteran B. Reeves Eason. Mystery out West as undercover agent Captain James Millican searches for stolen gold and investigates the killings supposedly committed by unjustly hanged gambler Reed Hadley. Producer Ron Ormond also collaborated on the screenplay with Arthur

ROUGHSHOD *(RKO Radio 1949) Finding love in the great outdoors, Gloria Grahame and Robert Sterling.*

St. Clair and Frank Wisbar, the supernatural element reflecting the latter's influence. No complaints with the rest of the cast, either, since it includes Henry Hull, Mary Beth Hughes, Fuzzy Knight, Victor Kilian, Margia Dean and Jason Robards (Sr.).

ROUGHSHOD (RKO Radio 1949)

Directed by Mark Robson (his last low budgeter). With some *film noir* elements and a story by Peter (*Saboteur*) Viertel, the tale's action occurs largely out of doors. Shot mainly at Sonora Pass in California's High Sierras in 1947, it concerns brothers Robert Sterling and Claude Jarman, Jr., as they herd horses and encounter saloon women and ex-convicts seeking revenge. Since the middle group consists of Gloria Grahame, Martha Hyer, Jeff Donnell and Myrna Dell and the last is headed by John Ireland, there's little doubt as to the superior quality of the production.

THE BARON OF ARIZONA (Lippert 1950)

Directed and written by Samuel Fuller, with cinematography by James Wong Howe. High-ranking character study with Vincent Price as the real life James Addison Reavis, who weaved an elaborate plan to pro-

THE BARON OF ARIZONA *(Lippert 1950) A fantastic scheme comes to its end, as Vladimir Sokoloff, Vincent Price and Ellen Drew discover to their regret.*

claim himself owner of the entire state of Arizona. Ellen Drew, Reed Hadley and Vladimir Sokoloff are sympathetic to the cause, to a point. The same material was twice used by Republic, for the John Wayne/Three Mesquiteers *Night Riders* (1939) with George Douglas as the swindler, and its remake, the Don "Red" Barry *Arizona Terrors* (1942) with Hadley in the role.

HILLS OF OKLAHOMA (Republic 1950) Directed
by R. G. Springsteen. A reworking of Gene Autry's *Call of the Canyon* (1942), using stock from Autry's *Sierra Sue* (1941) and the serial *King of the Texas Rangers* (1941), this came at the beginning of Republic's overuse of studio shooting and stock shots. Yet, the Rex Allen starrer—his third—is quite good in its blending of songs and action as rustlers dog a cattle drive. *Hills* boasts two heroines, Elisabeth Fraser and older Elisabeth Risdon; two comics, Fuzzy Knight and Roscoe Ates; and two main villains, Robert Emmett Keane and Robert Karnes.

KING OF THE BULLWHIP (Realart 1950)
Produced and directed by Ron Ormond. No other Lash La Rue feature exploits his prowess with a whip as this does. While not his best, the film does serve to make the legend indelible. Plot concerns Marshals La Rue and Al St. John's investigation of stolen gold bullion. Cast is as strong as the whip fights: Jack Holt, Tom Neal, Anne Gwynne, Dennis Moore, Michael Whalen, George J. Lewis. Filmed at Santa Susanna, with Lash also doubling as the masked, whip-wielding bandit El Azote.

THE RETURN OF JESSE JAMES (Lippert
1950) Directed by Arthur David Hilton. Even better than its inspiration, Sam Fuller's *I Shot Jesse James* (1949), which has the reputation. Many of the same actors have different roles here, Reed Hadley switching from Jesse to Frank James and John Ireland portraying a Jesse lookalike who cashes in on the resemblance. Quite good, with virtually everyone biting the dust. Top cast includes Ann Dvorak, Henry Hull and Hugh O'Brian. It served to bring together the comedy team of Tommy Noonan and Peter Marshall (latter a host of TV's "Hollywood Squares")—Noonan was Ireland's real-life half-brother, while Marshall is the brother of Joanne Dru, then Ireland's wife. The in-production ttitle of this one was *Return of the James Boys*.

SHORT GRASS (Allied Artists 1950) Directed by
Lesley Selander. Screenplay by Tom W. Blackburn, based on his book. Wide-ranging Rod Cameron vehicle with a fine performance by Johnny Mack Brown as the marshal (his Monogram series was still active). Title refers to the rich cattle grazing land coveted by ruthless rancher Morris Ankrum. Good action, although Cameron tends to let things happen to him rather than to force matters. Cathy Downs, Alan Hale, Jr., Jonathan Hale, Raymond Walburn and Harry Woods are in the cast.

HILLS OF OKLAHOMA *(Republic 1950) Robert Karnes and Rex Allen fight in an indoor setting, substituting for the sage.*

TRAIL OF ROBIN HOOD (Republic 1950) Directed by William Witney. Yet another Roy Rogers all-star extravaganza, this time in Trucolor. The plot concerns oldtime cowboy star Jack Holt and his dwindling Christmas tree business, hardly the stuff of legends, yet it's a good deal of fun. At a Western film convention, one of the hosts stated that his was what oaters were all about. The stellar cast includes Penny Edwards, Gordon Jones, Allan "Rocky" Lane, Monte Hale, Rex Allen, Tom Tyler, Tom Keene, William Farnum, Kermit Maynard, Ray (Crash) Corrigan, Foy Willing and The Riders of the Purple Sage, and George Chesebro in a funny bit as he tries to shed his villainous image.

THE VANISHING WESTERNER (Republic 1950) Directed by Philip Ford. Monte Hale's remake of Kirby Grant's *Lawless Breed* (see 1946 entry), possibly even better than the original. Bob Williams revised his script to fit Arthur Space into the dual roles, and to make way for Aline Towne, Paul Hurst, Roy Barcroft, Richard Anderson, William Phipps, Don Haggerty, Dick Curtis and Rand Brooks, as well. Some wagon action is stock from the Wayne-Corrigan-Terhune/Mesquiteers *Pals of the Saddle* (1938), while Monte takes time out to sing just one song, "There's No Use Worryin' " (Irwin Coster).

THE BUSHWHACKERS (Realart 1951) Directed by Rod Amateau. An intelligent script by Amateau and Tom Gries (Gries wrote and directed Charlton Heston's praised *Will Penny*, 1968) and an excellent cast make this a top attraction. Despite familiar characters, this is one of the best Westerns of the Fifties. Confederate veteran John Ireland arrives in Independence, Missouri, intending never again to use a gun. He finds that rancher Lon Chaney Jr.'s, men are forcing out settlers to claim their land for the railroad. Chaney is an arthritic despot, while Myrna Dell is his nasty, very independent daughter. Lawrence Tierney and Jack Elam are vicious badmen and Dorothy Malone the comely schoolteacher daughter of newsman Frank Marlowe. Malone and Tierney both started at RKO in 1943. Interestingly, both Ireland and Marshal Wayne Morris, in a fine performance, attempt to remain passive, Morris being more disinterested than dishonest. If the beautiful Malone wasn't the best actress to graduate from B Westerns, she was close.

LITTLE BIG HORN (Lippert 1951) Directed and written by Charles Marquis Warren. Grim, tough version of what happened on the way to Custer's Last Stand. A small detachment is torn apart by its own conflicts and the descending Sioux. Uncompromising and surprisingly violent. John Ireland again, Lloyd Bridges and

THE BUSHWHACKERS *(Realart 1951) Jack Elam is counting on Dorothy Malone's not shooting, but he's wrong.*

Marie Windsor form a triangle; Reed Hadley, Hugh O'Brian and Jim Davis offer support. First directorial effort for veteran Western writer Warren.

UTAH WAGON TRAIN (Republic 1951) Directed by Philip Ford. Descendants of the 1851 Colorado Trail pioneers participate in a commemorative wagon train. Wagonmaster Rex Allen learns that there's gold at the end of the trail in this fast-moving sagebrusher, filmed in Griffith Park. He gets to sing and Buddy Ebsen shows off his tap dancing skills, while Penny Edwards, Grant Withers, Roy Barcroft and Sarah Padden are also along for the ride.

HELLGATE (Lippert 1952) Directed and written by Charles Marquis Warren, from a story by him and producer John C. Champion. Another gritty Warren Western for Lippert, this concerns the hellish Hellgate Prison in New Mexico during the Civil War. Sadistic warden Ward Bond takes a particular dislike to innocent Sterling Hayden, who eventually helps combat an epidemic. Really a reworking of John Ford's *The Prisoner of Shark Island* (1936), the true story of Samuel Mudd, the doctor imprisoned for treating John Wilkes Booth after President Lincoln's death, *Hellgate* succeeds as a prison drama in Western garb, with a cast including Joan Leslie, James Arness, Peter Coe, Tim Carey, Kyle James (a.k.a. James Anderson).

THE LONE HAND (*Universal-International 1953*) *Joel McCrea can't tell son Jimmy Hunt that he's on secret assignment and faces the loss of his respect.*

THE ROAD TO DENVER (*Republic 1955*) *Lee J. Cobb, Karl Davis and Skip Homeier (seated) have John Payne at bay. Homeier is Payne's obviously wayward brother.*

OKLAHOMA ANNIE (Republic 1952) Directed by R. G. Springsteen, in Trucolor. One of the best of Judy Canova's musical Western comedies. Proclaimed Queen of the Cowgirls (a title more apt for Dale Evans), Judy plays a shopkeeper in Coffin Creek, a town suffering under Grant Withers' crooked gambling hall. New Sheriff John Russell and deputized Judy battle the bad guys, she masquerading as singer La Belle La Tour (the great Marion Martin, without billing, in her last film). Amidst the slapstick which calls for the ladies of the town to swing into action, Judy acquits herself as a blues singer, performing "Have You Ever Been Lonely" (George Brown-Peter De Rose) quite well while pining for heman Russell.

OLD OKLAHOMA PLAINS (Republic 1952) Directed by William Witney. Another good Rex Allen entry. With the B series Western winding down, Republic's writers (Albert DeMond, story; Milton Raison, screenplay) managed to concoct offbeat settings and plots. Set in 1926, this one concerns a race to determine if tanks will replace horses as conveyances for the U.S. Army. Roy Barcroft, ever the villain, is the horse breeder who sabotages the tank. Stock from *Army Girl* (1938) plus Slim Pickens, Elaine Edwards, Russell Hicks, and The Republic Rhythm Riders, also figure prominently.

THE LAST POSSE (Columbia 1953) Directed by Alfred Werker. After winning his Oscar for *All the King's Men* (1949) and then starring in *Born Yesterday* (1950), Broderick Crawford made as many Westerns and action pictures as he did near the beginning of his career. One of the best casts him as a boozing sheriff who redeems himself by joining a posse in pursuit of a band of bank robbers. In his quest, he contends with vicious Charles Bickford and the latter's stepson, John Derek. Told in flashbacks as the badly wounded Crawford listens to testimony, this has a downbeat ending and a strong cast to watch: Wanda Hendrix, Warner Anderson, Henry Hull, Skip Homeier, James Bell. The effective but uncredited musical score, directed by Ross DiMaggio, was the same as that used in all of Columbia's serials.

THE LONE HAND (Universal-International 1953) Directed by George Sherman. A pleasant Joel McCrea outdoor Technicolor feature, with emphasis on family relations. Joel and his idolizing son Jimmy Hunt are joined by Joel's new wife Barbara Hale as they settle down on a farm, but when he seemingly joins an outlaw gang, he loses their respect. One good scene has Jimmy mistaking big James Arness for Joel as the badman climbs a mountain to bring harm to the youngster. Alex

Nicol and Charles Drake ensure that all of the leading men are over six feet. Old Republic hand Sherman sees to it that things keep moving along nicely.

A MAN ALONE (Republic 1955) Directed by Ray Milland, who stars, in Trucolor. Milland had few films as a director; they were all interesting, being made with care, intelligence and a few offbeat touches. This, his first, also casts him as a gunfighter hiding in the cellar of the home of ailing Sheriff Ward Bond, falling in love with the lawman's daughter Mary Murphy, and avoiding the lynch mob that really should be going after sinister banker Raymond Burr. The cast also includes Lee Van Cleef and Alan Hale, Jr. During production, the film was called *The Gunman*.

THE ROAD TO DENVER (Republic 1955) Directed by Joe Kane, in Trucolor. Based on Bill Gulick's *Saturday Evening Post* story "Man from Texas," set in Colorado but filmed in Utah. Stage line operator John Payne contends with brother Skip Homeier, working for villainous Lee J. Cobb. Nice action, with Mona Freeman, Ray Middleton, Lee Van Cleef, Andy Clyde and Glenn Strange participating. Homeier's characterization of the wild younger brother could've been a basis for Kevin Costner's character in *Silverado* (1985).

BACKLASH (Universal-International 1956) Directed by John Sturges. With Richard Widmark and Donna Reed starring, can this be a B? As made by economy-mind Universal, certainly. Praised at the time for its sparkling dialogue, based on a Frank Gruber novel adapted by Borden Chase, this Technicolor film moves smoothly as the stars search for badman John McIntire and naturally fall in love during the quest. William Campbell, Barton MacLane and Harry Morgan are around to make things interesting, but the Widmark-Reed relationship is by far the best ingredient.

THE MAVERICK QUEEN (Republic 1956) Produced and directed by Joe Kane, in Naturama and Trucolor. The Zane Grey novel was published in 1950, eleven years after his death, completed by son Romer. It served as Republic's first offering in the short lived Naturama wide-screen process, making good use of the Durango and Silverton, Colorado, locations. Barbara Stanwyck, who loved the genre, stars as the head of an outlaw gang, The Wild Bunch. Undercover man Barry Sullivan infiltrates the hideout and proceeds to romance her. The characters of Butch Cassidy (Howard Petrie), Sundance (Scott Brady) and Cole Young (Jim Davis) are

BACKLASH *(Universal-International 1956) Battle of the sexes, Western style: participants, Donna Reed and Richard Widmark. Action, comedy, painted backdrops.*

THE MAVERICK QUEEN *(Republic 1956) A mortally wounded Barbara Stanwyck finds that she and Barry Sullivan won't enjoy a happy ending, after all.*

FORTY GUNS *(20th Century-Fox 1957) However, Stanwyck and Sullivan eventually find happiness in another setting.*

FURY AT SHOWDOWN *(United Artists 1957) John Derek protects Carolyn Craig in an adult Western that was designed for teenagers.*

portrayed less heroically than they were elsewhere. Mary Murphy and Wallace Ford complete the leading names of this top-rated effort. Pop singer Joni James sings the Ned Washington/Victor Young title song during the credits.

DECISION AT SUNDOWN (Columbia 1957)
Directed by Budd Boetticher. Excellent Randolph Scott revenge tale. His mission is simple—to kill John Carroll for stealing his wife. Along the way, however, he learns some disturbing truths. Produced by Scott and Harry Joe Brown, this is among the stalwart star's best and allows Carroll to steal the film as a thoroughly charming villain. Strong cast also: Karen Steele, Valerie French, Noah Beery, Jr., John Archer, Andrew Duggan, James Westerfield, John Litel, Ray Teal, Vaughn Taylor, Richard Deacon and, in a bit, every Western fan's favorite, Bob Steele.

FORTY GUNS (20th Century-Fox 1957)
Directed by Sam Fuller. Much admired Western stars Barbara Stanwyck as a ruthless, whip-wielding ranch owner who controls Cochise County, Arizona. The town of Tombstone becomes livelier when brothers Barry Sullivan, Gene Barry and Robert Dix (son of Richard) ride in. Sullivan, gunslinger turned lawman, and Stanwyck are naturally attracted—strong man, strong woman. Fuller uses a gun barrel to zoom in on gunsmith Eve Brent as Barry (Gene) glimpses her; other metaphors are in evidence. When Sullivan faces down Stanwyck's rotten brother John Ericson for killing Barry, Ericson uses his sister as a shield. Sullivan wounds her before gunning down Ericson, explaining that he aimed carefully only to get her out of the way. Originally, Fuller wanted him to shoot both sister and brother and filmed the ending with Stanwyck also dying. Although he was producer, director and writer, Fuller had to comply with a happier finale. Making good use of Joseph Biroc's black-and-white CinemaScope lensing, the filmmaker included a tribute to Stanwyck via the song "High Ridin' Woman" (Harold Adamson-Harry Sukman), sung by Jack "Jidge" Carroll. Dean Jagger gets third billing in this Western filmed more provocatively as *Woman With a Whip.*

FURY AT SHOWDOWN (United Artists 1957)
Directed by Gerd Oswald. An attempt to make a Western which appeals to teenagers and adults, with a youthful starring cast and good psychological touches. Young rancher John Derek desires to reestablish himself after a jail term for killing lawyer Gage Clarke's brother in self defense. Clarke retaliates by hiring a gunman, John Smith, to shoot down Derek's supportive brother, Nick Adams (in an appealing performance). Only jarring notes in this brooding sagebrush drama are Adams'

death and Derek's encounter with sweetheart Carolyn Craig as she swims, supposedly nude. That episode seems ludicrous rather than sexy. *Showdown Creek* was the film's production title.

THE TALL T (Columbia 1957) Directed by Budd Boetticher. Producers Randolph Scott and Harry Joe Brown again team with director Boetticher for a top Western, based on the *Argosy* magazine story "The Captive" by Elmore Leonard, adapted by Burt Kennedy. Although this has been touted as being Scott's best starrer, the Technicolor offering seems to be more of a fine film than a great one. Perhaps familiarity has lessened the impact. Ex-ranch foreman Scott is held hostage by Richard Boone and henchmen Henry Silva and Skip Homeier (as Billy Jack, no relation to the Tom

Laughlin character), along with newlyweds Maureen O'Sullivan and John Hubbard. Scott ultimately gains the upper hand, as well as O'Sullivan's hand. Title isn't quite explained, supposedly referring to the ranch which Scott had managed. Either *Captives* or *The Tall Rider*, the ones used during production, may have been better.

BULLWHIP (Allied Artists 1958) Directed by Harmon Jones. Guy Madison and Rhonda Fleming take top honors in this CinemaScope/Technicolor adventure. Madison, given his choice of hanging for a murder he didn't commit or marrying luscious Fleming, who needs a husband in order to claim her fur company, decides naturally to pursue the latter option—an enviable choice. He soon finds that Fleming's all business. With a whip to back her up, she makes Madison's job more

THE TALL T *(Columbia 1957) Maureen O'Sullivan, Randolph Scott and Richard Boone in a tense situation.*

THE LEGEND OF TOM DOOLEY (Columbia 1959) Directed by Ted Post. Produced and written by Stan Shpetner, based on the folk ballad "Tom Dooley." Cheaply made but well done retelling of the tragedy. Michael Landon, Richard Rust and Dee Pollock, three Confederate soldiers on a robbery and killing spree, learn the Civil War has ended and that they are fugitives. Jo Morrow and Jack Hogan are, respectively, Landon's love and nemesis, both leading him to his downfall. The Kingston Trio sing their popular title song during the credits. Landon, as Tom, didn't become a film star, but TV's *Bonanza* was only a few months away, and the rest for him was history.

NO NAME ON THE BULLET (Universal 1959) Directed by Jack Arnold. Cowboy star Audie Murphy was widely quoted as saying that he was performing under a disability because he couldn't act. His popular oaters prove otherwise and this, his finest moment, attests to that. He's cast against type as a baby-faced gunman, an ironic counterpart of his actual role in World War II as America's most decorated soldier. Lordsburg's citizens begin to crack under the strain when they realize that Murphy has arrived to gun down someone within their midst. Joan Evans, Charles Drake, Virginia Grey and future director Jerry Paris are involved. The film's title was also that of Murphy's posthumous biography, of 1989.

NO NAME ON THE BULLET *(Universal 1959) The end of a gunman's career—Audie Murphy's gun hand is permanently smashed.*

difficult. Women produced and wrote this extremely sexy Western—Helen Ainsworth and Adele Buffington— to add another dimension to the film. As he was then doing rather frequently, Frankie Laine sings the title song (by Hal Hooper and co-star James Griffith). Set in Kansas, *Bullwhip* was filmed in Sonora and Angels Camp, California.

THE BROKEN LAND (20th Century-Fox 1962) Directed by John Bushelman. Photographed in CinemaScope and DeLuxe Color by Floyd Crosby on location in Arizona. Kent Taylor had a long association with the Western genre, going back to the early Thirties, in later years switching from heroic to villainous parts, while retaining star status. Here, he's a sadistic marshal who runs the town his way. One element distinguishing *The Broken Land* is the fine performance by young Jack Nicholson as his prisoner.

GUNMAN'S WALK (Columbia 1958) Directed by Phil Karlson. Good, tough oater in CinemaScope and Technicolor. Hardbitten Wyoming rancher Van Heflin raises sons Tab Hunter and James Darren. The latter, a sensitive type, falling in love with half breed Kathryn Grant, unwittingly causes prejudice to rear its head. Hunter becomes a gunman and faces his father in a showdown. Frank Nugent's screenplay, based on a story by Ric Hardman, stresses the harsher aspects of frontier life. At the time, Hunter was something of a pop singing idol and he warbles "I'm a Runaway" (Fred Karger-Richard Quine) for his fans.

THE BOUNTY KILLER (Embassy 1965) Directed by Spencer Gordon Bennet. Superior adult Western tracing the journey of Dan Duryea from dude to vicious bounty hunter. The script was originally written by actor-scripter Leo Gordon as a vehicle for friend Mickey Rooney. Producer Alex Gordon (no relation) and his wife Ruth (no relation to the veteran actress) rewrote it, using just the basic concept; final credit is given to R. Alexander and Leo Gordon, the former being the producer's wife. It and its companion release feature, *Requiem for a Gunfighter*, were shot back to back on the Paramount lot and the Janss Ranch. Each cost $194,000, with financing coming from foreign deals and from Joseph E. Levine's Embassy Pictures. To satisfy the foreign financing, Duryea and Rod Cameron were given leads, along with Audrey Dalton. As in all his features, Alex Gordon then cast an array of veteran Western headliners, Buster Crabbe being particularly impressive as a gang leader. Others are Richard Arlen, Johnny Mack Brown, Fuzzy Knight, Bob Steele, Eddie Quillan, Edmund Cobb and the first cowboy star, Broncho Billy Anderson. The latter was given a royal treatment, even Elvis Presley being thrilled to meet the legendary actor. Anderson has a brief cameo, 47 years after his previous feature. Duryea's son Peter is cast as the bounty hunter who finally ends Dan's career. Shot in Techniscope and Technicolor, *The Bounty Killer* can stand by itself as the last truly great B Western.

THE BOUNTY KILLER *(Embassy 1965) Buster Crabbe, Richard Arlen and Fuzzy Knight surround the first Western hero, Broncho Billy Anderson. (Photo courtesy of Alex Gordon).*

FRANCES DEE

RUSSELL HOPTON *in* Mutiny in
the Big House *(Monogram 1939)*

SALLY BLANE

NIGEL BRUCE

PRESTON FOSTER

CHARLES QUIGLEY

JAYNE MANSFIELD

VICTOR SEN YUNG

HELL BOUND *(Tiffany 1931) Leo Carrillo initiates his Italian gangster portrayals by starring as softhearted Nick Cotrelli.*

ALIAS MARY SMITH *(Mayfair 1932) Asks Blanche Mehaffey, "Is it a nice jail?" when confronted by that prospect; Jack Grey and Henry B. Walthall are unmoved.*

CONVICTED (Supreme Features/Weiss Brothers/Artclass 1931) Directed by Christy Cabanne. An early talkie which solves the problems existing when filming aboard an ocean liner; veteran director and cast team up for a good murder mystery. On a Los Angeles-bound liner, actress Aileen Pringle is pursued by her producer, Richard Tucker, whose wife Dorothy Christy learns he has stolen funds. After playing poker with ex-convict Niles Welch, drunken Harry Myers and Jack Mower, Tucker is found knifed to death. Criminologist Jameson Thomas (a British actor recently arrived in the States) investigates. Annoyingly, this mystery proves to have two killers—ship's officer John Vosburgh (later Vosper) and radioman Lee Phelps (usually cast as a detective). Bill Elliott is one of the extras on deck. Satisfying example of how to produce a mystery in a different setting.

HELL BOUND (Tiffany 1931) Directed by Walter Lang. As a result of his casting as a good-hearted Italian gangster here, Los Angeles-born Leo Carrillo found himself forever typecast in similar roles or those calling for dialects. (In vaudeville, he was billed as The Italian Humorist, despite his Mexican ancestry.) When *Hell Bound* was released, the gangster film cycle was in full bloom and it was compared unfavorably to its predecessors, although the collaboration of some noted writers—Adele Comandini, Edward Dean Sullivan, Julien Josephson—make it seem more original than some of the others. Singer Lola Lane faints from pneumonia and malnutrition, thereby entering racketeer Carrillo's life. In order to prevent her testimony against him, Carrillo marries her (a wife couldn't then testify against a husband) in name only. Lane, however, really loves Lloyd Hughes, the handsome young doctor who nursed her back to health. Helene Chadwick, Richard Tucker and Gertrude Astor have other leading roles. Singer Russ Columbo composed the song "Is It Love?" for the film and is occasionally credited as appearing in it (he actually made few movies). A good entry from its era.

ALIAS MARY SMITH (Mayfair 1932) Directed by E. Mason Hopper. This shoestring crime drama which doesn't take itself too seriously is a prime example of how to stretch a budget. Well-known Henry B. Walthall and Alec B. Francis were hired for their name values; their scenes were shot quickly and then spread throughout the film. For shots of newspapers, headlines were printed over pages from *Variety*. As the villain, Mathew Betz does the best Edward G. Robinson imitation in a B feature. The plot gets underway when drunken playboy John Darrow saves Blanche Mehaffey from a purse snatcher and falls in love, while she attempts to prove gangster Betz guilty of murder. Wisecracking Gwen Lee, an MGM starlet, supplies laughs while reporter Raymond Hatton and stuttering photographer Ben Hall breeze in and out. When confronted with imprisonment, the comely Blanche inquires innocently, "Is it a nice jail?" [How can I explain my infatuation for Blanche Mehaffey, a pretty heroine of dozens of Bs who rarely rose above adequacy in her performances? This film was first viewed on TV about 1952; a 16mm print was acquired ten years later and enjoyed thereafter, being part of the Blanche Mehaffey Tribute at The CoOp in 1978, ten years after her passing. It's just one of those things that buffs often have for a performer.]

DOCKS OF SAN FRANCISCO *(Mayfair/Action 1932) A charming domestic interlude concerning Mary Nolan, Marjorie Beebe and John Davidson.*

THE DEATH KISS (World Wide 1932) Directed by Edwin L. Marin, his first after a long apprenticeship as an assistant director. Set at Tonart Studio, but filmed at Tiffany, this behind-the-scenes mystery has writer David Manners solving the killing of actor Edmund Burns. The murder takes place on the set of *The Death Kiss*, co-starring Adrienne Ames—Burns' former wife and beneficiary—under the direction of Edward Van Sloan. Studio manager Bela Lugosi and studio president Alexander Carr are among those who come under suspicion, while Vince Barnett, the dumb chief of studio police, "helps" Manners. Fascinating material devoted to the making and processing of films; the tinting of some scenes does exist on available 35mm prints. Much was made of the casting of three of the leads of Universal's *Dracula* (1931)—Manners, Lugosi, Van Sloan—but Bela's fans are disappointed by his secondary role. Based on the novel by Madelon St. Dennis, this deserves inclusion in any retrospective on Hollywood.

DOCKS OF SAN FRANCISCO (Action Pictures, later Mayfair 1932) Directed by George B. Seitz. Tragedy with a tragic star. Mary Nolan is the moll of small-time racketeer John Davidson; novelist Jason Robards attempts to reform her. One of Nolan's final films. (Nolan had been a Ziegfield Girl and a star of German silent features.) Stardom at Universal, MGM and Paramount led to a brace of quickies for independent companies. She lived only to age 42, dying in 1948. Comedy on the docks is supplied by Marjorie Beebe and German-born Max Davidson. This one is not to be confused with *San Francisco Docks* (see 1940 entry).

HELL'S HOUSE (Capital Film Exchange 1932) Directed and written by Howard Higgin. Here's a chance to see a pre-Warner Bros. teaming of Pat O'Brien and Bette Davis, although the film really belongs to juvenile Junior Durkin. The boy thinks O'Brien is a great guy, a friend of newspaper publisher Morgan Wallace. Actually, O'Brien's a bootlegger who lets Durkin do jail time for him. The title refers to the boys' reformatory where Durkin is sent, to endure the brutality of guard captain Hooper Atchley. Inmate Junior Coghlan, suffering a heart condition,

HELL'S HOUSE *(Capital 1932) Pat O'Brien and Bette Davis in a rare independent appearance before major stardom with Warner Bros.*

befriends Durkin, who escapes to confront O'Brien. As was the case during this period, Davis—as O'Brien's moll—is overshadowed by her costars; her forceful personality hadn't yet been exposed. Durkin, who won fame playing Huckleberry Finn, made only a few more films before his death at 20 in a 1935 auto accident. Also featured in *Hell's House*: Charley Grapewin and Emma Dunn.

PENGUIN POOL MURDER *(RKO Radio 1932) At the aquarium, teacher Edna May Oliver shows her class how to deal with pickpocket Joe Hermano (on floor). Students include Edith Fellows, left; Sid Miller, tall boy, right; Dorothy Vernon, far right, owns the purse that was stolen.*

PENGUIN POOL MURDER (RKO Radio 1932)

Directed by George Archainbaud. Executive producer, David O. Selznick. First of the Inspector Piper/Hildegarde Withers comedy mysteries and, all things considered, the best. This consideration acknowledges that the murderer's identity is so easy to guess that it must have been intentional. Film was based on the very first Piper/Withers novel, in 1931, by Stuart Palmer. She's a spinster schoolteacher (Palmer derived the character partially from his high school English teacher) and amateur sleuth and he's a gruff investigator for the New York City Police Department. They form an unbeatable team at solving crimes and insulting each other while hiding a mutual affection and admiration. In the hands of James Gleason and Edna May Oliver, the characters really come alive. At the aquarium with her class, Oliver finds the body of broker Guy Usher in the penguin tank. Suspects include unfaithful wife Mae Clarke, former lover Donald Cook, attorney Robert Armstrong and aquarium director Clarence H. Wilson. Willis Goldbeck's screenplay also uses a story by Lowell Brentano for inspiration. Combination of talents creates such interesting characters as mute pickpocket Joe Hermano (a real deaf mute), policeman Edgar Kennedy (whose head is completely shaven) and medical examiner Gustav Von Seyffertitz. In small parts: Rochelle Hudson and child actors Sid Miller and Edith Fellows. After two more entries, Miss Oliver was replaced first by Helen Broderick and then, ZaSu Pitts. Both were distinctly good in other roles, but not that of Hildegarde; Gleason remained constant. Final note: although the leads are planning to wed at film's end, then never do; conclusion is that this may not have been designed as the first of a series.

THE PRIDE OF THE LEGION a.k.a. THE BIG PAY-OFF (Mascot 1932)

Directed by Ford Beebe. Screenplay by Beebe and Peter B. Kyne, from Kyne's story "A Film Star's Holiday." In his first starring role, Victor Jory is in very good company as he faces death and finds redemption. As a policeman dismissed from the force for losing his nerve, Jory tries drowning and is rescued by a dog, Rin-Tin-Tin, Jr. The ex-cop finds work as a waiter and discovers he's in a den of thieves headed by Ralph Ince. Involved in the proceedings are such headliners as Barbara Kent, Sally Blane, Glenn Tryon, Matt Moore, J. Farrell MacDonald and Lucien Littlefield. Good police drama.

70,000 WITNESSES (Paramount 1932) Directed by Ralph Murphy. In this adaptation of the novel by Cortland Fitzsimmons, those of the title are football fans who see player Johnny Mack Brown collapse and die on the field. (Well cast, Brown had been a college football star at Alabama.) Inspector David Landau has the game replayed with Phillips Holmes—who has been accused of trying to throw it—in Brown's place. Only Holmes' slim build and sensitive nature prevent his audience acceptance as a gridiron star; other than that, the film's a well crafted mystery with a fine cast. Charlie Ruggles is the sports announcer and Dorothy Jordan plays the heroine, sister of the deceased and beloved of the hero; Lew Cody scores as Holmes' gambler-brother. The cast also features J. Farrell MacDonald, Kenneth Thomson, Guinn "Big Boy" Williams.

THE THIRTEENTH GUEST (Monogram 1932) Directed by Albert Ray. At the beginning of the mystery, Ginger Rogers is found murdered in an old house. This might not be so unusual, but she's the star. Before long, it develops that she's actually a double. The real Rogers and detective Lyle Talbot investigate the killing of her father at a dinner for thirteen guests some thirteen years before. Good "old house" mystery with such artists as Paul Hurst, Erville Alderson, James Eagles and the ever present J. Farrell MacDonald in the cast. Popular because of Ginger's later stardom, the film was remade as *The Mystery of the 13th Guest* (1943). Armitage Trail did the dialogue for the original and the mystery novel on which it was based.

THE CRIME OF THE CENTURY (Paramount 1933) Directed by William Beaudine. From the play *The Grootman Case* by Walter Maria Espe. Interesting premise has Dr. Jean Hersholt confessing to a crime before he commits it. He's hypnotized bank president Samuel S. Hinds into giving him $100,000 for Hersholt's demanding wife Wynne Gibson. When Hinds is killed, Hersholt naturally becomes the prime suspect and is arrested. Reporter Stuart Erwin (on a break from his usual dense characters) investigates and soon is romancing Hersholt's co-ed daughter Frances Dee. Robert

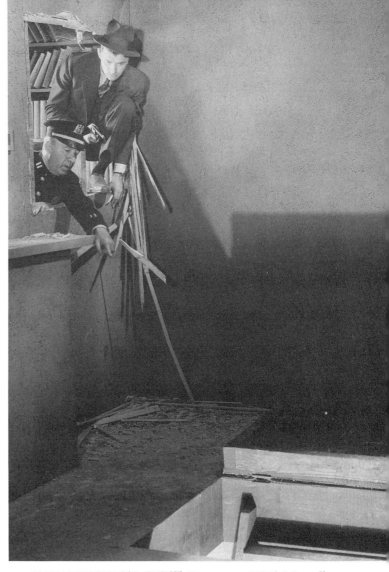

THE THIRTEENTH GUEST *(Monogram 1932) J. Farrell MacDonald and Lyle Talbot find the killer's base of operations in an old dark house.*

Elliott and David Landau are police officers; Gordon Westcott is Gibson's lover, and William Janney, Dee's brother. Long before William Castle thought of it, the action stops for a minute as the clues are reviewed. Of course, none actually give away the real killer, who also does in the vixenish Gibson.

THE SILK EXPRESS (Warner Bros. 1933) Directed by Ray Enright. After unscrupulous Arthur Hohl corners the silk market, manufacturers—to avoid his high rates—import raw silk by boat from Japan to Seattle, there transferred to a special express to New York. Neil Hamilton takes charge of the shipment and a train load of fabulous Warners types: Prof. Dudley Digges, who suffers from sleeping sickness; Digges' daughter Sheila Terry; lawyer Robert Barrat; Dr. Vernon Steele; conductor Arthur Byron; sheriff Guy Kibbee; tramp Allen Jenkins; phony detectives Harold Huber and G. Pat Collins. An unusual murder weapon is used—an icicle, which melts and leaves no evidence. Offbeat, as can be seen.

THE SPHINX *(Monogram 1933)* Lionel Atwill deals with Sheila Terry.

THE SPHINX (Monogram 1933) Directed by Phil Rosen. Rich philanthropist Lionel Atwill literally gets away with murder when it's proven in court that he's a deaf mute who could not have spoken to witness Luis Alberni. Reporters Theodore Newton and Sheila Terry investigate to discover that Atwill has a twin, an actual deaf mute, who's kept hidden. Long thought lost, the print of *The Sphinx* was found to be worth the wait. Featured are such good types as Paul Hurst, Paul Fix, Lucien Prival, Robert Ellis and George Hayes. When Monogram remade it as *The Phantom Killer* (1941), John Hamilton took over the Atwill roles, as emphasis shifted to leads Dick Purcell and Joan Woodbury.

A STUDY IN SCARLET (World Wide 1933) Directed by Edwin L. Marin. Sir Arthur Conan Doyle's Sherlock Holmes mystery, adapted by Robert Florey (who was to have directed), with continuity and dialogue by Reginald Owen. A member of The Scarlet Ring is found strangled on a train in London's Victoria Station. Made at the California Tiffany studios, with an almost all-British cast and a modern setting, this is a Holmes adaption with atmosphere in abundance. Reginald Owen is the famed sleuth—he also worked on the screenplay—and had the distinction of playing at various times both Holmes and Dr. Watson. (He had been Watson opposite Clive Brook in *Sherlock Holmes* the previous year.) Owens' Watson is Warburton Gamble, while Alan Mowbray plays Inspector Lastrade. A sturdy cast also numbers Anna May Wong, June Clyde, Alan Dinehart, John Warburton, J. M. Kerrigan, Doris Lloyd, Billy Bevan,

Leila Bennett, Halliwell Hobbes, Olaf Hytten and Hobart Cavanaugh among its members. Well done in its modest way, it is one of the most revived of all the early sound Holmes pictures.

TOMORROW AT SEVEN (RKO Radio 1933) Directed by Ray Enright. What seems to be a misdirected Warner Bros. film is actually an independent, made by Jefferson Pictures Corporation and distributed by RKO. That aside, it's highly entertaining, involving a mysterious killer, The Black Ace, who leaves an ace of spades for his intended victims and murders precisely at 7:00 PM. Wealthy Henry Stephenson is flying to his Louisiana plantation to take refuge after attempting to track down the murderer. On the plane with Stephenson's party, secretary Grant Mitchell is killed. At Stephenson's estate, writer Chester Morris, Mitchell's daughter Vivienne Osborne (sympathetic here), and dumb detectives Frank McHugh and Allen Jenkins encounter an assortment of strange people including coroner Charles Middleton. Ralph Spence's dialogue allows Jenkins to use some slang references to dope addicts, if anyone's paying attention. In the earlier days of television, the first two scenes were sometimes shown transposed.

CRIME OF HELEN STANLEY (Columbia 1934) Directed by D. Ross Lederman. Before playing Ellery Queen, Ralph Bellamy starred as Inspector Trent in four features also made at Columbia. The third, set in a movie studio, centers around the murder of star Gail Patrick. In the cast of suspects are Shirley Grey, Kane Richmond, Bradley Page, Vincent Sherman (later a director), Lucien Prival, Ward Bond and Clifford Jones (later Philip Trent), playing the assistant director. (Trent recalls that both he and Bellamy were afraid of heights and needed a crane to place them on a catwalk. An extra rather than a stuntman performed a jump and suffered a broken back.) Trent's most unusual encounter was with an extra on the night club set who began telling him of things in Trent's past and future. The extra later emerged as The Great Norvelle, a mentalist. Production title was *Murder in the Studio*. Remade as *Who Killed Gail Preston?* (see 1938 entry).

MURDER IN TRINIDAD (Fox 1934) Directed by Louis King. In his 1933 novel of the same name, writer-explorer John W. Vandercook conceived the character of Bertram Lynch as an investigator for the League of Nations. As played by Nigel Bruce, he seems a casual and rather unkempt man who proves to have keen methods of investigation. Amusingly, critics of the day called him a modern Sherlock Holmes, long before Bruce made a career of playing Holmes' associate, Dr. Watson, as a complete boob. Here, as Lynch, he arrives in Port of Spain to track diamond smugglers. A trail of murder leads him to a hideout in a crocodile-infested swamp. Heather Angel, Victor Jory, Douglas Walton, J. Carrol Naish, Claude King and Murray Kinnell figure in the action. Remade by 20th Century-Fox, with different characters and settings, as *Mr. Moto in Danger Island* (1939) with Peter Lorre and then as *Caribbean Mystery* (1945) with James Dunn.

THE NINTH GUEST (Columbia 1934) Directed by Roy William Neill. Predating Agatha Christie's *Ten Little Niggers* a.k.a. *And Then There Were None* in 1939, was Gwen Bristow and husband Bruce Manning's similarly plotted novel *The Invisible Host* (1930), which Owen Davis adapted into a play, *The Ninth Guest*, the same year. The 1934 feature taken from it has eight people invited to a penthouse where they find eight graves. Trapped by an electrically-charged gate, courtesy of their unknown host, they begin meeting mysterious ends. Those involved are college dean Samuel S. Hinds, radical Hardie Albright, socialite Nella Walker, political boss Edward Ellis, his friend Helen Flint, crooked broker Edwin Maxwell, author Donald Cook and Hollywood star Genevieve Tobin. No need to reveal who, if any, survive or how intriguing the screenplay by Garnett Weston proves to be.

THE CASE OF THE CURIOUS BRIDE (Warner Bros.-First National 1935) Directed by Michael Curtiz. Billed as a "Crime Club Picture," the second Perry Mason mystery starring Warren William was the American film debut of 25-year-old Errol Flynn. He plays the supposedly dead first husband of newlywed Margaret Lindsay, whom he's blackmailing. When Flynn is murdered, Lindsay is naturally suspect. A strong cast includes Claire Dodd as Della Street, Donald Woods, Barton MacLane, Allen Jenkins, Phillip Reed, Wini Shaw, Warren Hymer, Thomas Jackson and Mayo Methot. The screen Mason, as played by William, is much more fun-loving than his book and television counterparts. Based on the 1934 novel by Erle Stanley Gardner.

LADIES LOVE DANGER (Fox 1935) Directed by H. Bruce Humberstone. Daffy Mona Barrie bursts into playwright Gilbert Roland's apartment and promptly involves him   series of murders within a theatrical circle. Both charmed and perplexed by his intruder, Roland turns amateur sleuth to find out who's guilty. Police lieutenant John Wray and Sergeant Dick Foran also turn their attentions to such as Donald Cook, Adrienne Ames, Hardie Albright, Herbert Mundin, Ray Walker, etc. The story by Ilya Zorn, 23-year-old Broadway actress and

THE NINTH GUEST *(Columbia 1934) Genevieve Tobin and Donald Cook face danger together in an Agatha Christie kind of mystery, written by others.*

violinist, was scripted by noted author and playwright Samson Raphaelson, with help from Robert Ellis and Helen Logan. In keeping with her breeziness, Barrie wears a blonde wig and smart clothes by Royer. Enjoyable as both comedy and mystery, this was called *Secret Lives* while in production.

MYSTERIOUS MR. WONG (Monogram 1935) Directed by William Nigh. Based on the story "The Twelve Coins of Confucius" by Harry Stephen Keeler. Another old favorite from the early TV days, but not as exciting as it might be. Action and comedy mix for a fairly satisfying solution as reporter Wallace Ford and sweetheart Arline Judge investigate murders in San Francisco's Chinatown. They ultimately learn the killings are being perpetrated by Bela Lugosi, a mandarin who seeks the twelve Confucian coins which will enable him to rule over Keelat, a Chinese province. Wisecracks and ethnic slurs abound and there is some attention to such details as settings (Ernest Hickson) and music (directed by Abe Meyer). Billed as Bela (Dracula) Lugosi in the ads, the star occasionally loses his Chinese accent, but that's just part of the fun.

CHARLIE CHAN AT THE OPERA *(20th Century-Fox 1936) Backstage: Warner Oland as Charlie, William Demarest, Maurice Cass, Fred Kelsey and Guy Usher.*

EASY MONEY *(Invincible 1936) In an interior decorating establishment, Barbara Barondess and Allen Vincent clash with Noel Madison, boss of an insurance racket.*

CHARLIE CHAN AT THE OPERA (20th Century-Fox 1936) Directed by H. Bruce Humberstone. Of special interest in the Chan series are the strong presence of Boris Karloff as a deranged opera star and *Carnival*, a mini-opera composed especially for the film by Oscar Levant and William Kernell. Karloff escapes from an asylum to avenge himself on wife Margaret Irving and her lover Gregory Gaye, who had tried to kill him. During a performance of *Faust*, he appears as Mephistopheles, and shortly thereafter, Irving and Gaye are both stabbed. Warner Oland as Charlie doesn't readily accept Karloff's guilt and has the opera performed once more to force the hand of the actual killer. Keye Luke as Number One Son Lee joins a cast including Charlotte Henry, Thomas Beck, Nedda Harrigan, Frank Conroy, William Demarest, plus the voices of Tudor Williams dubbing for the singing Karloff (a sight to behold) and Zari Elmassian for Irving's soprano. One of the best of all Chan films and probably the best of the Olands. Based on Earl Derr Biggers' characters.

EASY MONEY (Invincible 1936) Directed by Phil Rosen. Well done exposé of the insurance racket, shot in seven days at Republic, has Noel Madison heading a gang operating out of his interior decorating establishment. Costarring is Barbara Barondess, who actually became an interior decorator and worked on the homes of scores of Hollywood celebs. Nominal stars Onslow Stevens and Kay Linaker do good work as they penetrate the gang, which includes Stevens' wayward brother Allen Vincent, who loves Barondess. Barbara Bedford portrays a victim of the gang; her planned accident results in her death. On TV, this one is known as *Final Payment*.

15 MAIDEN LANE (20th Century-Fox 1936) Directed by Allan Dwan. Slick entertainment about jewel thieves, with the title referring to New York's diamond district. To help her uncle Robert McWade's insurance agency, Claire Trevor allows her own diamond to serve as loot to gain entry into the gang. Heading the operation is Cesar Romero, as smooth an opportunist as ever lived. He and Trevor seem to be getting along quite well until police detective Lloyd Nolan comes to her rescue. An angered Romero shoots her down, not fatally, before his own fate is sealed. Oddest element of this Sol M. Wurtzel production is that Romero completely steals the film; he's graceful on the dance floor as he twirls Trevor on the slightest provocation; as the gang leader, he's not only charming and resourceful, but also a ruthless killer. The fact that no romance develops between Trevor and good guy Nolan shows that the filmmakers hoped that crime, for once, would pay. With Douglas Fowley, Lester Matthews and everyone's favorite female menace of the day, Natalie Moorhead.

HUMAN CARGO (20th Century-Fox 1936)

Directed by Allan Dwan. Based on the novel *I Will Be Faithful* by Kathleen Shepard, this was another collaboration among Dwan, producer Sol M. Wurtzel and star Claire Trevor. Although melodramatic, the story is handled in a light manner as debutante Trevor and reporter Brian Donlevy track a ring smuggling aliens into the country. Their quest takes them to Vancouver and back to Los Angeles. Along the way, she employs a French accent charmingly if unconvincingly. Second female lead is Rita Cansino (Hayworth), who was performing with her father in a dance act in Tijuana when signed for the film. Dwan remembered that she was quite nervous to be working on the set with so many professionals, although she'd done a few previous features. However, her role is of fairly short duration—she's bumped off by Ralf Harolde—and the dancing skills are employed all too briefly. The Jefferson Parker-Doris Malloy screenplay includes references to a hophead and a dope fiend, which always seems surprising in a mainstream Thirties production. Well done, and with a good cast in support—Alan Dinehart, Ralph Morgan, John McGuire, Morgan Wallace (watch out for him), Wade Boteler, Harry Woods and the marvelous Herman Bing as a ship's officer on the boat used by the smugglers.

MOONLIGHT MURDER (MGM 1936)

Directed by Edwin L. Marin. Set in the open air Hollywood Bowl (*Hollywood Bowl* was one of the film's production titles, along with *Murder Under the Stars* and *Murder in the Bowl*), this murder mystery with an operatic background offers the choral sequence of Verdi's *Il Trovatore*. Opera star Leo Carrillo is warned, by swami Pedro de Cordoba, he will die if he sings. When that warning comes to pass and his death proves to be murder, suspects include: prima donna Katharine Alexander, her conductor husband H. B. Warner, dancer Benita Hume, her husband and partner Duncan Renaldo, insane composer J. Carrol Naish, and ambitious singer Leonard Ceeley. Detective Chester Morris and Madge Evans, scientist-niece of Dr. Grant Mitchell, work backstage to sort out the clues. Apart from the setting and a particularly colorful cast— Frank McHugh as a valet, as well—there's an added treat. Renaldo and Carrillo, later films and TV's Cisco Kid and Pancho, play suspect and victim.

THE PREVIEW MURDER MYSTERY (Paramount 1936)

Directed by Robert Florey. Backstage dramas are always interesting, particularly Hollywood-themed murder mysteries and this one has quite a lot to recommend it. At the preview of his new film, *Song of the Toreador*, singer-actor Rod La Rocque is murdered. Suspicion falls on flamboyant director Ian Keith, until he also turns up dead. After night watchman Spencer

HUMAN CARGO *(20th Century-Fox 1936) Morgan Wallace, Edward Cooper and Harry Woods have Claire Trevor bound and gagged.*

Charters is stabbed, police lieutenant Thomas Jackson forbids anyone to leave the lot, including Reginald Denny and Frances Drake, the leads playing amateur sleuths who uncover the clues. The synopsis hardly conveys the many fascinating and funny bits of business. La Rocque has two roles, his voice being dubbed in his second part; he sings "Promise With a Kiss" (Leo Robin – Charles Kisco) and is dubbed in that instance, too. Silent stars Jack Mulhall, Bryant Washburn and Franklyn Farnum are cast as actors, while veteran comics Chester Conklin and Hank Mann make a shambles of a beauty contest in a movie sequence, composer Ralph Rainger and Charlie Ruggles make appearances at the preview, and Jack Norton, perennial drunk of scores of pictures, is seen as a comedy director. Most bizarre in the proceedings is the recreation of a scene from the German expressionistic classic *The Cabinet of Dr. Caligari* (1919); here, Wilfred Lucas (a Griffith player in the earliest days of film) is directing *Bat Man*. In the sequence, Henry Kleinbach (Brandon) as Bat Man and John George as his assistant, a gnome, are shown in a menacing light. The end of this segment is punctuated by a gag, proving that Florey could both bow to and mock the masters at the same time. Also in the cast are Gail Patrick, George Barbier, Conway Tearle, and Colin Tapley. Called simply *Preview* while in production, the film uses television as an accepted medium, long before that happened in reality.

BEHIND THE HEADLINES (RKO Radio 1937)

Directed by Richard Rosson. Lee Tracy again portrays a wisecracking reporter, but this melodrama is one with a difference, in that he works for a radio station, carrying a microphone so that he can broadcast news on the spot. His driver, Tom Kennedy, transmits from a broadcasting truck. Tracy's former newspaper employer, Philip Huston, hires Diana Gibson as a replacement and the two reporters become romantically involved while not for-

CITY GIRL *(20th Century-Fox 1937) The crowd watches Phyllis Brooks and Chick Chandler do The Shag before she turns to crime.*

NIGHT KEY *(Universal 1937) Jean Rogers and father Boris Karloff, who uses his night key invention to stop Alan Baxter's car and their kidnapping.*

getting their professional rivalry. When Donald Meek, a rogue government agent, plans to hijack a gold shipment en route to the new Federal Reserve at Fort Knox, Gibson is taken prisoner. She alerts Tracy and the authorities, including FBI Chief Selmer Jackson, via Tracy's broadcasting back-pack. (At the time, rambling reporters broadcast on the spot via radio transmitters. One kind was pocket sized and had a range of only a few blocks. The other, with a range of up to thirty miles, weighed several pounds and was strapped to the reporter's back. Neither could be picked up by an ordinary receiver. A truck, parked nearby, and equipped with powerful receiving and transmitting apparatus, picked up the reporter's voice and automatically relayed it to the broadcast station and then onto the airwaves. There was no need for connecting wires or telephone cables. Within range of the truck, the reporter could broadcast from a diving bell or an airplane.) J. Roy Hunt, a director of photography for RKO (and a colleague of *Behind the Headlines* cinematographer Russell Metty), was a radio enthusiast and loaned his own broadcasting truck to the studio. Radio direction finders, developed during World War I to locate enemy submarines, were employed for the rescue of Gibson at film's end. Meek, almost always in comedy roles, certainly makes for an interesting and tiny villain. Gibson, an artists' model and beauty contest winner (named, incidentally, for famed artist Charles Dana Gibson, creator of The Gibson Girl), worked exclusively for RKO and Universal and had leads in only four films and serials. Her years in Hollywood were brief and she retired to Key Largo, Florida.

CITY GIRL (20th Century-Fox 1937) Directed by Alfred Werker. Blonde Phyllis Brooks is the focal point of a tragedy that revolves around a waitress looking for a better life who forsakes Robert Wilcox, a promising young assistant district attorney, for Ricardo Cortez, a smooth gangster who offers the finer things. Unfortunately, with them comes a life of crime. Wanted for murder and jailbreaking, she resorts to plastic surgery before the inevitable end of this fast-moving tale that packs a lot into its sixty minutes. Before her downfall, a less-depressed Brooks does the shag, a dance of the day, with pal Chick Chandler, a breezy type of many films. Marjorie Main scores in a dramatic role as Brooks' mother, and Cortez continues in the gangster character mold he began in sound features after a lengthy career as a silent screen lover. Douglas Fowley and bad girls Esther Muir and Adrienne Ames also are in the cast, and in small roles are such later B headliners as Lon Chaney, Jr., Lynn Bari and Robert Lowery. The latter starred with Brooks in the Forties.

LONDON BY NIGHT (MGM 1937) Directed by William Thiele. Based on screenwriter George Oppenheimer's adaptation of the play *The Umbrella Man* by Will Scott. Viennese-born Thiele and art director Cedric Gibbons, a native New Yorker, combined talents to produce an atmospheric London by night with help from the fog machines. Irish reporter George Murphy investigates disappearances and murders linked to the mysterious Umbrella Man, operating by night in foggy Sundial Square. Some casting against type: George Zucco, usually a menace, is the hard-working police inspector; Virginia Field and Eddie Quillan employ Cockney accents as pub types who are brutally murdered; Rita Johnson, of Massachusetts, makes her film debut, not in one of her "other woman" roles, but as the sympathetic heroine whose welfare becomes Murphy's concern. Montagu Love, J. M. Kerrigan, Leonard Mudie and many from Hollywood's English colony also take part. Stealing the film—and giving away the plot—is Leo G. Carroll, who proves to be incredibly versatile. He's billed officially as Correy, secretary to Lord Love and sporting glasses. In addition, he portrays tobacconist Casey, who has disappeared; Von Krawitz, a friend of the latter, with mustache, glasses and a German accent; and, you guessed it, The Umbrella Man, also known as Mr. Rabbit, himself. It's quite a feat and he carries it off well. Unfortunately, he rarely had an opportunity to display so many facets of his talent and is today best remembered for his TV "Topper" and Mr. Waverly on "The Man From U.N.C.L.E." *The Umbrella* was the production title of this engaging mystery.

NIGHT KEY (Universal 1937) Directed by Lloyd Corrigan. The rotund character actor also directed some features, wrote many more and co-authored and directed the Oscar-winning short *La Cucaracha* (1934). Here is one of director Corrigan's best. Boris Karloff, in elderly makeup, is a victim of unscrupulous Samuel S. Hinds and lawyer Edwin Maxwell. Hinds steals an invisible beam alarm system Karloff has perfected just as he filched the alarm network which inventor Karloff had devised twenty years earlier. To discredit Hinds, Karloff uses a night key which breaks into the old system and renders it useless. Petty thief Hobart Cavanaugh wants to use the device to his advantage, but young gang leader Alan Baxter has bigger ideas. Acting as well as the action really scores: Karloff is fine as a sympathetic, not mad, scientist; Baxter nicely underplays his very interesting role; and Ward Bond shines as always in one of his many gangster portrayals. Cavanaugh wins a lot of laughs as a crook who wears as many articles of clothing as he can don during a shopping spree; it's a colorful characteriza-

tion. Warren Hull and Jean Rogers, as Karloff's daughter, are a handsome young couple. Frank Reicher and David Oliver also have parts. Although the Robert Presnell production has something of a science fiction aspect (sci-fi buffs could be disappointed), it qualifies as a gangster feature.

THE SHADOW (Columbia 1937) Directed by C. C. (Charles) Coleman, Jr. Very fast moving circus mystery, aided by Byron Robinson's rapid paced editing and a tentfull of suspects. Rita Hayworth won good notices for her playing of the harried heiress to a circus, who will lose it all to bareback rider Donald Kirke, hated by all, if she defaults on a loan made to her late father. Press agent Charles Quigley is a virile hero as he braves dangers to solve the killings plaguing the circus; at the time, the studio was touting him as a new Robert Taylor, but he never rose above B picture and serial stardom. Colorful suspects: hunchback animal trainer Dwight Frye; Rita's aunt Marjorie Main; fortune teller Bess Flowers; knife thrower Dick Curtis; boxer-turned-trouble shooter Marc Lawrence who stands out, but couldn't be guilty. The ending is as swift and bizarre as anything a scriptwriter could conceive, making this a really top mystery. Produced by Wallace MacDonald. Kudos to writers Milton Raison and Arthur T. Horman.

THE WESTLAND CASE (Universal 1937) Directed by Christy Cabanne. Based on Jonathan Latimer's 1935 novel *Headed for a Hearse*. This film was the first of Universal's "Crime Club" series, also the name of a group of Warner Bros. mysteries, and the first of three features with Preston Foster as detective Bill Crane and Frank Jenks as assistant Doc Williams. Foster is a Chicagoan

THE WESTLAND CASE *(Universal 1937) Barbara Pepper, resembling a famous star, and Clarence Wilson share pleasantries in a comedy-mystery.*

SCANDAL STREET *(Paramount 1938) Lew Ayres, Louise Campbell and Elizabeth Patterson share the effects of small-town gossip.*

WHO KILLED GAIL PRESTON? *(Columbia 1938) Rita Hayworth as a singer who's murdered and Robert Paige as a singing bandleader in prison garb.*

who'd rather drink and play games than solve crimes, but he takes on the case of Theodore Von Eltz, about to be executed for murdering his wife. Involved are Von Eltz's partners in a brokerage firm, George Meeker and Russell Hicks; bookkeeper Rollo Lloyd; secretary Astrid Allwyn; Von Eltz's sweetheart, Carol Hughes; gangster Tom Quinn. Putting all that aside, what really makes the film outstanding is the work of Barbara Pepper as Foster's buxom neighbor. She does the best, if never properly acknowledged, Mae West impersonation outside of the real thing. Clarence Wilson is a befuddled aide, Alice Belcher is Pepper's unlovely aunt and Ward Bond plays a convict. A comedy gem.

ARREST BULLDOG DRUMMOND! (Paramount 1938) Directed by James Hogan. Based on the 1926

Drummond story "The Final Count," by H. C. (Sapper) McNeile, this remains the liveliest of the Drummond series in which John Howard starred. Opposite him are H. B. Warner as Colonel Nielson, Reginald Denny as Algy, E. E. Clive as servant Tenny and Heather Angel as the patient fiancée Phyllis Clavering. She and Howard are about to wed, as they were in several of the installments, when he becomes involved in a plot to steal an atomic disintegrator capable of destroying explosives within a range of half a mile. Thick-lensed madman George Zucco has control of the device and Howard, who is suspected of the theft, pursues all the clues to an island colony. The fireworks explosion adds a great comic touch. Of course, no one would expect Drummond to wed as long as the series lasted and that certainly didn't happen in this case.

PRISON TRAIN (Equity 1938) Directed by Gordon Wiles. Starting in the industry as an art director, Wiles won an Academy Award for his work on Fox's *Transatlantic* (1931). In the mid-Thirties, he turned to producing and directing and specialized in crime and action features. Rather few directorial credits thereafter reflected a desire to alternate between his artistic crafts. In this early TV favorite, he combines skills to create a visually stunning and offbeat production. Racketeer Fred Keating runs a numbers operation and night club in Philadelphia, but after accidentally causing the death of drunken James Blakely, he is sent to Alcatraz. Odds are that he'll never reach there alive because Alexander Leftwich, his rival and the father of Blakely, sends assorted henchmen to dispose of him. Also aboard the train taking Keating to prison are his sister Linda Winters (later Dorothy Comingore, making her "official" debut in *Citizen Kane*), and federal agent Peter Potter (later the famed disk jockey). There are a few surprises in the casting, with a number of actors in larger roles than they normally had. Keating for one, playing a tough criminal, was often cast as a brash type with a sense of humor, while Clarence Muse, a talented black actor-composer-writer-director-producer-singer, is very much against type as a steward who's in reality a hitman. Nearly every scene is composed in a way that seems to be geometrically designed, with lines and circles dominating many shots. That and the train setting give rise to the speculation that *Prison Train* may have been influenced by the fascinating German film *Das Stahltier (The Steel Beast)*, made in 1935 by documentarian Willy Zielke—a masterpiece of shapes and sizes, carefully and artfully filmed. Bill Everson, who supplied the print of *Prison Train*, doubts that possibility as Zielke's film was made in Nazi Germany as a propaganda piece and then banned from release. And yet . . .

SCANDAL STREET (Paramount 1938) Directed by James Hogan. Based on Vera (*Laura*) Caspary's story "Suburb," this is an altogether lighthearted remake of the far more dramatic *The Night of June 13* (1932), showing how small-town gossip and fears can destroy a life. For the most part, *Scandal Street* (shot under the title *They Knew What Happened*) is a cheery affair, verging on slapstick as Louise Campbell—a new librarian—causes a great deal of gossip among people who have nothing better to do. Much of the humor revolves around the children who are performing a dance recital; ringleaders among the juvenile merrymakers are Virginia Weidler and Carl "Alfalfa" Switzer. When a murder occurs in town, Campbell becomes the prime suspect, having been the unwelcome object of victim Roscoe Karns' attention. Lew Ayres, as her beau, has limited footage despite top billing. (Campbell, widow of Horace McMahon, remembers Ayres as "pleasant and workman-like on the set," however large his role.) Small-town and small-minded types are delineated by such characters as Elizabeth Patterson, Edgar Kennedy, Porter Hall, Cecil Cunningham, Lucien Littlefield and Jan Duggan, all of whom knew their way around a comedy line. Three up-and-coming actresses in minor roles appear under their real names: Laraine Day (Laraine Johnson), Adrian Booth (Virginia Pound) and Ellen Drew (Terry Ray). Although the elements are in opposition to each other, the end result is a satisfying, somewhat offbeat affair.

WHO KILLED GAIL PRESTON? (Columbia 1938, but copyright 1937) Directed by Leon Barsha. This is a remake of *Crime of Helen Stanley* (see 1934 entry), with the action switched from a movie studio to a nightclub and songs added for spice. Since Rita Hayworth is the singer of the title and she's hated by all, it's only a matter of time until she's murdered, and that in the middle of one of her numbers. Don Terry is the police inspector on the case with his dumb assistant, Gene Morgan, and the first suspect, Dwight Frye, proves his innocence by falling to his death. Thereafter, suspicion falls on orchestra leader Robert Paige and sweetheart Wyn Cahoon, as well as Marc Lawrence, Arthur Loft and John Gallaudet. Opening resembles a prison film with convicts attempting an escape; it's merely a prelude to the first number, "12 O'Clock and All's Not Well" (Ben Oakland-Milton Drake), which Paige and the band render in prison-like outfits, along with Rita. The change of setting gives fresh life to the plot. *Murder in Swingtime* was its production title.

THE BIG GUY (Universal 1939) Directed by Arthur Lubin. (Reissued by Realart as *Warden of the Big House.*) Based on the story "No Power on Earth" by Wallace Sullivan and Richard K. Polimer, this prison movie has young convict Jackie Cooper being apprehended after a big-house break. In recapturing Cooper and his fellow

CHARLIE CHAN AT TREASURE ISLAND *(20th Century-Fox 1939) Wally Vernon, Sidney Toler as Charlie, Pauline Moore, Douglas Fowley, magician Cesar Romero in the best of the Chans.*

NICK CARTER, MASTER DETECTIVE *(MGM 1939)*
Walter Pidgeon and Rita Johnson as detective and his
stewardess interest.

escapees, guard captain Victor McLaglen decides to hide their loot and keep it for himself. Made acting warden, McLaglen wrestles with his conscience when Cooper is sentenced to death for a killing he didn't commit. Enhancing the fast-moving action is the presence of Ona Munson as McLaglen's wife and Peggy Moran as Cooper's hometown girl, plus Ed Brophy, Jonathan Hale, Russell Hicks, Edward Pawley and Murray Alper. In small parts are such later Universal headliners as Milburn Stone, Anne Gwynne and horror star Rondo Hatton as a convict. The tale was remade by Universal as *Behind the High Wall* (1956) with Tom Tully, John Gavin, Sylvia Sidney and Betty Lynn in the McLaglen, Cooper, Munson and Moran parts.

CHARLIE CHAN AT TREASURE ISLAND (20th Century-Fox 1939) Directed by Norman Foster. Generally regarded as the best of the Charlie Chan series; certainly the best of all those starring Sidney Toler, Warner Oland's replacement. Strains of "San Francisco" (Bronislau Kaper-Walter Jurmann-Gus Kahn) are heard before the story gets underway with shots of San Francisco's Treasure Island from the air and land. Writer Louis Jean Heydt (filmdom's eternal victim) dies on a plane, a supposed suicide, but Toler naturally suspects murder. Number Two son Victor Sen Yung is along to aid and obstruct honorable father in usual fashion. Magician Cesar Romero, performing on the island, is determined to prove that mystic Gerald Mohr is a fake, in the course of the investigation. Also mixed up in the mystery are Pauline Moore, Douglas Fowley, June Gale as Romero's jealous wife, Douglass Dumbrille, Billie Seward, Wally Vernon, Donald MacBride and Sally Blane (director Foster's real-life wife) as Heydt's widow. With a good deal of atmosphere and some nifty seance scenes, featuring Kay Linaker as the lady in ectoplasm, this presents a well concealed killer. One film from Hollywood's Golden Year which should be on the list of the best 1939 Bs.

THE ESCAPE (20th Century-Fox 1939) Directed by Ricardo Cortez. When actor Ricardo Cortez turned to directing briefly (1938-40), he specialized in crime dramas. Here's the best of the small group (seven films), shot under the title *Eastside, Westside*. At the wake of gangster Edward Norris, *New York Star News* reporter Jack Carson (then doing dramatic parts) learns of the deceased's past from Dr. Frank Reicher. In flashback, there follows a complicated but fascinating tale of crime and tangled family relationships. Top-billed Kane Richmond is the cop who tries to help Norris for the sake of the latter's sister Amanda Duff and father Henry Armetta. Norris is secretly wed to June Gale, their baby girl being adopted by District Attorney Richard Lane. When the gangster is confronted by the kidnapping of his baby by racketeer Nick Copeland, he attempts to rescue her. Although Norris is depicted as a cold-blooded killer, he manages to win a certain amount of sympathy because of his concern for the family. In the cast are Scotty Beckett, Jimmy Butler and Rex Downing as young brothers, Leona Roberts, Matt McHugh, Mary Gordon, Selmer Jackson, Thomas Jackson and studio contractee Robert Lowery, who a few years later most likely would have had Norris' role.

MUTINY IN THE BIG HOUSE (Monogram 1939) Directed by William Nigh. Associate producer, actor Grant Withers, a Monogram mainstay. If Warners made the best prison dramas, here's one of the best imitations, with Barton MacLane reprising a familiar role as the ringleader of the cons (alternate role, sadistic guard captain) and Charles Bickford excelling as the prison chaplain. Bickford's role of Father Joe Collins is dedicated to Father Patrick O'Neil, order of St. Benedict, hero of the famed 1929 prison break at Canon City, Colorado. Dennis Moore is the wayward youth who's torn between Bickford's guidance and MacLane's determination to stage an escape. Pat Moriarity is the warden of Westview Penitentiary, where the cons pass the time in song and dance: I. Stanford Jolley leads an all-girl (male convict) chorus and Charley Foy tap dances. William Royle has the MacLane role of the mean prison captain, while some of the guards in the all-male cast were recruited from Westerns: Dave O'Brien, Charles King, Wheeler Oakman. Also with Russell Hopton and Nigel de Brulier. Outstanding is the work of George Cleveland as the elderly inmate who can't adjust to life on the outside and decides to spend the rest of his days behind bars.

NICK CARTER, MASTER DETECTIVE (MGM 1939) Directed by Jacques Tourneur. Created in 1886, Nick Carter became the most prolific detective character in American fiction. Various writers contributed well over a thousand different Carter stories, bringing him a long way from the brilliant, clean-cut youth of Ormond G. Smith's conception. Actually, Smith merely outlined

the character and John Russell Coryell wrote the initial stories. Nick Carter as a screen character has undergone strange incarnations, dating back to the earliest silent days. French auteurist Tourneur directed the first of the MGM series with Canadian Walter Pidgeon as a dashing, older Nick. Called simply *Nick Carter* initially, this first film had only two sequels: *Phantom Raiders* and *Sky Murder* (both 1940), approximately as good as this. In the 1939 edition, Pidgeon is summoned by Addison Richards, head of the Radex Airplane Factory in Pasadena. There, engineer Henry Hull has perfected a 420 MPH "rocket ship," the object of spies who are smuggling out plans. Pidgeon isn't above killing one of his opponents, as he finishes off pilot Frank Faylen. Aiding Pidgeon in his investigation are air hostess Rita Johnson (only woman in the cast) and eccentric beekeeping amateur sleuth Donald Meek. Also recruited to fill other roles—Stanley Ridges, Henry Victor, Milburn Stone, Martin Kosleck, George Meeker, Don Castle, Richard Lane and Sterling Holloway as the bee catcher. Remember that World War II had barely begun, but spies were being given a Germanic background.

TELL NO TALES (MGM 1939) Directed by Leslie Fenton. After apprenticing with several short subjects, actor-turned-director Fenton made his feature bow with an intricate and intelligent though episodic story, aided by Peter Ballbusch's montage work. Editor Melvyn Douglas, struggling to save his newspaper from demise, follows up on a big story involving a kidnapping, obtaining one of the bills used as ransom and finding that it went through many hands. Each of the vignettes involving the bill is a tale in itself, the most compelling being that of a black boxer who was murdered. As the boxer's widow, Theresa Harris does exceptional work, and there are a number of impressive bits in this sequence, including Mantan Moreland and Madame Sul-Te-Wan. Louise Platt, the heroine, may hold the key to the plot as she heads a large and effective cast that features Gene Lockhart, Douglass Dumbrille (ever the villain, or is he?), Florence George, Zeffie Tilbury, Addison Richards, Esther Dale, Hobart Cavanaugh, Halliwell Hobbes, Sara Haden, Norman Willis and Clayton Moore, under the name Jack Carlton. Two days of filming were done in the *Los Angeles Daily News* plant. Production title for this gem was *One Hundred to One*.

THE WITNESS VANISHES (Universal 1939) Directed by Otis Garrett. From the novel *They Can't Hang Me*, which was also the film's production title. Final, not overly exciting entry in the "Crime Club" series; however, a good example of an indifferent film being saved by the playing of one actor. Edmund Lowe, in the lead, refuses to take anything seriously and makes his role fun; at one point, he imitates fellow actor Walter

TELL NO TALES *(MGM 1939) Seeking out kidnappers, Louise Platt and Melvyn Douglas spot one of the group.*

Kingsford, a feat in itself. Lowe and his associates at the newspaper *The London Sun* have owner Barlowe Borland committed to an asylum so that they can take over. When Borland escapes, Lowe finds his fellow executives are being bumped off while he manages to keep an unaccountably lighthearted attitude. Wendy Barrie, Borland's daughter, goes incognito and works with her beau, Lord Bruce Lester, to clear her father's name. Forrester Harvey, J. M. Kerrigan, Leyland Hodgson, Reginald Barlow, Anne Nagel and Hally Chester of "The Little Tough Guys" all take part in the proceedings.

BOWERY BOY (Republic 1940) Directed by William Morgan. This melodrama, from an original story by Sam Fuller and Sidney Sutherland, has nothing to do with Monogram's Bowery Boys, which didn't hit the screen until 1946. Title refers to Jimmy Lydon, a tough Bowery kid who opposes idealistic doctor Dennis O'Keefe and nurse Louise Campbell and their health clinic. Racketeers led by Roger Pryor not only prey on the

GAMBLING ON THE HIGH SEAS *(Warner Bros. 1940) Gambling on a high seas honeymoon are Jane Wyman and Wayne Morris.*

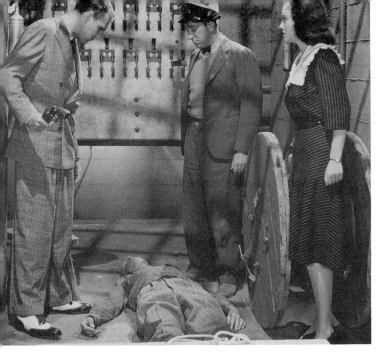

MEET THE WILDCAT *(Universal 1940) In Mexico City, Ralph Bellamy, Allen Jenkins and Margaret Lindsay take care of guard Robert O. Davis (Rudolph Anders); she's a reporter-photographer for* Squint *magazine.*

poor, but also cause an outbreak of food poisoning. O'Keefe then battles botulism as Lydon comes to his aid. Helen Vinson has a standard role as the society woman who'd take O'Keefe away from Campbell. Also in the cast: Paul Hurst, Ed Gargan, and Lydon's brother Ormund, 13, who plays his younger brother while older sibling Vincent, 18, acted as Jimmy's stand-in. A good directorial debut for fomer editor Morgan, who later went on to direct several Gene Autry Westerns in the Forties.

[When Louise Campbell visited The CoOp, she referred to Republic as a low class operation; the gathered throng—Republic lovers all—voiced disapproval of her opinion. Other than that, a good time was had by the Campbell-McMahon clan.]

GAMBLING ON THE HIGH SEAS (Warner Bros. 1940)

Directed by George Amy. A brief directorial interlude for Amy, who edited many of the Errol Flynn features, proving that he could adapt to the swift Warners style, which, perfected in the Thirties, lasted until the company stopped making short crime dramas in the mid-Forties. Off the New England coast, Gilbert Roland runs a crooked gambling ship, the S. S. Sylvania, which has become the target of a newspaper exposé. Reporter Wayne Morris enlists the aid of Roland's secretary, played by a very blonde Jane Wyman, and when a raid is staged, they photograph the devices rigged to fix the roulette wheels. Roland is a smooth villain, while Wyman exudes a sexiness to go with her new look. Also involved are Roger Pryor, John Litel and, as a reporter, George Reeves, some time before he became a more famous newsman named Clark Kent.

MEET THE WILDCAT (Universal 1940)

Directed by Arthur Lubin. Just eight days before the release of their first Ellery Queen picture for Columbia, Ralph Bellamy and Margaret Lindsay costarred in this diverting comedy mystery set in Mexico City, but made, of course, on Universal's all-purpose lot. The Wildcat of the title is a master art thief, sought by policeman Bellamy and reporter Lindsay, among others. When not getting in each other's way, as heroes and heroines often do in films of this type, the leads invariably find time to develop a fondness for each other. Joseph Schildkraut as a suave thief and Allen Jenkins, Jerome Cowan, Rudolph Anders (billed as Robert O. Davis), Iris Adrian, Frank Puglia, Reed Hadley and Gloria Franklin keep things on a fun level. A word for Stanley Cortez's photography— excellent.

PAROLE FIXER (Paramount 1940)

Directed by Robert Florey. Using the book *Persons in Hiding* by J. Edgar Hoover, Paramount had enough material for several films and the inspiration for others. They were so loaded with actors, mid-level names and future stars, that the films took on an episodic narrative. Crooks and cops shared equal screen time. The FBI headquarters and training center are featured in this installment, as lawyer Paul McGrath uses his influence to obtain paroles for undeserving convicts. One, Robert Paige, obtains a chauffeur's position as a prelude to kidnapping. Another, vicious Anthony Quinn, bumps off Jack Carson, the agent on his trail. William Henry more or less heads the cast as the agent determined to bring his colleague's killer to justice. A large contingent of performers supply greater and smaller roles with interest—Virginia Dale, Gertrude Michael, Richard Denning, Fay Helm, Harvey Stephens, Marjorie Gateson, Lyle Talbot, Louise Beavers and Charlotte Wynters. Florey packs the film with incident and fast-moving dramatics, all with an almost documentary feel.

THE SAINT TAKES OVER *(RKO Radio 1940) The Inspector, Jonathan Hale, is shown a hidden camera by The Saint, George Sanders.*

THE SAINT TAKES OVER (RKO Radio 1940)

Directed by Jack Hively. Here's yet another editor-turned-director who did well with crime films. George Sanders starred in both The Saint and The Falcon series until he, or the studio, tired of the characters. He was equally at home in portraying villainy or heroics, the latter with a sly attitude that seemed to say the character was getting away with more than one would realize. That is, Sanders' heroes always had something of the rogue in them. In this series entry, he's aided by Paul Guilfoyle as a former safecracker now a loyal assistant. Guilfoyle was particularly skilled at portraying the dumb hood, a part he usually played seriously. Sanders is concerned with the reputation of his inspector friend, Jonathan Hale, who has been accused of involvement in a racetrack scandal. Making an occasional appearance is Wendy Barrie, who had different roles in three of the Saint series and two of the Falcon's, all opposite Sanders. Cy Kendall is a particularly nasty head of the gang, while Morgan Conway (later filmdom's Dick Tracy just twice), Robert Emmett Keane, Roland Drew and James Burke also contribute to both sides of the law.

SAN FRANCISCO DOCKS (Universal 1940)

Directed by Arthur Lubin. Fast-paced crime thriller with surprisingly little wasted motion. As a longshoreman accused of killing waterfront character Joe Downing, Burgess Meredith, despite his star billing, is offscreen for long stretches as the plot speeds along. Unfortunately, the man who could free Meredith is Edward Pawley, an escapee from Alcatraz and the real murderer. Helping to prove Meredith's innocence are sweetheart Irene Hervey, her saloonkeeper father Raymond Walburn, priest Robert Armstrong, character Barry Fitzgerald and lawyer Lewis Howard. On the sidelines are beautician Esther Howard and Pawley's wife Esther Ralston, adding up to quite a cast. This was the veteran Ralston's last film and she made it memorable, engaging in a hair-pulling contest with the heroine. Wrote Ralston in 1989: "Irene Hervey and I did the fight scene without any prompting—she only said, 'Esther, please watch out for my false eyelashes.' My husband, Ted Lloyd (a columnist), had come to Hollywood and was sitting on the set watching this fight scene. He was so afraid I was going to make another film so he came to get me and take me home—I was sorry to give up my career but happy to please my husband." Thank you, Esther.

SAN FRANCISCO DOCKS (Universal 1940) On the set, Esther Ralston and Irene Hervey are cheered on by their husbands Allan Jones and Ted Lloyd, a columnist wed to Ralston, making her final film.

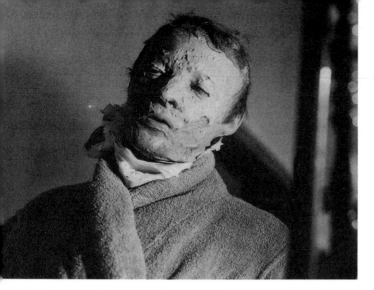

THE FACE BEHIND THE MASK *(Columbia 1941) In his hospital room, Peter Lorre views his burned face for the first time; the only glimpse of the makeup in the entire film.*

CONFESSIONS OF BOSTON BLACKIE (Columbia 1941)

Directed by Edward Dmytryk. Second of the 14-film series starring Chester Morris as the reformed thief is way above average, due to the Dmytryk touches, not to mention a good cast and an offbeat plot. Harriet Hilliard, in a rare excursion into drama, has commissioned Walter Soderling to sell her statue of Augustus Caesar. At the auction, she's wounded by Soderling's accomplice Ralph Theadore and Soderling is killed by the same bullet. Suspected of pulling the trigger, Morris flees the scene as the injured Hilliard is prepared to be stuffed inside the imitation statue which the conspirators, including Kenneth MacDonald, intended to sell. Billy Benedict has a funny bit as an ice cream vendor, while George E. Stone (The Runt), Richard Lane (Inspector John Faraday), Lloyd Corrigan (Arthur Manleder) and Walter Sande (Sgt. Mathews) turn up in their recurring Boston Blackie roles. Blackie, created by Jack Boyle, dates back to the late Teens, his screen character in this series embellished considerably by a light approach in the writing and in Morris' always enthused playing.

THE FACE BEHIND THE MASK (Columbia 1941)

Directed by Robert Florey. Produced by Wallace MacDonald. Based on a radio play by Thomas Edward O'Connell and scripted by Paul Jarrico and former actor Allen Vincent, this bizarre exercise offered Peter Lorre one of his best roles. There's a touch of horror, if not fantasy, to the tale of a man who wears a face mask to hide his scarred features. The film has just one quick shot of Lorre with the hideous face, but it pales in comparison to screen horrors of a later day. At the time, it made the necessary impact. Hungarian immigrant Lorre is horribly burned in a boarding house fire and contemplates suicide when he meets George E. Stone, a cheerful criminal. Beginning a life of crime, Lorre inveigles his way into James Seay's gang and soon takes it over. With a mask fitted over his face, to make himself presentable to the outside world, Lorre then falls in love with blind Evelyn Keyes (in a most appealing performance), and through her, finds happiness. Seay, thinking he's been cheated, causes Keyes' death in an attempt to kill Lorre. The Face then carries out his own revenge. Don Beddoe has a good role as a friendly police lieutenant, but Lorre excels in a role calling for both repulsion and compassion.

NO HANDS ON THE CLOCK (Paramount 1941)

Directed by Frank McDonald. Chester Morris is cast as detective Humphrey Campbell, a creation of mystery novelist Geoffrey Homes (Daniel Mainwaring), in this production by the "Two Dollar Bills"—William Pine and William Thomas. Jean Parker plays Morris' bride (called Louise Campbell, no relation to the actress). They rent a room at Reno's Truckee River Hotel, from which Morris begins investigating the kidnapping of rancher James Kirkwood's son, and soon finds that a bank robbery committed by Dick Purcell is somehow related to the case. Complicated mystery, but solidly cast and interestingly developed. Among the solid citizens are widow Rose Hobart, ranch foreman Rod Cameron, handyman Grant Withers, pianist George Lewis, moll Astrid Allwyn, bartender Jack Norton (the drunk gone sober) and undertaker Lorin Raker, who fashions rabbits from handkerchiefs. Across from the newlyweds' hotel is Edward Earle's mortuary. The handless clock rests here, because, as Earle explains, "Death is timeless"; something to ponder.

PAPER BULLETS *(PRC 1941) Members of a racket— Vince Barnett, Jack LaRue and Joan Woodbury. Picture is better known as* Gangs, Inc.

PAPER BULLETS a.k.a. CRIME INC. (NOT TO BE CONFUSED WITH 1945 ENTRY) (PRC 1941)

Directed by Phil Rosen. Reissued in 1943 as *Gangs, Inc.*, cashing in on Alan Ladd's success. While Ladd has a small role, the film itself is a good one, first to be produced by the King Brothers (then using their real name of Kozinsky), Maurice and Frank. In it, Joan Woodbury, who was raised in an orphanage, goes to prison for a hit-and-run accident committed by playboy Philip Trent. On her release, she forces herself into the graft operations of Trent's reformer father, George Pembroke. Triggerman Jack LaRue and henchman Vince Barnett assist Woodbury. At the time, Trent was being managed by Sue Carol, whose chief client was future husband Ladd. Initially, Ladd was to have taken the role of the playboy and Trent had been scheduled for the undercover agent who masquerades as his gangster double. They switched parts for good results; less than a year later, Ladd was at Paramount, set for major stardom. Rest of the cast features Linda Ware, John Archer, Gavin Gordon, William Halligan, Selmer Jackson, Kenneth Harlan and Bryant Washburn. One of the songs, "Blue Is the Day" was written by Maurice Kozinsky in collaboration with PRC tunesmiths Johnny Lange and Lew Porter. Film's original title refers to the votes which can shoot down dishonest politicians.

SLEEPERS WEST (20th Century-Fox 1941)

Directed by Eugene Forde. Lloyd Nolan starred as Brett Halliday's detective Michael Shayne in seven comedy-action features for Fox. Three were adapted from other works, including *Sleepers West,* second in the series. It was based on Frederick Nebel's 1933 novel *Sleepers East* which was first filmed under that title in 1934 with Preston Foster and Wynne Gibson. In the Nolan remake, the sleuth is escorting Mary Beth Hughes on a train from Denver to San Francisco, where she can clear a wrongly convicted murderer. Hampering Nolan's assignment are a train full of interested passengers, led by Lynn Bari, a reporter who once loved him, and detective Don Costello, hired to get rid of Hughes before she hits Frisco. Ed Brophy, Don Douglas and porter Mantan Moreland are others aboard. Making the film something a bit special are the scenes between Hughes and Louis Jean Heydt, who's thinking of leaving his wife. The two have a brief attraction, beautifully understated, which they enjoy for the moment before moving on. And this is accomplished without so much as an embrace. A good study in restraint, as Peverell Marley's camerawork contributes to the setting.

AFFAIRS OF JIMMY VALENTINE (Republic 1942)

Directed by Bernard Vorhaus. Conceived as a safecracker with charm, Jimmy Valentine was created by O. Henry in 1909. In subsequent plays and films, he was always portrayed as a reformed character who might have to use his skills for a good cause. The 1942 film, a remake of Republic's *The Return of Jimmy Valentine* (1936), starts with a radio program based on Valentine's exploits. When a reward of $100,000 is offered for the whereabouts of the real Valentine, the advertising agency sends Dennis O'Keefe and assistant, little George E. Stone, out into the field. After they run down leads to a

SLEEPERS WEST *(20th Century-Fox 1941) Lloyd Nolan, as Detective Michael Shayne, is confronted by crooked Don Costello, representing a gubernatorial candidate whose son is guilty of murder.*

small town, a series of murders commences; the shock is that Stone is the brutal killer. O'Keefe finds news editor Roman Bohnen to be Valentine, who has settled there with several of his former associates, to a life of respectability. John Alton's cinematography is exceptional and Vorhaus' fluid direction is hampered only by a musical score (directed by later Broadway producer Cy Feuer) which all too frequently plays up the comic aspects. A good cast delineates small-town types: Ruth Terry, Gloria Dickson, Harry Shannon, Spencer Charters, Roscoe Ates, Jed Prouty and Joe Cunningham. *Unforgotten Crime* is the film's TV title.

AFFAIRS OF JIMMY VALENTINE *(Republic 1942) Reporter Dennis O'Keefe is unaware that Ruth Terry is daughter of the man he's seeking, Jimmy Valentine (Roman Bohnen).*

THE FALCON TAKES OVER (RKO Radio 1942)

Directed by Irving Reis. George Sanders' third outing as The Falcon was an adaptation of Raymond Chandler's 1940 Philip Marlowe novel *Farewell, My Lovely.* With the setting changed from Beverly Hills to New York City, the

KID GLOVE KILLER *(MGM 1942)* Lee Bowman, in the title role, Marsha Hunt and Van Heflin amidst the wonders of modern crime detection.

MURDER IN THE BIG HOUSE *(Warner Bros. 1942)* Van Johnson, in his starring debut, and Ruth Ford face trouble.

action gets underway as wrestler and ex-convict Ward Bond wrecks a night spot, Club 13, in his attempts to find lost love Velma. The theft of Helen Gilbert's necklace and the uncovering of a seance racket revolving around psychic Turhan Bey are but two of the plot threads. The Frank Fenton-Lynn Root adaptation allows for Sanders' interaction with inspector James Gleason, The Falcon's assistant Allen Jenkins and others within and without the book. Lynn Bari, as a novice reporter, Anne Revere, Harry Shannon, Hans Conried and Selmer Jackson are all involved. Just two years later, the remake—*Murder, My Sweet* (also RKO)—changed Dick Powell's career. The Robert Mitchum version, *Farewell My Lovely* (Avco Embassy 1975), was well regarded, also, but the original has a lot to recommend.

KID GLOVE KILLER (MGM 1942) Directed by Fred Zinnemann. After making a number of shorts for MGM, including entries in the "Crime Does Not Pay" series, director Zinnemann made his American feature debut with a well rendered crime film. Bringing things full cycle, *Kid Glove Killer* was an expansion of the Oscar-nominated "Crime Does Not Pay" entry *They're Always Caught* (1938), directed by Harold S. Bucquet. Set in Chatsburg, *Kid Glove* revolves around Lee Bowman, lawyer, special prosecutor, radio commentator and campaign manager for successful mayoral candidate Samuel S. Hinds. Bowman also works for hoodlum John Litel and undermines everything Hinds is attempting to achieve. Bowman and police lab analyst Van Heflin are both interested in the latter's assistant Marsha Hunt and, when Bowman kills Hinds with a car bomb, Heflin is the expert who sorts out the clues leading to him. Heflin is quite animated as the brusque, dedicated, off-center analyst, a character ideal for the series—one which failed to materialize. Eddie Quillan goes dramatic as a suspect, and among the many bits is Ava Gardner, as a carhop kissing her husband (not Mickey Rooney). Production titles, *Then There Were Two* and *Along Came Murder.* Zinnemann quickly graduated to A features and in 1948 directed Heflin in a superb performance in *Act of Violence.*

MURDER IN THE BIG HOUSE (Warner Bros. 1942) Directed by B. Reeves Eason. Reissued in 1945 as *Born for Trouble,* after Van Johnson had become a top name at MGM. In his first starring role, but not at the studio with which he'd be forever identified, Van Johnson plays a cub reporter assigned to cover the execution of Michael Ames (later Tod Andrews). When Ames is killed via the headphones on a radio set, Johnson suspects murder and eventually is able to prove that the headphones were connected to the switch on the electric chair. Aiding Johnson is fellow reporter Faye

Emerson, later to become famous as an early television star. Roland Drew has a colorful role as Ames' partner in crime, faking death to further complicate the plot. Ruth Ford plays Drew's wife and George Meeker is the news ace whose boozing gives Johnson his big break. Told in Warners' swift style, it features such sterling players as Frank Wilcox, Joseph Crehan, Douglas Wood, William Gould and Pat McVey (who was also a better known TV name via his "Big Town" series).

SHERLOCK HOLMES AND THE SECRET WEAP-ON (Universal 1942) Directed by Roy William Neill. Based on Arthur Conan Doyle's 1903 story "The Adventure of the Dancing Men," this one went into production as *Sherlock Holmes Fights Back*. When Universal revived the Sherlock Holmes films after two major productions from 20th Century-Fox, the settings were updated to wartime as the definitive deductive duo operated in contemporary settings. They were, of course, Basil Rathbone as the fabulous sleuth and Nigel Bruce as his Dr. Watson. This, second of the 12 in the Universal series, was the first to be directed by Neill, who helmed all of the succeeding entries. It also introduced the recurring characters of Inspector Lestrade, played with perpetual petulance by Dennis Hoey, and Professor Moriarty, done in the magnificently malevolent style of Lionel Atwill. The story begins when Rathbone, disguised as a book peddler, thwarts a Nazi plot to abduct Swiss inventor William Post, Jr. Removing him from Zurich to England, Rathbone then must help protect Post's bomb sight. The British Air Ministry is anxious to keep the plans out of Gestapo hands, but Atwill steps in to betray his country by aiding the enemy. At one point, during a confrontation with Atwill, Rathbone finds himself strapped to an operating table, his blood being drained from his body drop by drop. Atwill sees this as a good means of not only torturing but also eliminating Rathbone, although of course that would never happen. The memorable torture scene elevates the film above others in the group. With Kaaren Verne, Phillip Van Zandt, Paul Fix, Robert O. Davis (a.k.a. Rudolph Anders) and, naturally, Mary Gordon as housekeeper Mrs. Hudson.

STREET OF CHANCE (Paramount 1942) Directed by Jack Hively. This is called in some circles the best B picture ever made, while others think it's more than a B feature. In any case, it's a fine adaptation (by Garrett Fort) of Cornell Woolrich's 1941 novel *The Black Curtain,* delving into the darker aspects of life. Burgess Meredith finds himself on a street, completely unaware of who he is and what he's doing. An encounter with Claire Trevor at a boarding house is a key to fitting all of the pieces together, and he learns that he has a wife, Louise Platt, and is involved in a murder. In a well-played

Basil Rathbone and Nigel Bruce perform on the "Sherlock Holmes" radio show on the Mutual Network in 1943. See Sherlock Holmes And The Secret Weapon *(1942 entry).*

scene, he has to communicate with Adeline de Walt Reynolds, a paralyzed, wheelchair-bound old woman who witnessed the murder. Jerome Cowan, Frieda Inescort, Sheldon Leonard, Arthur Loft and Ann Doran have roles in this top mystery, and although the identity of the killer may be predictable, the path leading to the denouement is a compelling one.

DANGEROUS BLONDES (Columbia 1943) Directed by Leigh Jason. Funny and involved comedy-mystery adapted from the story "If the Shroud Fits" by Kelley Roos, with Allyn Joslyn and Evelyn Keyes as a mystery writer and his wife who prefer solving crimes. Killings plague Edmund Lowe's fashion photography studio, after secretary Anita Louise reports that someone tried to murder her there. Mary Forbes, aunt of Lowe's

DANGEROUS BLONDES (Columbia 1943) *Murder mystery with Evelyn Keyes, Bess Flowers, Edmund Lowe, John Hubbard, Michael Duane. Known as Queen of the Dress Extras, Bess had not merely a supporting role but was a prime suspect.*

THE FALCON STRIKES BACK *(RKO Radio 1943) Intruder Rita Corday forces herself upon Tom Conway and his hangover in a Falcon adventure. She was also known as Paula Corday and Paule Croset.*

UNKNOWN GUEST *(Monogram 1943) Even when telephoning, Victor Jory has a sinister look.*

wife Ann Savage, is stabbed and evidence points to older model Bess Flowers, an apparent suicide. Inspector Frank Craven, whom Joslyn is fond of besting, is satisfied that the case is closed—until Savage turns up dead. Nice set pieces: Joslyn spills luminous paint on himself and glows in the dark; Horace McMahon and Dwight Frye (in his last screen appearance) are briefly menacing at a nightclub; announcer Don Wilson plays himself and spoofs his craft. Typically good supporting cast: John Hubbard, Michael Duane, William Demarest, Hobart Cavanaugh, Frank Sully, Lynn Merrick, Stanley Brown, John Abbott, Minerva Urecal and Ray Teal. During production this was called first *Restless Lady,* then *The Case of the Dangerous Blondes.* In 1944, Joslyn and Keyes did a sequel of sorts, *Strange Affair,* as different characters but with similar sleuthing interests.

THE FALCON STRIKES BACK (RKO Radio 1943) Directed by Edward Dmytryk. Having inherited

the role of suave sleuth The Falcon from his brother George Sanders, with whom he appeared in *The Falcon's Brother* (1942)—art imitating life—Tom Conway made his first solo effort. As one of the best in the series, extending until 1946 with the star, this revolves around a $250,000 war bond robbery. Following a strange encounter with a saloon that becomes a knitting center, Conway arrives incognito at Pinecrest Lodge. His contact Rita Corday is promptly killed and a houseful of suspects is discovered. These people are: manager Harriet Hilliard, her ex-convict/male nurse husband Erford Gage, wealthy but ill Andre Charlot, miserly puppeteer Edgar Kennedy, and knitting center head Wynne Gibson. Most prove to be other than what they pretend, as Conway finds out, enlisting the aid of reporter Jane Randolph and houseboy Richard Loo. The usually slapstick-prone Kennedy does well with his dramatic role as an unsavory character, and part of the film's bizarre charm revolves around his puppets, performing "Bluebeard," with a Goofy caricature giving the tag line (Goofy was a character creation of Walt Disney, then releasing through RKO). Another interesting bit concerned the introduction of a character at the film's end, which set up a situation in the next entry. Here it's Jean Brooks, unbilled, who had a lead in the follow-up film, *The Falcon in Danger* (1943). Cliff Edwards, Cliff Clark, Ed Gargan, Byron Foulger, Joan Barclay, Olin Howlin, Eddie Dunn, Frank Faylen, Jack Norton and The Velma Dawson Puppets also are in the cast of *The Falcon Strikes Back.*

MURDER ON THE WATERFRONT (Warner Bros. 1943) Directed by B. Reaves Eason. Based on the play *Without Warning* by Ralph Spenser Zink, this is a reworking of Boris Karloff's *The Invisible Menace* (1938). Even the armed services weren't immune to murder mysteries during the war; this quickie (Warners' shortest feature at a spare 51 minutes) is rather savage in its violence as killings occur on a naval base. A secret thermostat belonging to the Navy is the object of a Nazi saboteur who proves to be a member of the military. Sailor Warren Douglas, scoring in his none-too-bright characterization, is intent upon having some time with bride Joan Winfield as the troops are being entertained by various acts—among them, knife-thrower Don Costello (doubled by expert Steve Clemento) and wife-assistant Ruth Ford. Surgeon John Loder immediately becomes a chief suspect and seemingly everyone is put under scrutiny: Bill Crago, James Flavin, Bill Kennedy, William B. Davidson, DeWolfe (William) Hopper, Frank Mayo, Fred Kelsey and hula dancer Mary Landa, who performs to "In Waikiki" (Arthur Schwartz and Johnny Mercer, from 1941's *Navy Blues*). Fast and brutal, it was called *The Navy Gets Rough* during production.

UNKNOWN GUEST (Monogram 1943) Directed by Kurt Neumann. King Brothers Production with a music

score by Dimitri Tiomkin. Suspenseful mystery with Victor Jory as a presumed murderer, on the run after a shooting in a cafe, hiding out at The Happy Hunting Lodge run by his miserly aunt and uncle, Nora Cecil and Lee "Lasses" White. Waitress Pamela Blake is told by Jory that he's in charge during their absence. His actions and the arrival of Paul Fix and Ray Walker, supposed hunters who may be gunmen, arouse the suspicions of Sheriff Emory Parnell, realtor Harry Hayden and Blake. Soon Jory's moll Veda Ann Borg shows up and they have a falling out after he accuses her of informing on him. Blake begins playing up to him, falling in love, and then starts to realize that Jory may have killed his relatives and buried the bodies in the wine cellar. Suspense builds nicely as Jory handles all questions with a sneer or nasty crack. Blessed with a deep and distinctive voice, Jory was equally well cast as tough heroes or tougher villains. The cast is peopled with many familiar faces, mostly in small parts: Bernard Gorcey, Frank Faylen, Dick Rich, Emmett Lynn, Paul Porcasi, Jody Gilbert and Edwin Mills. *I Was a Criminal* was the production title, and it's very good of its type.

GIRL IN THE CASE (Columbia 1944) Directed by William Berke. Lawyer Edmund Lowe is in the process of buying an anniversary present for wife Janis Carter when Robert Scott hires him. Since Lowe is an expert at picking locks, he's asked to open an old chest and, in so doing, becomes involves with enemy agents led by Richard Hale. Funny happenings, with Stanley Clements a standout as Lowe's juvenile assistant. The main problem is that Lowe, good as he is, proves to be much too old for the beautiful Carter (53 to her 26). On the other hand, it may just be a film ahead of its time. Robert B. Williams and Carole Mathews are also in the cast.

NINE GIRLS (Columbia 1944) Directed by Leigh Jason. Based on the play by Wilfrid H. Pettitt. Mystery is secondary to comedy, as the wisecracks fly and the killer

NINE GIRLS *(Columbia 1944) Standing: Jeff Donnell, Jinx Falkenburg, Anita Louise, Nina Foch, Lynn Merrick, Marcia Mae Jones, Shirley Mills. Seated: Leslie Brooks, William Demarest and Evelyn Keyes. All in a day's work.*

WHEN STRANGERS MARRY *(Monogram 1944) Involved in a murder case, Robert Mitchum and Kim Hunter. The missing Dean Jagger is suspect.*

revealed long before the end. The nine are sorority sisters at a California college, reduced by one when not-well-liked Anita Louise is done in. The other eight, all suspect: future teacher Evelyn Keyes, medical student Jinx Falkenburg, Louise's relation Leslie Brooks, drama student Lynn Merrick, athlete Jeff Donnell, top student Nina Foch, and new pledges Shirley Mills and Marcia Mae Jones, with Ann Harding as their chaperone. After the murder, captain Willard Robertson and detective William Demarest arrive on the scene. Since the women dominate, only Demarest among the male contingent has a chance to shine and resorts to pratfalls when the occasion demands. Lester Matthews as Louise's father and Grady Sutton as a photographer round out the cast. Considering all of the young talent on hand, only one could really be considered a newcomer: Nina Foch, in her second film. The others were varying degrees of veterans: Louise and Jones had made silent films, the former as a child and the latter as a baby; Keyes had debuted in 1938, top model Falkenburg made films as early as 1936, Donnell had worked steadily since 1942, and Mills had starred in the exploitation feature *Child Bride* (1938), which called for nudity. The other two had worked before name changes: Leslie Brooks was show-girl Lorraine Gettman as early as 1941 and Lynn, formerly Marilyn, Merrick went back to 1940, often as a Western heroine. As many a critic said, these nine were good company.

WHEN STRANGERS MARRY (Monogram 1944) Directed by William Castle. Production title, *I Married a Stranger*; 1947 reissue one, *Betrayed,* with third-billed Robert Mitchum elevated to star position. Made in just ten days and praised highly, this tight thriller has good production values by the King Brothers, a score by Dimitri Tiomkin and a script on which Philip Yordan worked. The last named wrote and produced Humphrey Bogart's final film, *The Harder They Fall* (1956). Waitress Kim Hunter (in the third of her too few films) arrives in

New York to meet Dean Jagger, the husband she barely knows, and finds that he may be involved in the murder of Dick Elliott, who was attending a convention. Salesman Mitchum, an old flame of Hunter's, and police lieutenant Neil Hamilton try to assist her in searching for the missing Jagger, whose absence may be an indication of his guilt. A trip through Harlem's jazz joints provides good diversion from the suspense. Interesting camerawork by Ira Morgan, a PRC and Monogram regular, includes a borrowing from Hitchcock's *The 39 Steps:* a screaming mouth is quickly cut into the blast of a train whistle from a tunnel. Martin Cohn's editing shouldn't be overlooked in this instance. In a tiny part, one of her first, is Rhonda Fleming, a few years before she was a gorgeous lead in many action features, including *Out of the Past* (1947), costarring with Jane Greer and Mitchum.

ALLOTMENT WIVES a.k.a. WOMAN IN THE CASE (Monogram 1945) Directed by William Nigh. In 1945 and 1946, Thirties star Kay Francis co-produced (with partner Jeffrey Bernerd) and starred in three features for Monogram release, her last screen efforts. Second of these was a surprisingly good crime melodrama which allowed her to be totally unsympathetic and fascinating at the same time. The film begins as a mini-documentary, introducing the governmental Office of Dependency Benefits which supported the dependents of servicemen. Although released months after war's end, it was clear that benefits were necessary until all of the military personnel returned home. Kay plays a San Francisco socialite, head of a servicemen's canteen, proprietress of a beauty salon, and chief of a bigamy racket in which young women marry servicemen for their allotment checks. Amidst all this activity, she attempts to raise her rebellious daughter Teala Loring. To expose the racket, Army major Paul Kelly goes undercover as a reporter (another surprise derives from the lack of a romantic attachment between Kelly and Francis). An old acquaintance, Gertrude Michael, threatens to reveal Kay's humble origins and also to lead Loring further astray. Kay's cold-blooded killing of Michael erases any sympathy her character might have gained. Otto Kruger is ever suave and ever crafty as Kay's highly supportive associate and Selmer Jackson, usually a solid citizen, has a colorful role as a cultured member of the crime ring. Anthony Warde also goes against type as a law officer, while Bernard Nedell and Matty Fain are true to their typecasting as criminals. Although she comes to a well deserved end, Kay Francis rewards herself with a memorable exit line.

CRIME, INC. (PRC 1945) Directed by Lew Landers. Based on the book by Martin Mooney, who also co-produced. Some casting surprises here as well: Leo Carrillo portrays a gangster without resorting to an

accent; Lionel Atwill is a member of a crime ring rather than the homicidal fiend he seemed to enjoy playing; and Grant Mitchell and Sheldon Leonard switch sides, with the former as a criminal and the latter as a police captain. Star Tom Neal appears to be portraying author Mooney, as a crime reporter who finds that racketeering is big business and has been organized by some of the most respected citizens in his city. Matters begin to heat up when Neal chooses jail rather than revealing the source of his stories. Also, affable hood Danny Morton is shot to death while seated in a wax museum electric chair; he's the brother of Neal's sweetheart Martha Tilton, a singer. She and Virginia Vale share the honors on the four songs written by the teams of Jay Livingston and Ray Evans, Marla Shelton (the actress) and Nacio Herb Brown. A better than normal cast participates: Harry Shannon, Don Beddoe, George Meeker, Michael Mark, Stanley Price, Robert Strange and Emmett Vogan. Set in New York, site of most of the better gangster dramas. [At the CoOp on a Friday the 13th in 1973, as a tribute to Tom Neal. One wag, impressed by the cast and production, termed *Crime, Inc.* "the *Gone With the Wind* of PRC."]

DETOUR *(PRC 1945) The title says it all: Tom Neal and Ann Savage.*

ALLOTMENT WIVES *(Monogram 1945) Racketeers Otto Kruger and Kay Francis are shocked to find her daughter Teala Loring turning wayward; best of the three Francis-produced features of 1945-6.*

DETOUR (PRC 1945) Directed by Edgar G. Ulmer. Screenplay by Martin Goldsmith, from his 1939 novel. The very best film ever made by PRC, by general consensus. A hero beset by fate and a heroine consumed by greed and evil might be descriptive of stars Tom Neal

and Ann Savage; actually antihero and villainess are simpler terms. A piano player's attempts to reach his sweetheart a continent away is also a terse plot synopsis. Neal, in New York, hitchhikes to Los Angeles to join girlfriend Claudia Drake, a singer, and is picked up by Edmund MacDonald, who seems to have problems of his own. When MacDonald dies accidentally, Neal panics and fears he'll be charged with murder. Actually, the unconscious man fell out of the car and struck his head on a rock when Neal opened the door. As fate would have it, Neal later picks up his own hitchhiker, Ann Savage, a nasty type who had earlier been given a lift by MacDonald. Knowing that the dead man was heir to a fortune, she forces Neal into carrying on an impersonation. Later, he attempts to stop her from making a phone call and accidentally strangles her with the cord. Now responsible for two deaths, Neal awaits his true fate, the detour he couldn't avoid. Moody photography by Benjamin Kline makes this six-day wonder a visual treat. Drake warbles the 1927 standard "I Can't Believe that You're in Love With Me" (Jimmy McHugh-Clarence Gaskill). The volatile Neal, a former boxer, could have predicted his own fate from this film: he served time for the accidental killing of his last wife and died shortly after being paroled, in 1972. (For 1990 release, a remake of *Detour* was shot in Missouri by film historian-distributor-director Wade Williams. Its stars: Lee Lavish, in the Savage role, and, in an intriguing twist, Tom Neal, Jr.)

DILLINGER (Monogram 1945) Directed by Max Nosseck. Top-rated crime thriller which established Lawrence Tierney as a screen tough guy, starring with Anne Jeffreys, fellow contract player at RKO, she on loan out and he between contracts. After the King Brothers production, they returned to the home studio for better assignments. Tierney, of course, is John Dillinger, in jail for petty theft, where he meets a gang composed of

DILLINGER *(Monogram 1945) Anne Jeffreys and Law-rence Tierney in a top rated crime drama. Background banner is an anachronism: Monogram released* Barefoot Boy *in 1938, four years after Dillinger's death.*

Edmund Lowe, Eduardo Ciannelli, Elisha Cook, Jr., and Marc Lawrence (obviously an all-star prison). Once released, they get together to stage several successful bank robberies. Tierney takes over the leadership from Lowe and makes Jeffreys his moll. Back in stir again, Tierney escapes to kill Lowe, who he suspects had fingered him, and then disposes of accomplice Ralph Lewis, the new favorite of Jeffreys. At this, she becomes the infamous Lady in Red and sets him up for killing by the FBI as they leave a Chicago movie house. The theater, The Biograph, placed a commemorative plaque to record the event for posterity. Tierney does well by director Nosseck, a Polish-born moviemaker who also guided him through three other films. This version of the Dillinger legend is better than the 1973 concoction from AIP, with Warren Oates playing him as a more rustic killer, and it even brought an Oscar nomination to Philip Yordan for Best Original Screenplay. Australian Constance Worth, who starred at RKO in her American debut (*China Passage,* 1937) and had a number of bits there through 1949, has a brief role.

THE GREAT FLAMARION (Republic 1945)

Directed by Anthony Mann. Vaudeville as murder melodrama, with settings in Mexico City, San Francisco and Chicago. Marksman Erich von Stroheim has as assistants Mary Beth Hughes and husband Dan Duryea. When Hughes arouses his interest, von Stroheim arranges an "accidental" death for her spouse, but when Hughes spurns him and goes off in tandem with Stephen Barclay, joining his bicycle act, a humiliated von Stroheim proceeds to strangle her, realizing that women have always been his downfall. Mann uses lighting to achieve a murky backstage atmosphere, and also includes such elements as: songs written by Faith Watson and Lester Allen, cartwheels by composer/comic Allen, Mexican dances by Fred Velasco and Carmen Lopez, and Mexican songs sung by Tony Farrell. It was all based on a character in "Big Shot" (a double meaning title), a *Collier's* magazine story by Vicki (*Grand Hotel*) Baum.

MY NAME IS JULIA ROSS (Columbia 1945)

Directed by Joseph H. Lewis. Considered to be among the best of the *film noir* school, this is a modern day "old house" mystery with marvelous visuals. Innocent Nina Foch, hired as a secretary, becomes a pawn in a plot by evil George Macready to get his murdered wife's inheritance. German actor Roland Varno is Foch's sweetheart and sweet old Dame May Whitty portrays Macready's wealthy mother with a sinister quality unsuspected by her admirers. It wasn't altogether apparent at the time, but *Dead of Winter* (1987), the suspenser with Mary Steenburgen and Roddy McDowall, was a remake, the star playing three roles, including Julie Rose.

MY NAME IS JULIA ROSS *(Columbia 1945) Up to no good: Anita Bolster (aka Sharp-Bolster), Leonard Mudie and Dame May Whitty.*

THE POWER OF THE WHISTLER *(Columbia 1945)*
Performing in the best of its series are Richard Dix, Janis Carter and Jeff Donnell.

THE POWER OF THE WHISTLER (Columbia 1945) Directed by Lew Landers. The CBS radio program "The Whistler," tales of suspense, led to an eight film series and later a syndicated television series. The Whistler was a shadowy figure with a deep voice who narrated the stories. Richard Dix starred in all but one of the features, making his last appearances in varied roles (a detective, an artist, head of a trucking company). The third entry, and best of the group, casts him as an amnesiac with Janis Carter foreseeing death in his future, during a Greenwich Village encounter. She, sister Jeff Donnell and Donnell's fiance, Loren Tindall, piece together Dix's past and come up with a startling discovery: he's a homicidal maniac. Colorful characters, including Tala Birell, John Abbott, Kenneth MacDonald and I. Stanford Jolley (once Warren William's stand-in), and a well-developed plot move things along to a smash climax. One of Dix's most impressive portrayals.

RIVER GANG (Universal 1945) Produced and directed by Charles David, from the story "Fairy Tale Murder" which he wrote with Hugh Gray. Screenplay by Leslie Charteris. Stylish melodrama, verging on fantasy, one of just two American films by French director David (the other: *Lady on a Train* in 1945 with future wife Deanna Durbin). Gloria Jean believes in fantasy, while her uncle John Qualen, an antique dealer, is more realistic and gives musical instruments as protection to Keefe Brasselle's gang, so they won't break his shop windows. Irish cop Bill Goodwin comes on the scene to investigate after peg-legged Sheldon Leonard, unrecognizable underneath his makeup, sells a cursed Stradivarius violin and is crushed to death under a carlift. Brasselle, here making his film debut at 21, displays the brashness he used as his style. Vince Barnett oddly enough plays another peg-leg, an organ grinder. A good deal of offbeat casting helps put this into a class of under-appreciated features.

THE SCARLET CLUE (Monogram 1945) Directed by Phil Rosen. Contemporary technology makes this the best of the Monogram Charlie Chan features. Radar secrets are sought at a radio center, which houses a TV studio and a research lab and where phone messages are answered via a teletype. A body which fell through a trap door in an elevator is found in the laboratory weather tunnel and poisonous gas is released by a shortwave beam. Aiding Sidney Toler are Number Three Son Benson Fong and chauffeur Mantan Moreland, who, naturally, tangles with the disguised killer. Suspects abound: unpleasant radio producer Virginia Brissac, meek secretary Milton Kibbee, actress Helen Devereaux, actress-blackmailer Janet Shaw, station manager I. Stanford Jolley, announcer Reid Kilpatrick, actor Jack Norton,

employee Charles Jordan, Swedish washwoman Victoria Faust, Shakespearean actor and monster portrayer Leonard Mudie. (On the radio, Norton plays women's roles, but for television, he does his specialty, a drunk—certainly as bizarre as it sounds.)

BEHIND THE MASK a.k.a. THE SHADOW IN BEHIND THE MASK (Monogram 1946) Directed by Phil Karlson. Lamont Cranston, The Shadow, began as a hero of pulp fiction, became a fictional radio personality and ultimately switched to films. In 1937-38, former silent star Rod LaRocque had two Shadow outings, one poor, one fair. The 1940 serial featured Victor Jory. Then, in 1946, Kane Richmond made three entertaining fea-

BEHIND THE MASK *(Monogram 1946) Dorothea Kent and Barbara Reed (Read) are shocked by George Chandler's reaction to Kane Richmond's brutality, but the men are reconstructing a murder in this Shadow installment.*

MURDER IN THE MUSIC HALL *(Republic 1946)*
William Marshall and Vera Hruba Ralston find Edward Norris' body next to the Music Hall.

tures with the accent on comedy, whenever the melodrama didn't intrude. In the second of the three, Richmond postpones his marriage to sweetheart Barbara Reed to tackle an important case. Blackmailing columnist Robert Shayne has been murdered, bookie Marjorie Hoshelle being just one of his victims. Complicating Richmond's investigation is the knowledge that an impersonator of The Shadow is apparently guilty. Pierre Watkin as Commissioner Weston starred in all three films with Richmond and Reed. For this entry, George Chandler is chauffeur Shrevvie (as in Shreveport), Dorothea Kent is his silly girl Jennie, and Joseph Crehan plays Inspector Cardona. This comedy-mystery also included June Clyde, James Cardwell, Joyce Compton, Ed Gargan, and a jazz and organ score directed by Edward Kay. *The Shadow's Shadow* was the in-production title.

THE GLASS ALIBI (Republic 1946)

Produced and directed by W. Lee Wilder. Film master Billy Wilder's often forgotten brother alternated between crime and science fiction themes in his film work. This, his first American effort, is unquestionably his best—an ironic, adult tale worthy of Billy himself. Although Paul Kelly gets first billing, Douglas Fowley takes top honors, playing an opportunistic reporter who persuades wealthy Santa Monican Maris Wrixon to marry him. He and girlfriend Anne Gwynne are planning on Wrixon soon succumbing to her heart ailment, leaving them to enjoy her money. Renewed by love, Wrixon finds her condition improving, prompting an impatient Fowley to plot the "perfect" murder, but homicide detective Kelly is able to provide an unexpected twist that lets him nab the killer. A sharp screenplay and spicy dialogue are provided by the equally forgotten Mindret Lord.

HER ADVENTUROUS NIGHT (Universal 1946)

Directed by John Rawlins. Comedy mystery with an adolescent twist. Imaginative Scotty Beckett, 14-year-old son of Dennis O'Keefe and Helen Walker (latter was about 25 at the time), is caught trying to bring his father's gun into school. Long before that became a serious real-life problem, it was introduced as a comic element. Having long been suspicious of principal Tom Powers, Beckett embellishes a story about events surrounding a fifteen-year-old crime. In flashback, O'Keefe is seen as a telephone lineman as he encounters Walker, who's eloping. Mutual dislike naturally turns to love as the two are thrown together by Powers, who's hiding from the police after a robbery and killing. The three find shelter at Charles Judels' home, where O'Keefe attempts to overpower Powers, who flees. Back to the present, Beckett feels it's up to him to bring the real culprit to justice and he lays a trap. While the young actor dominates the surrounding story, he naturally is nowhere to be found in the main part of the proceedings. O'Keefe and Walker age not a bit from one era to another, but the improbability of the whole affair doesn't intrude on the fun. Other leading roles are played by Fuzzy Knight, Milburn Stone, Betty Compson, Bennie Bartlett and Peggy Webber.

MURDER IN THE MUSIC HALL (Republic 1946)

Directed by John English. Reissued in 1951 as *Midnight Melody*. Actually, it's murder next to the Music Hall, as producer-blackmailer Edward Norris is stabbed to death in his penthouse. With a wealth of song and ice skating numbers woven into the plot, it's appropriate that his demise is at a piano. The much-maligned Vera Hruba Ralston stars in one of her best films, displaying her skating skills in ice numbers directed by Fanchon, with a cast and production elaborate enough to consider this an A. Music Hall ice ballerina Ralston and orchestra leader William Marshall (not the later black exploitation star) find the body. Suspects under Inspector William Gargan's scrutiny: showgirls Helen Walker, Ann Rutherford and Julie Bishop (a good lineup right there), socialite and ex-ice performer Nancy Kelly, her columnist-husband Jerome Cowan, stage manager Frank Orth and, of course, Jack LaRue. There's a highly effective scene with a blind man to provide a false lead. Fay McKenzie has a singing bit. A Republic treat.

MYSTERIOUS INTRUDER (Columbia 1946)

Directed by William Castle. For the fifth of "The Whistler" series, Richard Dix gives his finest latter day performance. Once a major star of silents and early sound films, he had headed the casts of many B Westerns before finding work in the low-budgeted Columbia series. Rather than merely showing up for work and

HER ADVENTUROUS NIGHT
(Universal 1946) Bank robber Tom Powers, telephone lineman Dennis O'Keefe and Charles Judels protecting his wine vat.

NIGHT EDITOR *(Columbia 1946) Covering up their involvement in a crime are Janis Carter and William Gargan.*

reading his lines, he regularly put forth an admirable effort in his characterizations. Playing a private investigator, he isn't above some unethical practices in tracking down two very valuable Jenny Lind recordings. There's a high mortality rate among the cast: Paul E. Burns, Mike Mazurki, Helen Mowery, Harlan Briggs, Pamela Blake, Barton MacLane, Nina Vale, Regis Toomey, Charles Lane and Kathleen Howard. Despite the plethora of B movie talent, Dix makes the film his.

NIGHT EDITOR (Columbia 1946) Directed by Henry Levin. Based on the story "Inside Story" by Scott Littleton, as presented on the "Night Editor" radio program created by Hal Burdick. Offbeat detective story, with a nice guy hero turning bad for a no-good woman. The twist here is that such a solid citizen as William

SO DARK THE NIGHT *(Columbia 1946) Micheline Cheirel and Steven Geray share brief happiness, as he later investigates her murder in one of the best psychological mysteries ever.*

Gargan portrays that part. Fitting into the structure of the radio show, the film begins with Charles D. Brown, night editor of the *New York Star,* trying to straighten out wayward young reporter Coulter Irwin by recalling the story of police lieutenant Gargan, happily married to Jeff Donnell until he meets socialite Janis Carter, wife of older Roy Gordon. Gargan and Carter begin stepping out on their spouses and one night, while parked on a deserted road, they witness a killing. Neither want to reveal what they know, fearing a scandal, but Gargan finds that Carter knows the murderer, Frank Wilcox, a banker. Since she's blackmailing Wilcox, Carter provides Gargan with an alibi. After confessing his involvement, Gargan attempts to persuade Carter to do the same but, in the middle of a kiss, she stabs him. A twist ending reveals that it wasn't the climax of Gargan's story. (So identified with the detective genre was William Gargan that he was also starring at the time as an investigator on radio's "I Deal in Crime.") Good acting all around, particularly by Carter and Donnell as the bad and good influences in a man's life.

SO DARK THE NIGHT (Columbia 1946) Directed by Joseph H. Lewis. A melodrama of particular distinction, superbly designed and photographed (by Burnett Guffey). The leads are played by actors generally seen in secondary parts. Making the most of his starring role is Steven Geray, Czech-born veteran of the Hungarian stage and British screen, as a senior inspector of the French Surete. Taking a much delayed vacation in the countryside, he stops at the inn run by Eugene Borden and Ann Codee and promptly falls in love with their daughter, comely young Micheline Cheirel. For a time, he believes that the much younger Cheirel returns that affection until she runs off with her true love, farmer Paul Marion. Realizing that happiness wasn't meant for him, especially at his age, Geray is soon confronted by the double murder of Cheirel and Marion and later by that of the mercenary Codee. Actor Geray is as good as both the stylish lighting and dazzling photography. Among a mixed cast of both French and American actors is one Theodore Gottlieb, a strange-looking young actor later famed as the stranger-acting monologist Brother Theodore.

STEP BY STEP (RKO Radio 1946) Directed by Phil Rosen. Nicely turned out melodramatics, reuniting Lawrence Tierney and Anne Jeffreys from *Dillinger* (see 1945 entry) in a lighter vein. Ex-marine Tierney and secretary Jeffreys meet on a Malibu beach, and spend a full reel in just their bathing suits before becoming involved in a plot by ex-Nazis to steal valuable government papers. Along the way, they hide out at colorful George Cleveland's motel colony, while dodging such baddies as

Lowell Gilmore, Jason Robards (Sr.) and Myrna Dell. Young actors Phil Warren, Lee Bonnell, Robert Clarke and Tommy Noonan, then part of the RKO family, play bits. Even as a hero, Tierney always managed to be menacing, although this is his most sympathetic part.

THE UNKNOWN (Columbia 1946) Directed by Henry Levin. The "I Love a Mystery" series originated on radio in 1939, created and written by Carlton E. Morse. It was entirely different from his previous hit, "One Man's Family," although three of that series' actors had the leads on the mystery show. The main characters were Jack Packard, of superior intelligence; Doc Long, a master locksmith; and Reggie York, an Englishman with incredible strength (at one time, Tony Randall had this part on radio). The three Columbia features of 1945-46 eliminated the part of Reggie and concentrated on the offbeat aspects of Jack and Doc's cases. Jim Bannon was Jack and Barton Yarborough (later Jack Webb's original partner on the "Dragnet" radio and TV series) repeated his radio characterization of the Texan, Doc. In this excellent last of a three-film series, which was produced by Wallace MacDonald, heirs to a fortune arrive at a mansion for the reading of a will, but only one—top-billed Karen Morley—appears to be normal. Bannon and Yarborough are called in to investigate strange doings, including the cry of a seemingly nonexistent baby and the presence of an ax murderer. This particular script was an adaptation of the radio episode titled "Faith, Hope and Charity Sisters." Jeff Donnell, Robert Wilcox, Robert Scott (Mark Roberts), James Bell, Wilton Graff, Helen Freeman, Russell Hicks and Robert Stevens (Kellard) also appear in this compact drama, production title of which was *The Coffin*.

DICK TRACY'S DILEMMA (RKO Radio 1947) Directed by John Rawlins. Production title, *Dick Tracy vs. the Claw.* Originating in 1931 as a comic strip, Dick Tracy has passed into legend as fiction's most resourceful police detective. Creator Chester Gould kept up with the latest technology for the pursuit of criminals and invented numerous gadgets. For the third of four feature films made from the strip, Ralph Byrd returned to the role he had originated in the Dick Tracy serials, four Republic cliffhangers, 1937-41. Morgan Conway played Tracy in the first two features, but Byrd *was* Tracy to movie buffs. (He also had the part in the one-season TV series made just before his death in 1952.) Kay Christopher portrayed his Tess Trueheart, while Lyle Latell continued in the role of partner Pat Patton—the only one to repeat his character in all four features. Fur robbers and killers concern Byrd in *Dilemma,* especially their vicious leader Jack Lambert. He's The Claw, who kills with the hook he has in place of a hand. Other colorful characters in this entry include

DICK TRACY'S DILEMMA *(RKO Radio 1947) Harry Harvey, Ralph Byrd (as Tracy) and Lyle Latell get down to police work.*

Ian Keith as hammy Vitamin Flintheart, Bernadene Hayes as Longshot Lillie, and Jimmy Conlin as phony blind man Sightless. Each of the Tracy features provided stock footage for the others in the series, part of the films' unconscious appeal. Seen originally in 1947, the film left an impression on buffs by the demise of The Claw, electrocuted when his hook hit a high tension wire.

THE GUILTY (Monogram 1947) Directed by John Reinhardt. Based on Cornell Woolrich's short story "He Looked like Murder," later entitled "Two Fellows in a Furnished Room." Intriguingly complex tale, as are all good Woolriches, in which Don Castle recalls his search for the killer of girlfriend Bonita Granville's twin sister (also Granville). Although the two had distinct personalities, he really isn't sure which one was killed or who may be guilty. It could have been Wally Cassell or John Litel, who were both involved with the women, or even police detective Regis Toomey. For once, the outcome is as unpredictable as anyone could wish. This was the first film to be produced by Texas oilman Jack Wrather who was to marry Bonita Granville just prior to the film's release. They became partners in the Wrather Corporation, producing the "Lone Ranger" and "Lassie" series for television, had four children and remained wed for life.

HIGH TIDE (Monogram 1947) Directed by John Reinhardt. Based on the story "Inside Job" by Raoul Whitfield, this is a good adult drama of corruption concerning gangsters and a newspaper empire, produced by Jack Wrather. Two men trapped in a wrecked car on a beach find the tide threatening to engulf them. In flashback, we learn that the younger man, Don Castle, is a none-too-ethical private investigator called to Los Angeles by editor Lee Tracy, his companion in the car, who has been threatened for articles condemning An-

HIGH TIDE *(Monogram 1947) Publisher Douglas Walton is restrained by Lee Tracy, his editor, in a dispute with detective Don Castle, once involved with Julie Bishop, Walton's wife.*

thony Warde's criminal activities. Publisher Douglas Walton, also the object of threats, is married to ambitious Julie Bishop, Castle's old flame. Secretary Annabel Shaw would like Castle to keep away from Bishop's clutches. When Walton is killed and Tracy wounded, police inspector Regis Toomey determines to prove Castle guilty. Tracy, in his last starring film (his only later appearance was in *The Best Man* in 1964), is as dynamic as ever, while Castle—once considered a younger version of Clark Gable—portrays a solidly shady hero. Veteran Francis Ford has a nice bit, as does Argentina Brunetti as a gangland widow. In an interview I had with the Wrathers in 1979, when they were announcing production on the large-scale *The Legend of the Lone Ranger* (1981), they reminisced about their earlier work and this film in particular (after I'd made a point of saying that it was one of my favorites). Don Castle had been close to them and was best man at their wedding. At the time of *High Tide,* he was part owner of a commercial 16mm film production company headed by Wrather. Later switching from acting to producing, Castle was associate producer for the "Lassie" TV show. He died following a traffic accident in 1966 at age 47.

SHOOT TO KILL (Screen Guild 1947) Produced and directed by William Berke. Reissued as *Police Reporter.* Interesting gangland drama, told in flashback from her hospital bed by Susan (Luana) Walters, the wife of gangster Douglas Blackley, framed by the mob for trying to move in on its rackets. (Blackley was better known as Robert Kent.) Walters had obtained a position as secretary to assistant district attorney Edmund MacDonald, who is in league with rackets kingpin Nestor Paiva, and the evidence she uncovers on her boss is turned over to reporter Russell Wade (who didn't resort to a later name change). Together, they attempt to expose MacDonald and clear Blackley. Vince Barnett, the bald comedian, has a brief bit as a janitor in the courtroom around which much of the action revolves, while Gene

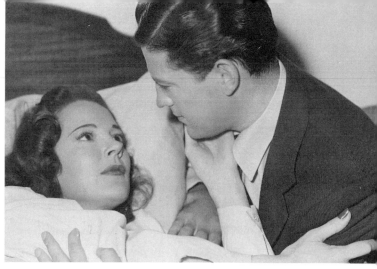

SHOOT TO KILL *(Screen Guild 1947) From her hospital bed, Susan (Luana) Walters confers with Russell Wade.*

Rodgers is seen doing his specialty, playing piano at a nightclub. A Lippert presentation, before that production company also became a distributor.

CLOSE-UP *(Eagle-Lion 1948) Alan Baxter, with a silencer, pursues Richard Kollmar, a Nazi war criminal, to the foot of 93rd Street and the East River in New York.*

CLOSE-UP (Eagle-Lion 1948) Directed by Jack Donohue. New York locales offer good background to an unusual tale of a former Nazi being pursued through postwar Manhattan. While making a fashion shoot, newsreel cameraman Alan Baxter unknowingly catches Richard Kollmar, the Nazi, on film. Thereafter, the film becomes of interest to those aiding Kollmar's flight. Reporter Virginia Gilmore proves to be a member of the gang of Nazis, headed by sadistic Philip Huston. At the insistence of New York police authorities when the script was submitted for approval, Huston is portrayed as a former actor rather than an ex-policeman as originally written (story by James Poe, screenplay by John Bright, Max Wilk, Donohue). In the course of the action, Baxter proves himself to be an energetic hero by transferring from one moving ferryboat to another (close inspection will show that the boats are actually moving slowly, but the effect is achieved). Gilmore was at the time Mrs. Yul Brynner, while Kollmar—once radio's Boston Blackie—also had a better known spouse, columnist Dorothy Kilgallen with whom he had a husband-and-wife radio show; this was his only movie. Broadway comedian Joey Faye plays Baxter's comic sidekick, while Sid Melton, who was to become a regular in most of Lippert's features, went for laughs as a cabbie. Canadian-born Western actor Kenne Duncan, in what could be his only East Coast feature, appears briefly as a detective. Many of the locales seen in the film have changed considerably, so the Marathon Pictures production takes on an historical significance unintended at the time the film was made. The distributor's Manhattan office serves as the headquarters for Argus Newsreel.

HE WALKED BY NIGHT (Eagle-Lion 1948) Directed by Alfred Werker and uncredited Anthony Mann. Based on a true case and filmed to a great extent in the giant drainage pipes of Los Angeles' County Flood Control System. Officer John McGuire is killed by Richard Basehart, a vicious thief of superior intelligence. Captain Roy Roberts and detective Scott Brady lead the manhunt for Basehart, finally trapping him in the storm drains. Excellent semi-documentary whose realism had a profound effect on featured actor Jack Webb, who was said to have based his successful "Dragnet" series (radio-TV-films) on the happenings depicted. Narrated by Reed Hadley, the feature offers a host of familiar faces for easy identification: Whit Bissell, James Cardwell, TV's Jack Bailey, Byron Foulger and wife Dorothy Adams, Wally Vernon, Ann Doran, Harlan Warde, Lyle Latell, Frank Cady, Robert Bice, John Dehner, Kenneth Tobey, Jane Adams, even Carlotta Monti—formerly associated with W. C. Fields. Los Angeles Police Chief Bradley appears as himself. Called *29 Clues* while in production, it remains one of the best films of its kind in any category.

HE WALKED BY NIGHT *(Eagle-Lion 1948) Richard Basehart is about to murder radio patrolman John McGuire, prompting a massive manhunt.*

GUN CRAZY *(United Artists 1949) Following her aborted stardom in* Forever Amber *(she was replaced by Linda Darnell) and his appearance in Hitchcock's* Rope, *Peggy Cummins and John Dall had their best roles as a Bonnie and Clyde duo.*

FOLLOW ME QUIETLY (RKO Radio 1949) Directed by Richard Fleischer and uncredited Anthony Mann. Story by Mann and Francis Rosenwald; screenplay by Lillie Hayward. Running just an hour, this tight little B tells a terrific story about a daring murderer who considers himself judge and executioner. As played by ugly Edwin Max, he calls himself The Judge. Detective William Lundigan takes the case and participates in a truly bizarre scene in which a life-size dummy of the killer is suddenly replaced by The Judge himself, at police headquarters. It isn't logical, just unnerving. Dorothy Patrick costars as a working woman, reporter for a magazine that specializes in sensational photos of crime cases, and as Lundigan's romantic interest. Paul Guilfoyle plays the husband of a strangulation victim; Douglas Spencer, a psycho pseudo-judge; Jeff Corey, a police assistant, and Max as the killer. Coincidentally, Guilfoyle costarred in another 1949 film, called *The Judge.* Climactic chase through a gas plant is similar to that in the classic serial *Daredevils of the Red Circle* (1939).

GUN CRAZY, formerly DEADLY IS THE FEMALE (United Artists 1949) Directed by Joseph H. Lewis. Based on the *Saturday Evening Post* story "Gun Crazy" by MacKinlay Kantor, with a screenplay by Kantor and Millard Kaufman, this is an updated retelling of the Bonnie and Clyde saga, with a pair of star-crossed lovers turning to crime because of their expert marksmanship. John Dall, played at age seven by Mickey Little and at 14 by Rusty (Russ) Tamblyn, loves guns and teaches himself to be an expert shot. He soon falls for Peggy Cummins, a sharpshooter with Berry Kroeger's carnival, and teaming up, they become bank robbers (one theft, shot entirely from the back seat of the getaway car, is a realistic touch very much ahead of its time). Although cold-blooded Cummins kills without emotion, Dall can't bring himself to shoot anyone—until the showdown. Boyhood friends Harry Lewis and Nedrick Young play an important part in that decision. Morris Carnovsky has a small part as the judge who sentences Tamblyn for his gun craze, while singer Frances Irwin introduces "Mad About You" (Victor Young-Ned Washington), which sums up the Dall-Cummins relationship. Russell Harlan's fluid camera uses such locales as Los Angeles' Great Armour Packing Plant; Montrose, for the bank robbery, and the mountains of Baldwin Estates for the climax. Technical adviser was Al Jennings, the 85-year-old train robber of another day, obviously an ideal choice. The drama originally had been scheduled for Allied Artists release.

TRAPPED (Eagle-Lion 1949) Directed by Richard Fleischer. Made with the cooperation of the Treasury

Department, this taut melodrama concerns the tracking down of a counterfeiting ring. The plan goes into motion when T-man John Hoyt infiltrates the gang as counterfeiter Lloyd Bridges is allowed to escape as a means of smoking out its members. Odd casting has Hoyt, usually a sinister type, here playing the heroic undercover man and Bridges, the nice guy, as a hardened criminal. Ill-fated (in real life) Barbara Payton is seen as an ill-fated cigarette girl. Some interesting locales give punch to the action scenes.

ARMORED CAR ROBBERY (RKO Radio 1950)

Directed by Richard Fleischer. The last of Fleischer's handful of fine crime capers before he went on to major assignments is among his best work—a taut, realistic drama. William Talman is the cold-blooded head of a ring which robs an armored car at Los Angeles' Wrigley Field, its final stop. Police lieutenant Charles McGraw takes a personal interest in the case as he and associates—Don McGuire, James Flavin, et al.—track down Talman and gang—Douglas Fowley, Steve Brodie and Gene Evans. Stripper Adele Jergens, Talman's girlfriend, becomes a pawn in McGraw's efforts to trap the gang leader, who dies a spectacular death. James Bush and Anne Nagel, leads in earlier B efforts, here have bits; in support is Don Haggerty, star of one of TV's earliest filmed detective shows, "Cases of Eddie Drake" (1952).

MYSTERY STREET (MGM 1950)

Directed by John Sturges. For his MGM debut, Sturges was given one more low budgeter to prove his worth, along with the talents of a top cast, a screenplay by Richard Brooks (soon to direct, also) and Sydney Boehm, based on a story by Leonard Spigelgass (who won an Oscar nomination for it), and John Alton's photography of Boston and surrounding areas. The results: a well-made thriller singled out for special recognition. It begins on a surprisingly tawdry note when Edmon Ryan, a Cape Cod man of position, finds that his prostitute mistress Jan Sterling is pregnant, shoots her, and throws the body in the ocean. Hispanic police lieutenant Ricardo Montalban of the Barnstable, Massachusetts, police force, investigates when the remains are found. Aiding him is Bruce Bennett, chief medical researcher for the Department of Legal Medicine of Harvard University's Medical School. With just a skeleton as evidence, Bennett and associates begin reconstructing Sterling's identity. Marshall Thompson, married to Sally Forrest, is implicated, but Montalban realizes that he was only trying to help Sterling rather than harm her. Then Ryan has to deal with Elsa Lanchester, Sterling's gin-loving landlady, who begins dabbling in blackmail. Some social comment along with the detective work concerns the subtleties of class distinction. With Betsy Blair, Willard Waterman,

TRAPPED *(Eagle-Lion 1949) In a prearranged escape, FBI guard Robert Karnes allows himself to be overpowered by Lloyd Bridges, a counterfeiter. The Bureau wants Bridges to lead them to his associates.*

MYSTERY STREET *(MGM 1950) Elsa Lanchester discovers the price of blackmail at the hands of brutal Edmon Ryan in a Massachusetts-set mystery.*

Walter Burke, King Donovan, Ned Glass and the silent screen's Matt Moore and May McAvoy.

SIDESHOW (Monogram 1950)

Directed by Jean Yarbrough. Last starring role of Don McGuire and among the last films of the actor who would eventually receive

SIDESHOW *(Monogram 1950) More mayhem lurks as Don McGuire carries a pursuit through a wax museum.*

SOUTHSIDE 1-1000 *(Allied Artists/Monogram 1950) One-time Warners mainstays in lighter roles, George Tobias and Don DeFore find themselves on opposite sides of the law.*

credit as one of the original writers on Dustin Hoffman's *Tootsie* (1982). He's an undercover treasury agent who traces the source of jewel smuggling to a carnival, where he encounters sideshow operators John Abbott and Ray Walker, cooch dancer Tracey Roberts, and such comic types as Eddie Quillan, Iris Adrian and Jimmy Conlin. The trail eventually leads McGuire to a pursuit through a wax museum. Nicely done, but really short on mystery.

THE SLEEPING CITY (Universal-International 1950)
Directed by George Sherman. Shot entirely in New York City, under the title *Web of the City,* largely at Bellevue Hospital. Star Richard Conte points out in the foreword that none of these events actually took place at Bellevue, but the Jo Eisinger story and screenplay has the air of reality to it. Drugs are the cause of deaths at the hospital, including doctor Alex Nicol's suicide. Undercover agent Conte, posing as an intern, finds that nurse Coleen Gray—to whom he's attracted—is involved. Richard Taber, who also appeared with Conte in *Under the Gun* (1950), has a colorful role as an elevator operator. John Alexander, Peggy Dow and such New York types as Robert Strauss, Jack Lescoulie (later the famed TV announcer), Dort Clark and James Daly have roles. Well regarded and one of the first Hollywood-based productions intended to be shot entirely in New York City, according to director Sherman.

SOUTHSIDE 1-1000 (Allied Artists/Monogram 1950)
Directed by Boris Ingster, who also co-scripted with Leo Townsend. Another documentary-like depiction of the cracking of a counterfeiting ring, narrated by Gerald Mohr, was based on the actual case of an engraver making plates in prison. The story was written by Milton M. Raison and by Bert C. Brown, who had been in charge of the Secret Service's Chicago office for two decades. Taken from U.S. Secret Service files, the King Brothers production uses Washington, D.C., San Quentin and Los Angeles for effective backgrounds. Convict Morris Ankrum has smuggled the plates out of prison, so enter agent Don DeFore as an undercover man. Posing as an Eastern operator, he journeys to the West Coast for the purchase of a large amount of bills. A romance with Andrea King ends with the revelation of her involvement in the ring. DeFore and George Tobias (said to have mastered 36 dialects) were usually associated with comic roles and here do admirable work in serious parts, the latter as a vicious killer. Ingster shows a fascination for heights by staging death scenes around high places, with double-crossing Barry Kelley (who

WESTERN PACIFIC AGENT *(Lippert 1950) Robber Mickey Knox, The West Coast Kid, hits his grocer father Morris Carnovsky with a jar after being accused of a murder.*

replaced Paul Douglas on Broadway in *Born Yesterday*) being pushed through a 12-story window. The climax was shot at L.A.'s Angels Flight (a.k.a. Angels Leap), a 50-year-old cable line on which a tram transported passengers on a track 100 yards long and some 40 yards in the air. Kippee Valez sings "Je T'Aime" (Fritz Rotter-Harold Stern). DeFore, King and Tobias coincidentally all had been Warner Bros. players in the Forties.

WESTERN PACIFIC AGENT (Lippert 1950)
Directed by Sam Newfield. After years with PRC, the prolific Newfield switched to Lippert with brother Sigmund Neufeld producing, as always. One of the brothers' very best is this crime drama in which the heroes become secondary to the villain. Filmed largely at Oroville in the Feather River country of Northern California, it introduced the Western Pacific Railroad's new super streamliner the Zephyr Vista Dome. Some scenes were shot on the train's San Francisco-to-Chicago run. Aboard is Jason Robards (Sr.), oddly unbilled as the narrator of the story, telling it to fellow passenger Vera Marshe. Ex-convict Mickey Knox has been mistreating his father Morris Carnovsky, a hardworking grocer, and demanding money. Intent upon stealing a fruit pickers' payroll, Knox kills bridge tender Anthony Jochim and paymaster Robert Lowery, then flees. Lowery's sister Sheila Ryan helps special agent Kent Taylor in his search for the murderer. Sid Melton tries to supply some comedy, while Western villain Charles King turns up briefly as a vagrant. Knox's acting was highly praised for its intensity; he's so rotten that he tries to kill the decent Carnovsky. A distinguished stage actor, Carnovsky made limited film appearances, and doesn't give the impression that he's inhibited by such modest circumstances as this low-budget Lippert winner.

WOMEN FROM HEADQUARTERS a.k.a. WOMAN FROM HEADQUARTERS (Republic 1950)
Directed by George Blair. Very good police drama, made with the full cooperation of the L.A.P.D., revolves around lady cops. Twelve female graduates of the L.A. Police Academy in Elysian Park appear in the training scenes filmed there, while Sergeant Mary Galton served as technical adviser. Rookie Virginia Huston not only attempts to reform wayward Barbra Fuller, mixed up with hoodlum Norman Budd, but also helps sergeant Robert Rockwell, with whom she's romantically involved, to smash a drug ring. Jack Kruschen and, as a very authentic looking policewoman, Frances Charles, who was in other films, are in support. Fuller, from radio's "One Man's Family," was typecast as a blonde menace. Luther Crockett's police chief is based on the real Chief William A. Worton. Some realistic touches lift this above the usual run of films of the day, particularly those from action oriented Republic.

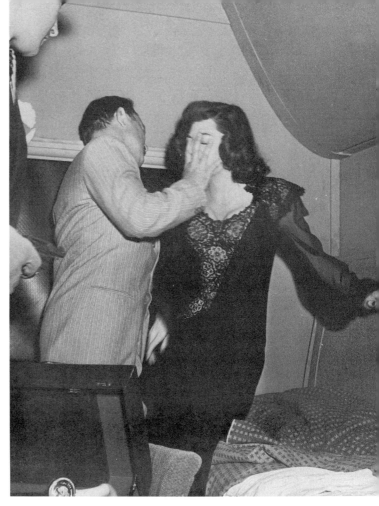

THE NARROW MARGIN *(RKO Radio 1952) In close quarters (a train compartment), Peter Virgo and David Clarke treat Marie Windsor as criminals would.*

THE NARROW MARGIN (RKO Radio 1952)
Directed by Richard Fleischer. A sleeper in its day and still highly effective, it was made for just $230,000 under the production title *Target*. Earl Felton's taut screenplay, from an Oscar-nominated story by Martin Goldsmith and Jack Leonard, sets the action aboard a Chicago-Los Angeles train, as police sergeant Charles McGraw escorts gangster's widow Marie Windsor to testify at a trial. He must protect her from the gang that killed his partner Don Beddoe. Meanwhile, he's become friendly with fellow passenger Jacqueline White and her (hilariously) obnoxious son Gordon Gebert. A sinister fat man, Paul Maxey, also presents a problem as McGraw relies on brute strength as well as cunning to outwit the team of David Clarke, Peter Virgo and unbilled Peter Brocco. No music is used, except as natural background on the radio or the jazz records Windsor plays in her cramped compartment. Windsor appeared in some of the best *films noir* of the period: *Force of Evil* (1948), *The Sniper* (1952), *The Killing* (1956), and in this claustrophobic classic, matches McGraw's tough performance, asking no sympathy and receiving none. Remade in 1990 with Gene Hackman.

THE BURGLAR *(Columbia 1957) A pensive couple in a moody crime drama, Dan Duryea and Martha Vickers.*

THE BURGLAR (Columbia 1957) Directed by Paul Wendkos. Screenplay by David Goodis, based on his novel. In this moody crime drama, filmed almost entirely in Philadelphia, with some footage of Atlantic City, Dan Duryea gives a fine performance as the American equivalent of a doomed French hero. He heads a burglary gang which includes his half-sister Jayne Mansfield, Mickey Shaughnessy and Peter Capell. They plan to steal the jewels of spiritualist Phoebe Mackay, while Martha Vickers and crooked cop Stewart Bradley intend to then relieve Duryea's crew of the gems. The brooding camerawork of Don Malkames and some highly imaginative special effects—particularly in the flashback scenes in which Richard Emery and Andrea McLaughlin portray Duryea and Mansfield as children—make this something unusual and extremely effective. By contrast, the French-Italian remake, *The Burglars* (1972) with Jean-Paul Belmondo, Omar Sharif and Dyan Cannon, while action-packed, is played with a light touch.

THE GIRL IN BLACK STOCKINGS (United Artists 1957) Directed by Howard Koch. Based on the

story "Wanton Murder" by Peter Godfrey, called simply *Black Stockings* while in production, and filmed in Kanab, Utah. The title character is a corpse at the beginning of the mystery, which is rife with suspects having hidden motives and neurotic personalities. Set at Three Lakes, a Utah resort, it concerns mutilation murders of beautiful women with the swimming pool a handy dumping ground. Hollywood lawyer Lex Barker, virtually the only non-suspect, turns detective late in the proceedings. In the cast, and therefore under suspicion, are inhibited secretary Anne Bancroft, alcoholic ex-star John Holland, model Mamie Van Doren, paralyzed lodge owner Ron Randell, his protective sister Marie Windsor, Indian handyman Larry Chance, millworker Gerald Frank, telephone worker Diana Vandervlis, detective Gene O'Donnell, sheriff John Dehner, and Stuart Whitman—who has a personal stake in the investigation. In a rare film appearance, Dan Blocker (soon to be riding the Ponderosa as Hoss in TV's "Bonanza") plays a larcenous bartender (adding to the observation that no one can be trusted).

SHORT CUT TO HELL (Paramount 1957) Directed by James Cagney. W. R. Burnett's screenplay for *This Gun for Hire* (1942), from Graham Greene's novel, originally published in England in 1936 as *A Gun for Sale,* served as source material. Cagney appears in the prologue and the trailer for this, his only directing job, produced by his good friend A. C. Lyles, known for his star-packed low-budgeters. This is a good remake of the classic original, which made a star of Alan Ladd as the hired killer. Unfortunately, Robert Ivers didn't have Ladd's charisma nor did Georgann Johnson in Veronica Lake's part. After being paid in stolen money for two murders, Ivers sets out to take revenge upon Jacques Aubuchon, the man who hired him, and, in so doing, kidnaps Johnson, a girlfriend of William Bishop, the detective investigating the killings. Gradually, Johnson begins to help Ivers and not just to save herself. Also with Yvette Vickers (said to be a Cagney discovery), Peter Baldwin, Murvyn Vye and Milton Frome. Originally in VistaVision, this was producer Lyles' first and best effort, as tough as would be expected from the dynamic Cagney.

THE BONNIE PARKER STORY (American International 1958) Directed by William Witney. Far removed from *Bonnie and Clyde* (1967), with Dorothy Provine as waitress Bonnie wed to Richard Bakalyan, as bank robber Duke Jefferson, serving time in Texas. Jack Hogan as Guy Darrow becomes the main man in her life

THE GIRL IN BLACK STOCKINGS *(United Artists 1957) Reacting to the discovery of a body are Marie Windsor, Diana Vandervlis (Van Der Vlis) and Mamie Van Doren.*

when she joins him and his brother, played by Joseph Turkel, for their own crime ring. Turkel is killed, Bakalyan is freed from jail and then gunned down in an armored car robbery, and Provine grows hard and hateful of all men. Texas Ranger Douglas Kennedy sets up a roadblock which spells the end for Provine and Hogan. Narration by Vince Williams attempts to give it an air of authenticity, but the action and Provine's performance overcome that. Bob Steele has a bit as an armored car guard. Originally in Superama, subtitled *The Female Monster*, and released with *Machine Gun Kelly* (see below).

THE COOL AND THE CRAZY (American International 1958)

Directed by William Witney. Filmed in Kansas City, this seemingly ordinary youth-gang-gets-hooked melodrama benefits from the outstanding performance of Scott Marlowe. He plays a teen addict and drug pusher for supplier Marvin J. Rosen, and takes over Dick Jones' gang. One of its members, Richard Bakalyan, falls for sweet Gigi Perreau, and is nearly killed by Marlowe. The latter does succeed in murdering Rosen,

SHORT CUT TO HELL *(Paramount 1957) Cops Joe Bassett and Hugh Lawrence, Georgann Johnson, Milton Frome and Peter Baldwin surround Robert Ivers on the ground in a remake of* This Gun For Hire *(1942).*

who refuses to supply more dope on credit. Before coming to a sorry end, Marlowe shows how to deal with plot and budget restrictions by his acting, used to better advantage in a later TV career. Title song, appropriate to the times, is by Bill Nolan and Ronnie Norman. Originally released with *Dragstrip Riot,* featuring Fay Wray.

THE CRY BABY KILLER *(Allied Artists 1958) Starring in his first film, Jack Nicholson is a crazy, mixed-up kid who holds Smoki Whitfield and mother Barbara Knudson hostage.*

THE CRY BABY KILLER (Allied Artists 1958)

Directed by Justus Addiss. Screenplay by Leo Gordon and Melvin Levy, based on Gordon's story. In his film debut in the title role, 21-year-old Jack Nicholson works with Roger Corman for the first time. Nicholson really isn't a killer, but he does shoot nasty Brett Halsey and pal James Fillmore over Carolyn Mitchell, Jack's girl. Hiding in a storeroom with a gun, Nicholson holds black worker Jordan (Smoki) Whitfield and Barbara Knudson and her baby as hostages. Police lieutenant Harry Lauter, outside, attempts to persuade Nicholson to surrender, as TV cameras add to the circus-like atmosphere. Executive producer Corman is seen as Joe, a TV crewman, while author Gordon and Corman regular Bruno VeSota appear as radicals. Dick Kallman also appears, to sing "Cry Baby Cry," which he wrote. Suspenseful little thriller, set at night in and around the drive-in restaurant and teen hangout, presents a capable performance by Nicholson, who had to wait another dozen years before finding major stardom. Originally released with *Hot Car Girl,* produced by Gene Corman (Roger's brother).

MACHINE GUN KELLY (American International 1958)

Produced and directed by Roger Corman. This was the year in which Charles Bronson became a star of action films, although it would take another decade for him to gain international recognition; with this film, Roger Corman began receiving attention from the European critics. A good throwback to the gangster films of the Thirties, this boasts a leading character who wasn't overly exploited. Bronson plays Kelly as a conscienceless killer, but his moll Susan Cabot displays the real brains. After dabbling in bank robbery, they decide that kidnapping is an easier way to make a good deal of money (little Lori Martin, later on TV's "National Velvet," is their victim). Cowardly gang member Morey Amsterdam, who picks up the ransom, proves Bronson's undoing by informing on him to the police. Although he kills Amsterdam, Bronson surrenders (as did the real Ma-

MACHINE GUN KELLY *(American International 1958) Charles Bronson has the title role in an early starring effort.*

chine Gun Kelly) rather than go down fighting. Amsterdam, usually a comic, has an interesting role, as does Connie Gilchrist as a madame. Other unsavory types are provided by Jack Lambert, Wally Campo, Barboura Morris, Frank De Kova and Richard Devon. Originally released in Superama with *The Bonnie Parker Story* (as above).

THE CRIMSON KIMONO (Columbia 1959)

Produced, directed and written by Samuel Fuller. Interracial love and anti-female sentiment are just two ingredients of the maverick moviemaker's interesting crime drama. Los Angeles' Little Tokyo district comes under scrutiny as detectives and longtime friends James Shigeta and Glenn Corbett investigate the murder of stripper Gloria Pall. Art teacher Victoria Shaw, a near victim of the killer, provides assistance and comfort to the detectives, both being attracted to her. Corbett finds that she prefers the Japanese Shigeta (in his U.S. debut). The two men fight over her, but Shigeta prevails and the pals forget their differences to solve the killing. Anna Lee has a great part as a kooky artist, quite a departure for this charming but usually reserved British veteran. Probably by design, Fuller cast four varying nationalities in the leads: English-born Lee, Shigeta (from Hawaii), Shaw (from Australia) and Corbett (from the good old U.S. of A.). Some Fuller veterans are featured, along with Paul Dubov, Jaclynne Greene, Neyle Morrow and Walter Burke.

WICKED, WICKED (United National Pictures/ MGM 1973)

Produced, directed and written by Richard L. Bare. An offbeat comedy mystery in Metrocolor and Duo-Vision—a split screen process in which two separate actions are shown, in this case events either happening at the same time or from different points of view. It was shot at the historic Hotel del Coronado in

WICKED, WICKED *(MGM 1973) In time honored fashion, Randolph Roberts disguises himself before committing a crime.*

Coronado, California (recognizable as the Florida setting of *Some Like It Hot,* 1959). Here, blonde guests are savagely murdered. Called the Grandview Hotel in the film, the beachfront residence becomes a deathtrap for Diane McBain, first stabbing victim. Security officer David Bailey suspects foul play when McBain disappears, but manager Roger Bowen feels that she's left without paying the bill. Things become complicated when singer Tiffany Bolling, Bailey's former wife, arrives to perform, in a blonde wig. Handyman Randolph Roberts is unmasked to the audience halfway through, as the killer. Police sergeant Scott Brady, however, suspects waiter Edd Byrnes. Bailey, meanwhile, assisted by chief electrician Arthur O'Connell, guards Bolling, who nearly becomes the next victim. Madeleine Sherwood, a penniless ex-actress, isn't so fortunate. At intervals, Maryesther Denver plays the organ score which has become identified with the silent classic *The Phantom of the Opera* (1925). Lots of film clips and references to please the real buff. Comedy tends to predominate, even in the dismemberment scenes (film was rated PG). Bailey, in a rare starring assignment, is more familiar for his many TV commercials.

THE CRIMSON KIMONO *(Columbia 1959) Artist Victoria Shaw is a house guest of policemen James Shigeta and Glenn Corbett, becoming friendly with the former.*

GRACE BRADLEY

ROBERT WILCOX *in* Island of
Doomed Men *(Columbia 1940)*

LEWIS HOWARD

RALPH BELLAMY

ELISSA LANDI

MARION MARTIN

GALE SONDERGAARD

THE SEA GHOST (Peerless 1931) Directed by William Nigh. Two silent stars in a kind of last stand: Alan Hale, Sr., in his final starring role as a hero and Laura La Plante in her last American starrer, before toplining some British pictures through 1935. The adventure, set in 1925 New Orleans, casts Hale as a disgraced World War I naval officer now the captain of a salvage ship and La Plante as the man-hating owner of a cabaret and heir to a fortune. Peter Erkelenz is a former German submarine commander searching for salvation, not salvage. Comedy comes from Claud Allister as the silly Englishman and from Hale's manhandling of shyster lawyer Clarence Wilson. Reissued by Astor in 1939 around the outbreak of World War II as *U-67* with a prologue emphasizing German submarine warfare.

OUT OF SINGAPORE (Goldsmith-William Steiner 1932) Directed by Charles Hutchison. TV title: *Gangsters of the Sea*. Adventure saga, directed by a star of silent serials, with three former silent film players in the male leads. Noah Beery is the notorious first mate of captain Montagu Love's ship, while heroic George Walsh portrays the second mate, in love with Love's daughter Miriam Seegar. The real action comes from Dorothy Burgess as the Lorelei luring men to their deaths; she performs a sexy dance for the lowlife sailors, knowing that they'll all be blown out of the water. Snowflake and Jimmy Aubrey supply some comedy.

TRAPPED IN TIA JUANA (Mayfair 1932) Directed by Wallace W. Fox. Hilariously inept action comedy-drama-romance, with none of the above. Duncan Renaldo stars as a young American army officer and his long lost twin, a Mexican bandit, struggling with an appropriate vocal inflection in the former part. Although he seemed to have a natural Latin accent, he was actually Romanian. Almost a reel is wasted as the Mexican Renaldo and his guest-captive Edwina Booth prepare coffee and tortillas. If anything, the film proves that Booth did not suffer a fatal illness following *Trader Horn* (1931), the MGM epic which also starred Renaldo. [So bad it's a joke, this was shown at the Club—where it was called "Trapped at the CoOp."]

THE BIG CAGE (Universal 1933) Directed by Kurt Neuman. In his film debut, circus star Clyde Beatty, 29, is billed as the youngest living animal trainer as he works lions and tigers together in one cage for the first time. Based on the book by Beatty and Edward Anthony, adapted by Ferdinand Reyher and Anthony, the story has Clyde adopting little Mickey Rooney, son of drunken trainer Raymond Hatton (whom Beatty doubles in the

THE SEA GHOST (Peerless 1931) Aboard the salvage ship Scavenger, lovely Laura La Plante is about to break into, rather than out of, a cabin.

OUT OF SINGAPORE (Goldsmith-William Steiner 1932) Mate Noah Beery and captain Montagu Love are up to no good, as Dorothy Burgess learns.

TRAPPED IN TIA JUANA (Mayfair 1932) Captive in the bandit's lair—Edwina Booth and Duncan Renaldo in an actionless adventure.

BLIND ADVENTURE *(RKO Radio 1933) Uninvited guests at a London house party, Roland Young—a burglar—and Helen Mack attempt to get past the hostess, Lady Laura Hope Crews. Comedy and adventure.*

KING OF THE JUNGLE *(Paramount 1933) Buster Crabbe and Frances Dee as a pseudo-Tarzan and a fully clothed Jane, in an American setting.*

tiger attack). The all-action feature also stars Anita Page, Wallace Ford, Robert McWade, and the comedy team of Andy Devine and Vince Barnett, and has bits by Walter Brennan and Louise Beavers.

BLIND ADVENTURE (RKO Radio 1933) Directed by Ernest B. Schoedsack. The production team of *King Kong* and *Son of Kong*—including executive producer Merian C. Cooper and scripter Ruth Rose—collaborated on a comedy thriller (*In the Fog* was its production title) set in the fog of London's West End. American Robert Armstrong (star of both *Kongs*) stumbles into a den of extortionists having papers of international significance. The gang is headed by, surprisingly, Ralph Bellamy, just before his good guy image took hold. Helen Mack (who was in *Son of Kong*) heads the impressive cast: John Miljan, Laura Hope Crews, Henry Stephenson, Marjorie Gateson, Beryl Mercer and George K. Arthur. Stealing the whole film, however, is Roland Young as a slippery Cockney who pilfers other things as well. Some of the dialogue was by an uncredited Robert Benchley.

HIGH GEAR a.k.a. THE BIG THRILL (Goldsmith-Hollywood Pictures 1933) Directed by Leigh Jason, who provided the screenplay, along with Rex Taylor and Charles Saxton. Familiar plot, made fresh by the handling: racer James Murray accidentally causes the death of mechanic Mike Donlin, puts Donlin's son Jackie Searl through military school, and regains his lost nerve by helping to save the boy's life. Joan Marsh is the reporter/love interest, Theodore Von Eltz her scandal-loving columnist/beau. Genuinely fine are young Searl in a rare sympathetic performance and the comedy of Yiddish dialectician Eddie Lambert. The tragic Murray (star of the silent classic *The Crowd*, 1928) was on a real-life downward spiral; his marriage to bit actress Marion Sayers (who plays Mamie) lasted for just a short time after the feature's completion.

KING OF THE JUNGLE (Paramount 1933) Directed by H. Bruce Humberstone and Max Marcin. Based on Charles Thurley Stoneham's novel *The Lion's Way*, the Buster Crabbe starrer is a Tarzan adventure under a different name. In Africa, orphaned Ronnie Cosbey is raised by a lioness and grows into Kaspa, the Lion Man (Crabbe). Taken to America by a circus, he escapes and learns to speak English from pretty kindergarten teacher Frances Dee. Returning to the circus, he becomes a star animal trainer—the beasts are his old friends—and saves the day when a fire started by roustabout Warner Richmond causes a stampede. Buster's first starring film came as a result of his 1932

Olympic Gold Medal for swimming; at the time, he was an $8-a-week stock clerk in a Los Angeles clothing store. Sidney Toler, Douglass Dumbrille, Irving Pichel, Robert Barrat, Nydia Westman and some anti-native sentiment figure in. Postscripts: Crabbe did star as Tarzan, in the 1933 serial *Tarzan the Fearless*, and the fire footage from *King* later turned up in Paramount's *Caged Fury* (see 1948 entry), again with Buster.

LAUGHING AT LIFE *(Mascot 1933) As South American revolutionaries, Frankie Darro and Victor McLaglen. One of the best of Thirties adventures.*

LAUGHING AT LIFE (Mascot 1933) Directed by Ford Beebe, from his original story. Production title: *I'll Be Hanged.* Exuberant adventure epic, one of the best independents of the Thirties, starring Victor McLaglen as a worldwide adventurer. Always on the go for excitement, he graduates from seeing action in World War I to supervising a Mexican revolution. While McLaglen naturally dominates, the cast has many names, some on-screen for only seconds. William (Stage) Boyd, Regis Toomey, Ruth Hall and Frankie Darro have more important parts, and the support includes Conchita Montenegro, Lois Wilson, Henry B. Walthall, Guinn (Big Boy) Williams, Ivan Lebedeff, Noah Beery, J. Farrell MacDonald, Tully Marshall, Henry Armetta, Irving Bacon, Pat O'Malley and William Desmond. The action's nonstop as we last see McLaglen riding from danger, but that final shot actually has Yakima Canutt as his riding double.

COME ON MARINES! (Paramount 1934) Directed by Henry Hathaway. Very sexy and funny service comedy-adventure with Richard Arlen leading the Marines to the rescue of ladies in their late teens, stranded on an island. There are enticing shots of Ida Lupino, Ann Sheridan, Toby Wing, Lona Andre, et al., bathing in their scanties and less enticing shots of the Marines (Roscoe Karns, Fuzzy Knight, et al.) imitating them and then having to dress in the girls' frocks. Grace Bradley's dance in a leather outfit, in front of mirrors, adds an almost surreal touch to the pre-Code proceedings.

COME ON MARINES! *(Paramount 1934) Comedy and adventure with Ann Sheridan, Ida Lupino, stalwart Richard Arlen and Toby Wing, bordering on a Marine's fantasy.*

CRIMSON ROMANCE *(Mascot 1934) The low budget version of* Hell's Angels *with James Bush and Ben Lyon in a good World War I adventure.*

CONFLICT *(Universal 1936) John Wayne prepares for battle, with Eddie Borden as second. Best of six Wayne action features.*

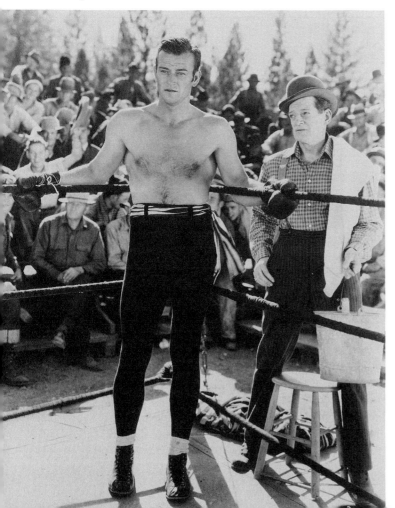

CRIMSON ROMANCE (Mascot 1934) Directed by David Howard. Serviceable B version of the classic *Hell's Angels* (1930) with Ben Lyon in a sympathetic variation of his original part and Erich von Stroheim as the sadistic field commander, the role he should have played in the original. In 1916, Lyon and German pal James Bush join the German Air Corps. When America enters the conflict, Lyon has to forsake Bush and return to his true loyalty. Outstanding, apart from von Stroheim, are drunken Hardie Albright and cowardly William Bakewell as German flyers. Bakewell and Vince Barnett were veterans of the other World War I classic, *All Quiet on the Western Front* (1930). Also in the cast: comical Herman Bing, Jason Robards (Sr.), Sari Maritza, Bodil Rosing—the women are secondary. A Mascot Master Production.

HONG KONG NIGHTS (Walter Futter-First Division 1935) Directed by E. Mason Hopper. Some unusual elements distinguish this actioner, beginning with Tom Keene playing himself (a distinction usually reserved for Western stars, but rarely in other films). Leading lady Wera Engels is Trina Vidor, the last name being that of the director of Keene's major film *Our Daily Bread* (1934), King Vidor. Keene and Warren Hymer are customs agents pursuing gun smugglers led by Cornelius Keefe in Macao. Hymer disappears before the climax, shot on a remote part of Catalina Island, where Keene and Engels bravely face what may be their final danger. A small cast is a minor drawback.

LADIES CRAVE EXCITEMENT (Mascot 1935) Directed by Nick Grinde. Another good Mascot release, combining action and comedy with a typically outstanding cast. Hotshot newsreel cameramen Norman Foster and Eric Linden scramble to keep ahead of a rival agency in the filming of assorted events and disasters and aren't above staging footage for Foster's conception, "March of Events," which might possibly be a familiar practice to latter-day television newsmen. Evalyn Knapp is the excitement-seeking heroine and Esther Ralston the beautiful blonde secretary. Jason Robards and George Hayes are featured and an unbilled Milburn Stone and Marie Wilson turn up as a sailor and his girl. It took two real cameramen, Ernest Miller and William Nobles, to film the events, while one editor—later director Joseph H. Lewis—cut it all together.

PURSUIT (MGM 1935) Directed by Edwin L. Marin. Based on "Gallant Highway," a novel-length story by Lawrence G. Blochman, in *Complete* Magazine, and filmed on highways between San Francisco and Mexico. Living up to its title, the MGM film is the fast-moving account of attempts by pilot Chester Morris and detective Sally Eilers to protect little Scotty Beckett from self-serving relatives. Many conveyances are used as Scotty (of Our Gang) dresses as a girl and dons blackface along with his costars. C. Henry Gordon and Henry Travers supply villainy, and Dorothy Peterson motherly support in this colorful outing.

CONFLICT (Universal 1936) Directed by David Howard. Based on Jack London's novel *The Abysmal Brute,* this one had the production title, *The Showdown.* It is a remake of the Universal silent *The Abysmal Brute* (1923) starring Reginald Denny in a somewhat different story. Second and best of John Wayne's six action adventures from producer Trem Carr, one of two period pieces, and the only one of the six not written directly for the screen. Making this tops is Wayne's performance as a con man reformed by love. He's a logger about to throw a fight with boxer Ward Bond, his partner in crime. Reporter Jean Rogers has to disguise herself as a man to see the fight, as women were then barred from such exhibitions—but she's fetching either way. Filmed in the Sonora area, with Harry Woods, Tommy Bupp and Eddie Borden in the cast. Others in the 1936-37 Wayne series, all worthwhile: *The Sea Spoilers, California Straight Ahead, I Cover the War, Idol of the Crowds* and the pirate saga *Adventure's End.*

I COVER CHINATOWN (Banner-William Steiner 1936) Directed by and starring Norman Foster. One of the most enjoyable comedy melodramas of the decade; Foster's last film as a leading actor and first as director. His work led to a 20th Century-Fox contract and a long career helming A and B features. Remarkably, it was previewed less than two months after filming began (under the title *The Trunk Murder*) in San Francisco, with nice shots of Chinatown, Fisherman's Wharf, the Embarcadero, Market Street, and the Oakland Bay Bridge. The Harry Hamilton plot: Foster is the guide and Vince Barnett the driver of a tour bus through San Francisco's Chinatown. On board is Elaine Shepard, whose sister Polly Ann Young (Foster's actual sister-in-law), has just been strangled by husband Theodore Von Eltz. The latter and brother Edward Emerson receive stolen goods at their Chinatown jewelry store. Arthur Lake has some irrelevant comedy spots on his way to becoming Dagwood Bumstead, and The Royal Hawaiians perform. Leading lady Shepard also changed careers, in real life becoming a news correspondent and writing a book amusingly titled *Forgive Us Our Press Passes.*

THE SPEED REPORTER (Reliable 1936) Produced and directed by Bernard B. Ray. TV title: *Dead Line*. To

I COVER CHINATOWN *(Banner-William Steiner 1936) Elaine Shepard, Norman Foster and Vince Barnett in the feature which turned Foster into a director.*

say that any of Richard Talmadge's talkies were among his best is a mistake, since they were crudely made and designed solely to show off his acrobatic skills. In this, he's a newsman out to get the goods on a supposed group of reformers. A silent screen stuntman who also starred on his own, Talmadge became a second unit director (handling action scenes) on big budget features. His vague accent—he was born in Switzerland—and shy-grinning style of acting were endearing, if nothing else. Luana Walters, Richard Cramer, Bob Walker (not the MGM star), Earl Dwire and, as Renfrew, Frank Crane (no relation to Renfrew of the Royal Mounted), are in the cast whose members manage to mangle pronunciations of that character name.

THE SPEED REPORTER *(Reliable 1936) Mixing it up are Richard Cramer, Richard Talmadge and George Chesebro in a Talmadge special.*

ARCTIC FURY *(RKO/Plymouth Productions 1949) New footage for the reissue of* Tundra *(Burroughs-Tarzan 1936) with Merrill McCormick reprising his old role, joined by Gloria Petroff and Eve Miller.*

YELLOW CARGO *(Pacific Pictures-Grand National 1936) In the !ineup are most of the leads: Claudia Dell, Jack LaRue, Vince Barnett and series stars Eleanor Hunt and Conrad Nagel.*

STRAIGHT FROM THE SHOULDER (Paramount 1936) First feature directed by former editor Stuart Heisler. Also the debut of its leading lady, Katherine Locke, 25, who did few films. Pleasantly filmed on some of the locations used for *The Trail of the Lonesome Pine* (1936), this programmer (shot under the title *Johnny Gets His Gun*) combines action with family elements. Commercial artist Ralph Bellamy witnesses a robbery-murder, is shot in an effort to stop his testimony, and hides out with son David Holt at Andy Clyde's lakeside home. Clyde and Locke, both crack shots, teach the boy to use a rifle; then gangsters Noel Madison and Bert Hanlon arrive to silence Bellamy. Onslow Stevens, Paul Fix, Jack Mulhall also appear, but Chick Chandler doesn't, despite his erroneous billing.

TUNDRA (Burroughs-Tarzan 1936) Directed and written by Norman Dawn, who also photographed with Jacob and Edward Kull. Subtitled *A Saga of the Alaskan*

Wilderness, and based on the experiences of Dr. Thomas Barlow, Alaska's flying doctor, as well as those of the Dearholt, Stout and Cohen film expedition. As fascinating for its history as its visuals, *Tundra* was reportedly started by Carl Laemmle under his regime at Universal, with seven months of filming in the Alaskan wilds. The foreword defines the area as a thousand miles of wilderness, from the Yukon to the Arctic Ocean, with snow, glaciers and green forests. Much footage originated in the silent documentary *Alaskan Adventures* (Pathe 1926) and Dr. Arnold Fanck's Greenland-made *SOS Iceberg* (Universal 1933). From the latter comes the footage of the air, glacier and Eskimo village scenes. *Tundra's* new shots feature Del Cambre and bear cubs Tom and Jerry coping with the elements in a quest for food and shelter. Cambre, an All-American football star-coach, acted briefly and was working for National Screen Service at the time of his death in 1958 at 48; this was his only lead. In 1949, a re-edited version called *Arctic Fury* was released by RKO/Plymouth Productions with new credits and additional footage of Eve Miller and Gloria Petroff playing Cambre's previously unseen wife and daughter. Merrill McCormick repeated his old role of Mac, the trapper, telling the story of the lost doctor (although Dan Riss narrated the by-then old, old footage). Fred R. Feitshans, Jr., directed the few new scenes. In any form, a treat for the kids.

CIRCUS GIRL *(Republic 1937) Circus hazards: apprentice June Travis is told by aerialist Bob Livingston that Betty Compson hasn't been badly harmed by a tiger mauling.*

wrote the Hollywood horror tale *The Day of the Locust.* Truckers Ralph Byrd and Ward Bond drive a load of dynamite needed for the demolition of a dam. Bond, for a change of pace, is a good guy and the hero's pal. Leading lady Doris Weston, a nightclub and radio singer, does some songs; a year earlier, she was starring with Dick Powell in Warner Bros.' *The Singing Marine.*

YELLOW CARGO (Pacific Pictures-Grand National 1936) Directed and written by Crane Wilbur, who also appears. First and best of the four G-men epics starring Conrad Nagel and Eleanor Hunt, here investigating a film production company suspected of smuggling in Chinese aliens—hence the (derogatory) title. Jack LaRue, naturally, heads the gang, with Claudia Dell as a comely assistant. Vince Barnett provides laughs and the Catalina Island exteriors are certainly scenic.

CIRCUS GIRL (Republic 1937) Directed by John H. Auer. Bob Livingston and June Travis made a popular Republic team and this is their best pairing. Footage of the aerial action and the daredevil costumes themselves were later recycled into features and serials. Travis here weds jealous Donald Cook, who tries to kill rival and fellow trapeze artist Livingston. Betty Compson and Charlie Murray of the silent era have good parts and the impressive flying scenes are undertaken by the Escalante Family, doubling for the three leads.

BORN TO BE WILD (Republic 1938) Directed by Joe Kane. The French *Wages of Fear* (1953) owes its inspiration to this and other action features of the era. Novelist Nathanael West provided the script and some sardonic dialogue for Robert Emmett Keane; he later

ROAD DEMON (20th Century-Fox 1938) Directed by Otto Brower. Second in the little known "Sports Adventure" series featuring Henry Armetta as Papa Gambini. This has a lot to recommend it, starting with Armetta's always exasperated character. Lon Chaney, Jr., plays a racing driver and the great Bill (Bojangles) Robinson is seen as the manager of a garage. Hollywood

BORN TO BE WILD *(Republic 1938) Tying up Ralph Byrd and Doris Weston for a happy ending is Ward Bond in a rare good guy assignment.*

FIVE CAME BACK *(RKO Radio 1939) Lucille Ball, Joseph Calleia, C. Aubrey Smith, Allen Jenkins (on the ground), and Chester Morris: not all of the five who return.*

mores being what they were, Robinson constantly refers to the unseen owner of the garage, making it clear that a black couldn't be in charge. Robinson was cut out of several big Fox musicals but here has a totally irrelevant—and most welcome—tap dance amidst tire irons and spares. Johnny Pirrone, Jr., accompanies him on the accordion and also does "The William Tell Overture" during the early truck race. Brower cleverly uses speeded-up photography to make the action look faster than it is in reality. Plot revolves around storekeeper Armetta's investment in a racing car driven by brash Henry Arthur. The only drawbacks to total enjoyment of the comedy and action are Arthur's atrocious performance and leading lady Joan Valerie's only slightly better one (she was previously known as Helen Valkis). Others in the series, also directed by Brower, are *Speed to Burn* (1938) and *Winner Take All* (1939).

FIVE CAME BACK (RKO Radio 1939) Directed by John Farrow. Richard Carroll's story was adapted by Jerry Cady, Dalton Trumbo and Nathanael West, turning a $225,000 effort into one of RKO's hits of the year. Lucille Ball wasn't quite a major star but the Thirties were primarily a learning period for her. Here, she's one of the passengers on The Silver Queen, a Los Angeles-to-Panama clipper which crashes in the jungle. Chester Morris and Kent Taylor are the pilots who attempt to keep order, ever aware that headhunters are nearby. Struggling for survival are John Carradine, Wendy Barrie, Joseph Calleia, Allen Jenkins, Patric Knowles, C. Aubrey Smith, Elisabeth Risdon and Casey Johnson. Farrow remade his film for RKO as *Back From Eternity* (1956) with a bigger budget and cast and less satisfying results.

THE GOOSE STEP a.k.a. BEASTS OF BERLIN (PDC, later PRC 1939) Directed by Sherman Scott (Sam Newfield). Alternate title: *Hitler—Beast of Berlin.* Based on Shepard Taube's story "Goose Step," this was heavily censored in its day, when America was still unsure of how to deal with Hitler. The story has Roland Drew leading a band of underground anti-Nazi activists. Steffi Duna and Greta Granstedt are the leading ladies of record, heading a large cast. Less effective now than it might have been, this was one of the earliest efforts of Producers Releasing Corporation, when it was briefly known as Producers Distributing Corporation. The title was again changed, to *Hell's Devils* in 1943, when it was reissued with *Paper Bullets,* or *Gangs, Inc.* (see Crime entry), to cash in on the new fame of Alan Ladd, who was featured in both.

MYSTERY PLANE (Monogram 1939) Directed by George Waggner. The first film of a series is not necessarily the best, but this one qualifies. World War I ace Hal Forrest created the comic strip "Tailspin Tommy," which had spawned two Universal serials. Producer Paul Malvern crafted a four feature series from the character, all released in 1939 by Monogram and each starring John Trent, Milburn Stone, Marjorie Reynolds and Jason Robards (Sr.). In *Mystery Plane* (formerly called *Sky Pilot*), Trent, a former real-life TWA transport pilot, was appearing in his first pilot role, with his character inventing a bombing system which interests not only the Army, but also a gang of criminals headed by Lucien Littlefield. Their pilot is Peter George Lynn, a war hero-turned-alcoholic. Lynn's excellent performance distinguished this from the ordinary programmer; he was never better than as the washed up flyer who discovers his humanity by remembering that he was Trent's idol when the latter was a boy. Polly Ann Young and Tommy Bupp, as the young Tommy, are also in the cast. Making the film even more authentic is the use of stunt flyer Tex Rankin as supervisor of the aerial scenes.

SECRET SERVICE OF THE AIR (Warner Bros. 1939) Directed by Noel Smith. Production title: *Secret Service in the Air.* Screenplay by Raymond Schrock, from his story "Murder Plane." Ronald Reagan's four "Secret Service" features cast him as Lt. Brass Bancroft, airline pilot turned treasury agent. Supposedly based on the files of former Secret Service Chief William H. Moran, the wild plots had Reagan going undercover to trap those who'd cheat Uncle Sam. This, first and (once more) best, set the formula followed in the balance of the 1939-40 output, *Code of the Secret Service, Smashing the Money Ring* and *Murder in the Air.* Eddie Foy, Jr., was the comic sidekick/assistant, while John Litel and Joe King alternated as the treasury chief. The initial entry takes a roundabout path as Reagan and Foy track James Stephenson's alien smuggling ring. In an incredible scene, pilot John Ridgely dumps a planeload of men to their deaths—one an undercover agent, John Harron. Although Reagan and Ila Rhodes are about to wed at film's end, the star's romantic interests in the other series entries are virtually nonexistent; Foy romances Margot Stevenson in *Ring* and has Helen Lynd for a fiancée in the final entry. This first film presents Reagan, although partially doubled, doing some impressive stunt work in a barroom brawl; he actually says "well" as he would in a more famous later role in Washington.

I TAKE THIS OATH (PRC 1940) Directed by Sherman Scott (Sam Newfield). Production title, *Sons of the Finest;* reissued as *Police Rookie.* When police officer Robert Homans is killed, his son Gordon Jones joins the force. Then Jones learns that Sam Flint, uncle of Jones' best friend Craig Reynolds, is responsible. Good police drama with interesting training scenes to give it a realistic air. J. Farrell MacDonald is promoted to police inspector here, while the distaff side is represented by Joyce Compton, Mary Gordon and Veda Ann Borg (mistakenly billed *Van* Borg on the credits).

ISLAND OF DOOMED MEN (Columbia 1940) Directed by Charles Barton, produced by former actor Wallace MacDonald. Undercover agent Robert Wilcox, posing as a con, infiltrates sadistic Peter Lorre's Dead Man's Island. There, ex-convicts are forced into slave labor. Rather stylish thriller with Rochelle Hudson as the only woman in sight, wed, curiously, to Lorre. Typical Columbia cast: George E. Stone, Don Beddoe, Charles Middleton, Bruce Bennett and Kenneth MacDonald. Wilcox, cast mainly in action films, was a later real-life husband of the equally ill-fated Diana Barrymore.

PRIDE OF THE BOWERY (Monogram 1940) Directed by Joseph H. Lewis. Last of the few films depicting the government's Civilian Conservation Corps. Others with the CCC as background were Paramount's *It's a Great Life* (1935) and Monogram's *Blazing Barriers* (1937). During the Depression, FDR created the agency, known initially as the Emergency Conversation Work, to help in reforestation and flood control. It was designed to help unemployed young men and war veterans, under enlistments of six months with a nominal pay of $22 a month. For the fourth of the East Side Kids comedy adventures (basically a rewrite of Warners' *On Dress Parade,* 1939, with Leo Gorcey and Billy Halop), the CCC serves as an outlet for amateur boxer Gorcey's pugilistic pursuits. Robert Cline's photography combines beautiful outdoor work with inferior interiors, the fight scenes being presented in fast motion to make them seem more

ISLAND OF DOOMED MEN *(Columbia 1940) As the head of a penal colony, of sorts, Peter Lorre is as menacing as usual.*

exciting. David Gorcey (Leo's brother), Donald Haines and Bobby Jordan make up the gang, and future regulars Bobby Stone and Sunshine Sammy Morrison are cast as enlistees. A pleasant surprise is the work of Mary Ainslee, a genuinely talented leading lady. The CCC was disbanded in 1941, due to the war effort; attempts to revive the idea in the late Eighties were unsuccessful.

YOU'RE NOT SO TOUGH (Universal 1940) Directed by Joe May. Assistant Director, Phil Karlstein (Karlson). Based on Maxwell Aley's story "Son of Mama Posita." While the East Side Kids were cavorting at Monogram, in a parallel universe, or Universal, the Dead End Kids were operating with a rival gang—Billy Halop, Huntz Hall, Gabriel Dell, Bernard Punsly and Bobby Jordan, again. *You're Not So Tough,* shot in the Salinas Valley, is blessed with imaginative touches and entertaining ingredients, and opens with a great visual shot as The Kids appear to be traveling by jalopy. Then, Elwood Bredell's camera pulls back to reveal that they're riding on a flatcar. As vagrants, The Kids become workers on Rosina Galli's ranch and fight the competition. Halop pretends to be the kindhearted Galli's son, then changes from a Little Tough Guy into a solid citizen. Nan Grey and Henry Armetta have top roles; David Gorcey, Hally Chester and Harris Berger, all of whom would figure prominently in these films, have small ones.

BOMBAY CLIPPER (Universal 1941) Directed by John Rawlins. Entertaining programmer with William Gargan as a correspondent who'd rather chase down a story than stay with bride Irene Hervey. They board the Bombay Clipper, on which are spies determined to steal industrial diamonds worth millions. Turhan Bey and

BOMBAY CLIPPER *(Universal 1941) Truman Bradley and Maria Montez are menaced by the shadow of Turhan Bey in an adventure spiced with comedy.*

Maria Montez, who would shortly costar in a number of exotic adventures at the studio, have supporting roles, but veteran character actors Lloyd Corrigan and Mary Gordon take acting honors, the latter in particular as a resourceful old lady. Philip Trent, as a disgraced pilot, saves the day by bringing in the Clipper which has become crippled. This was a reunion for the two heroes, who had both appeared in their first play in stock in Staten Island, with Gargan as leading man and Trent as the juvenile.

FORCED LANDING (Paramount 1941) Directed by Gordon Wiles. In 1941, Richard Arlen starred in three aviation-themed actioners for producers Pine-Thomas, *Flying Blind, Power Drive* and this. Set in a South Pacific island republic, *Forced Landing* pits pilot Arlen against colonel Nils Asther, general John Miljan and rebel J. Carrol Naish, and romancing Eva Gabor—in her film debut—in the process. Evelyn Brent, Mikhail Rasumny and Victor Varconi add an international flavor to the production, its villains being of dubious origin because of a fear of offending nationalities in countries where the film would play. Giving the feature a visual flair are the careful direction of Wiles, taking time out from his regular duties as an Oscar-winning art director, and the camera work of John Alton.

FORCED LANDING *(Paramount 1941) A general, John Miljan, forces attentions on Evelyn Brent, a housekeeper. Actually, there is no such scene in the film.*

THE GREAT TRAIN ROBBERY (Republic 1941) Produced and directed by Joseph Kane. Topnotch; the best B action feature of its day. Not a Western despite the title and setting and the casting of Bob Steele as star, playing a railroad detective out to stop crooked brother Milburn Stone and to rescue singer Claire Carleton. The opening borrows from *Beau Geste,* as an unusual situation is presented before events unfold in flashback. The Comanche, carrying a gold shipment, is stolen—the whole train. Fascinating twists and a top cast including Yakima Canutt, Monte Blue, Philip Trent. Remade as a Western, *The Last Bandit* (1949) with Bill Elliott.

HARMON OF MICHIGAN (Columbia 1941) Directed by Charles Barton. Produced by Wallace Mac-Donald. Why, you ask, is this virtually the only sports film in the book, possibly in the wrong category? It isn't because Tom Harmon, the football star who was Michigan's All-American halfback of 1940, plays himself, but rather that his character is presented as less than sympathetic. Surprisingly enough, Harmon is shown using illegal tactics to win, upon becoming a coach. Forest Evashevski, his teammate, portrays himself, as

THE GREAT TRAIN ROBBERY *(Republic 1941) Milburn Stone, Philip Trent, Bob Steele and Jack Ingram participate in one of the great action pictures.*

does Bill Henry (no relation to the actor), former sports editor of the *Los Angeles Times,* who sets the action in motion. Up-and-coming Larry Parks and Lloyd Bridges have supporting roles and Oscar O'Shea portrays Harmon's mentor and rival. In the film, Harmon marries fictitious college sweetheart Anita Louise; in reality, he wed Universal starlet Elyse Knox, became a top sportscaster and father of Mark, Kelly and Kristin—all performers. He died in 1990. Sidelight: Eighties star Mark Harmon had been a football hero at UCLA and had once intended to be a lawyer.

HIT THE ROAD (Universal 1941)

Directed by Joe May. The Dead End Kids, one more time. However, this qualifies as more than the ordinary because of the presence of Barton MacLane, Gladys George and Evelyn Ankers. MacLane plays Jimmy Valentine, an ex-convict who was a friend of the dead fathers of the Kids—Billy Halop, Huntz Hall, Gabriel Dell, Bernard Punsly—and provides a shelter for them at his ranch. George and Ankers are his wife and daughter. Also cast: Shemp Howard, Bobs Watson, John Harmon, Walter Kingsford. There were no more Dead End Kids pictures after 1943, the East Side Kids having taken over, to be succeeded by the Bowery Boys in 1946.

RAIDERS OF THE DESERT (Universal 1941)

Directed by John Rawlins. Liveliest and funniest of the Richard Arlen-Andy Devine comedy actioners made between 1939 and 1941. The boys stow away to what they think will be California, but wind up in Arabia (Arlen isn't necessarily the brighter of the two). They journey to the fictional Libertahd, where sheik Ralf Harolde opposes all attempts to modernize the area. Arlen romances secretary Linda Hayes and Devine tries his luck with Maria Montez. Providing menace is Turhan Bey, but the film is stolen by Lewis Howard as an opportunistic cab driver. His rich comic performance is a gem; unfortunately, he never managed to make a name for himself and died young. Howard's brother John is an accomplished New York film writer-historian. *Raiders* features a bit of stock from *I Cover the War* (1937) with John Wayne and Don Barclay visible in a truck.

SWAMP WOMAN a.k.a. SWAMP LADY (PRC 1941)

Directed by Elmer Clifton. Film debut of striptease artist Ann Corio, who does a brief dance ending with falling leaves. She's practicing her torrid terpsichore in cheap clubs before seeking refuge in her Everglades birthplace because of a murder, there fighting with her uneducated niece Mary Hull over the affections of Jack LaRue. Hull subsequently switches her attention to escaped convict Richard Deane. The film's nearly nonexistent production values give it a realistic

HARMON OF MICHIGAN *(Columbia 1941) Football great Tom Harmon as himself, Anita Louise as his fictitious wife in a sports feature.*

RAIDERS OF THE DESERT *(Universal 1941) An Arlen-Devine comedy adventure with Lewis Howard, who steals top honors, Sheila Darcy (later Mrs. Preston Foster), Andy Devine and Richard Arlen. Set in old Libertahd.*

air, making it seem a better offering than the same year's slicker *Swamp Water.* Ian MacDonald, whom the whole town fears in *High Noon* (1952), impresses as a tough police lieutenant, LaRue has a good time with his colorful character and Jimmy Aubrey almost plays it straight as the key to Jay Novello's guilt. Corio, who made only five films, all Bs, sings "You Surprise Me" (Eddie Cherkose-Jacques Press). Backgrounds shot in Georgia's Okefenokee Swamp.

FLY-BY-NIGHT (Paramount 1942)

Directed by Robert Siodmak. Fine lighthearted thriller, with as much comedy as excitement. Pathologist Richard Carlson kidnaps commercial artist Nancy Kelly in an effort to prove that he didn't kill spy Martin Kosleck (in a rare sympathetic role). The effort involves stealing a car from a moving auto carrier, going through a forced marriage and feigning insanity to gain access to a sanitarium which

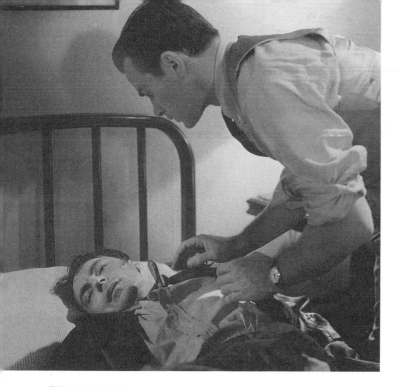

FLY-BY-NIGHT *(Paramount 1942) In his hotel room, Richard Carlson finds Martin Kosleck stabbed with the former's surgical knife; Kosleck in a rare sympathetic appearance.*

holds the secret to G-32. Albert Basserman is head of the enemy spy ring, with Walter Kingsford and Miles Mander also involved. Marion Martin is ludicrously cast as a glamorous nurse. A good effort from a director who would go on to bigger things (*The Killers, The Dark Mirror, Criss Cross*). Publicity stated that, due to Pearl Harbor, there was no longer a problem with identifying the nationality of the villains. Star Kelly was then a young veteran, having film-debuted in 1925 at age four, making 52 pictures in the East before arriving in Hollywood. She'd also supplied the voice of Eleanor Roosevelt on radio's "The March of Time." Production title: *Dangerous Holiday.*

HITLER—DEAD OR ALIVE (Charles House/Ben Judell/States Rights 1942) Directed by Nick Grinde. The title refers to an actual $1-million offer for the Fuehrer by an American businessman. In the film, he's played by Russell Hicks and the takers are ex-convicts Ward Bond, Paul Fix and Warren Hymer, joining the Canadian Air Force, parachuting into Germany with pilot Bruce Edwards, and infiltrating a reception for Hitler by posing as musicians. Played more for comedy than drama, it does wind up as tragedy. Bond is good in a rare starring role and comedian Bobby Watson plays Hitler (as he often would) as a sniveling coward. Dorothy Tree supplies some diversion as an underground operative. The casual use of Dachau as a concentration camp in one scene is startling, since the world was then unaware of the horrors committed therein.

HITLER'S CHILDREN (RKO Radio 1942) Directed by Edward Dmytryk. Based on Gregor Ziemer's book *Education for Death,* and made for just $205,000, this World War II shocker grossed more than sixteen times that amount, becoming one of the biggest surprise hits in RKO history. The Edward A. Golden (appropriate) production took advantage of lax wartime restrictions by concentrating on the women who were forced to bear children for the Nazi cause. Professor Kent Smith narrates the story of American born Tim Holt, a Nazi youth, and German born Bonita Granville, an American, beginning in 1933 Berlin. Granville is to be sterilized for her anti-Nazi sentiments and Holt, loving her, prevents Granville's being whipped. Together they face death. Powerful in its day and still persuasive. Richard Martin, later Holt's sidekick in Westerns, and Ann Summers, leading lady in two Holt oaters, have small parts. Otto Kruger, H. B. Warner, Lloyd Corrigan, Hans Conried, Peter Van Eyck and Nancy Gates have larger roles. Incredibly, this grossed more in its day than either *King Kong* or *Top Hat* originally.

WRECKING CREW *(Paramount 1942) Chester Morris and Richard Arlen (who made quite a few films) ready to wreck parts of Los Angeles.*

WRECKING CREW (Paramount 1942) Directed by Frank McDonald. Fast Pine-Thomas thriller with a then-fresh building demolition background, using recent stock shots for emphasis. Tale is an old one: gang boss Richard Arlen and worker Chester Morris, who seems to be a jinx, battle over Jean Parker. A twist has salty Esther Dale as the owner of the demolition company. Joe Sawyer, Alexander Granach, Evelyn Brent, Nigel de Brulier, Jody Gilbert, Byron Foulger and a host of familiar Pine-Thomas players show up for work and do it professionally.

CORREGIDOR (PRC 1943) Directed by Willian Nigh, written by Edgar G. Ulmer and Doris Malloy. Stagebound, with stock footage, but genuinely effective retelling of the gallant stand against Japanese forces in Corregidor in the spring of 1942. In an underground hospital, doctors Otto Kruger, Elissa Landi and Donald Woods form a romantic triangle while struggling to save lives. With Frank Jenks, Wanda McKay, Rick Vallin, Ian Keith and Ruby Dandridge in strong roles. Last film of Venice-born Landi, a major star of the Thirties who died of cancer in 1948, at 43. In addition to being a novelist, she made an acting impact in *The Warrior's Husband* and DeMille's *The Sign of the Cross*.

HITLER'S MADMAN, formerly HITLER'S HANGMAN (PRC/MGM 1943) Directed by Douglas Sirk, the American debut for a German director. Suggested by Bart Lytton's story "Hangman's Village" and inspired by Edna St. Vincent Millay's poem "The Murder of Lidice," as well as the good wishes of Eleanor Roosevelt, this is a true story. In retaliation for the killing of Reichs Protector Reinhard Heydrich, the Nazis under Commandant Heinrich Himmler ordered the execution of all the men of Lidice, Czechoslovakia, on June 10, 1942, and the women and children shipped to concentration camps. Sirk's film started out to be a PRC release, but MGM picked it up and additional scenes were shot. John Carradine as Heydrich and Howard Freeman as Himmler head a mixed cast, including Alan Curtis, Patricia Morison, Ralph Morgan, comic Edgar Kennedy, Western actors John Merton and Dennis Moore, starlets Ava Gardner and Frances Rafferty. The tragedy transcends such shortcomings as Carradine's repudiation of Hitler, uncharacteristic of Heydrich.

ISLE OF FORGOTTEN SINS (PRC 1943) Directed and written by Edgar G. Ulmer. A camp classic, more for the incredible editing of Charles Henkel, Jr., than for its plot. The sky in back of a boat, an obvious backdrop, has visible creases; Gale Sondergaard loses an earring which reappears in succeeding shots; divers obviously squat on their knees as they descend into the water of a studio tank. It's a lighthearted adventure, however, with few in the cast taking things too seriously as John Carradine

CORREGIDOR *(PRC 1943) Mixed ethnic types portray Japanese, defeated in hand-to-hand combat at the fortress; based on World War II engagements.*

ISLE OF FORGOTTEN SINS *(PRC 1943) Costars Rick Vallin, Sidney Toler and Veda Ann Borg, two thirds more attractive than the leads.*

dives for $3 million in gold on the sunken Tropic Star. Title refers to Sondergaard's South Seas cabaret. One classic scene has Veda Ann Borg in black wig singing "Sleepy Island Moon" (June Sillman/Carroll-Leo Erdody), as Buster Crabbe and Ann Corio are shown in a swimming scene from *Jungle Siren* (1942). Carradine and Frank Fenton as his sometime friend get into the spirit by doing the drinking song "Whiskey Johnny." With an interesting cast: Sidney Toler (before resuming his Charlie Chan role), Rick Vallin, Tala Birell, Betty Amann. Shot under the title *Tidal Wave*, it later was reissued as *Monsoon*.

173

HITLER'S MADMAN (PRC/MGM 1943) The people of Lidice: Elizabeth Russell, Kenner G. Kemp (rear), Blanche Yurka, children Richard and Betty Jean Nichols.

NIGHT TRAIN TO MEMPHIS (Republic 1946) The local people who sold their river land to the railroad attack its construction camp.

CAGED FURY *(Paramount 1948) Sheila Ryan and Richard Denning, wild animal trainers, confront murderous clown Buster Crabbe.*

[Sondergaard, on vacation from Universal, was persuaded by PRC to star, on the promise that the film would only be seen in small towns. Many years later, a good friend, Eric Spilker, arranged a screening for her. Afterwards, she said, "Now that we've seen it, we'll never have to mention it again. We've had our laughs."]

NIGHT TRAIN TO MEMPHIS (Republic 1946)

Directed by Lesley Selander. All of Republic's best elements are featured: Western settings, action, comedy, songs, romance, homespun philosophy, crime and redemption, fights and a touch of religion along with the sentimentality. Allan Lane returns to his Tennessee mountain home of Tranquility to find brother Roy Acuff working for the hated railroad which Lane holds responsible for his unjust prison term. The brothers have a falling out over comely Adele Mara, daughter of Joseph Crehan, incognito president of the line who wants the land in the vicinity for a right of way. An explosive brawl takes the edge off the too obvious rear projection scenes. Although the title song is sung almost constantly, Acuff (accompanied by his Smoky Mountain Boys) is most effective warbling "No One Will Ever Know" after losing Mara to the less sympathetic Lane. Except for Emma Dunn, most of the cast do comic turns—track inspector Irving Bacon, black maid Nina Mae McKinney (the sexy sensation of *Hallelujah,* 1929), villains Roy Barcroft and Kenne Duncan. Filming was done at Lake Big Bear, California.

TARZAN AND THE LEOPARD WOMAN (*RKO Radio 1946*) As the latter, Acquanetta leads the Leopard Men in a ritual.

SWAMP FIRE (Paramount 1946) Directed by William H. Pine. A Pine-Thomas production, this is notable as the only non-jungle feature to star Johnny Weissmuller and the first time he and Buster Crabbe co-starred. The two Olympic swim champions met again in the Jungle Jim adventure *Captive Girl* (1950)—in both, Buster is the villain, a role he always enjoyed playing despite his heroic image. In *Swamp Fire,* shell-shocked Navy veteran Weissmuller and trapper Crabbe have it out in the Cajun country of the Mississippi bayous. Crabbe employed an accent for his first villainous part in some years. He had been Tarzan just once, to Weissmuller's sixteen years in the role. With Virginia Grey, Carol Thurston, Edwin Maxwell and a teenaged David Janssen as Johnny's young brother.

TARZAN AND THE LEOPARD WOMAN (RKO Radio 1946, but copyrighted 1945) Directed by Kurt Neumann. For one of his last Tarzans, Johnny Weissmuller has Brenda Joyce as Jane, Johnny Sheffield as Boy, and the ever present Cheta the monkey. He also has the interesting (Burnu) Acquanetta as the high priestess of a leopard-worshiping cult, using the animal's claws to kill those who would bring civilization to the jungle. Depending on your source, Acquanetta (in the last of her few leading roles) was either of black or American Indian origin. Edgar Barrier, Tommy Cook, Dennis Hoey, Anthony Caruso, George J. Lewis and Doris Lloyd create an international flavor with their presences in one of the most exotic of the Ape Man series.

CAGED FURY (Paramount 1948) Directed by William Berke. Excellent Pine-Thomas production with a particularly fine performance by Buster Crabbe as a murderous clown. The nastier the role, the better he liked it, Buster always felt. He eliminates animal tamer Mary Beth Hughes, forcing her partner Richard Denning to train Sheila Ryan as a replacement. Both men fall for Ryan, but Crabbe is soon found out. He returns to cause a fire—stock from the Crabbe starrer *King of the Jungle* (see 1933 entry)—and his own death. Only the very cheap production, resembling an early telefilm, mars the effect.

HIGHWAY 13 (Lippert-Screen Guild 1948) Directed by William Berke. Low or no budget quickie, fast moving and entertaining in spite of that. Robert Lowery is a trucker who discovers that supposed accidents are really attempts to force a large transportation company out of business. Unusual aspect of the Maurice Tombragel screenplay is that the heads of the gang are Michael Whalen, a woman—Maris Wrixon—and a sweet old man—Clem Bevans. As an undercover detective,

HIGHWAY 13 *(Lippert-Screen Guild 1948) Trucker Robert Lowery is given a dangerous ride by Clem Bevans.*

Gaylord (Steve) Pendleton has a smashing scene in which he's crushed to death by a truck while working in a warehouse. Familiar faces: Pamela Blake, Dan Seymour (not a bad guy for a change), Mary Gordon and Lyle Talbot.

THUNDER IN THE PINES (Lippert-Screen Guild 1948) Directed by Robert Edwards. Played for laughs and with a good amount of stock, this logging saga pits George (Superman) Reeves against Ralph (Dick Tracy) Byrd, with Denise Darcel as the prize. Saloonkeeper and landowner Lyle Talbot, wanting everything, has Greg McClure sabotage both camps. However, Talbot's discarded girlfriend Marion Martin sees that Talbot doesn't cheat, as usual, in the climactic poker game. The first leading role for Darcel, who sings "Oh, Susannah" (Stephen Foster) in French and English, following her American debut in Warners' *To the Victor* (1948). Originally in Sepiatone, with Michael Whalen, Roscoe Ates and Vince Barnett in the cast.
[At the CoOp in 1975 as the opening of a "Strippers on the Screen" show, along with *Queen of Burlesque* (1946) with Rose La Rose, and Ann Corio in *Swamp Woman* (see 1941 entry). By then, Darcel was performing a strip act in clubs.]

THE BIG CAT (Eagle Lion 1949) Directed by Phil Karlson. Technicolor locales enhance a well-plotted (Morton Grant-Dorothy Yost) tale set in the Rocky Mountains of 1932. City lad Lon McCallister forsakes mean uncle Forrest Tucker and goes to live with his mother's old sweetheart, Preston Foster. The Foster-Tucker feud erupts in a well-staged fight on the lake, while McCallister tangles with his cousins Skip Homeier and Gene Reynolds. Foster's sudden death by a cougar he's trying to kill sets the youth out to destroy the big cat. Peggy Ann Garner supplies the romantic interest, with Irving Bacon and Sara Haden as her parents. Tucker's aging mountaineer characterization was in dramatic contrast to his usual parts as a rugged individual of much younger appearance. Filmed in Utah.

THE BIG CAT *(Eagle-Lion 1949) Cousins Skip Homeier and Lon McCallister participate in an old mountain feud; filmed in Utah in Technicolor.*

THE STEEL HELMET *(Lippert 1951) A Korean War classic, with James Edwards, William Chun and Gene Evans, guided by novice director Sam Fuller.*

THE STEEL HELMET (Lippert 1951) Produced, directed and written by Sam Fuller. For his first war film, Fuller created a tale of the Korean conflict that stands as a classic, focusing not on glamour or glory, only survival. Tough Gene Evans is a cynical World War II veteran who doesn't let sentiment cloud his vision and survives because he knows all the traps and shows no mercy. The actor played an extension of this character in Fuller's next bigger budgeted film *Fixed Bayonets!* (1951) for 20th Century-Fox. Although Evans tends to dominate and the others perform as ensemble players, James Edwards is also outstanding as a weary black medic, chain smoking out of boredom for the futility of war. With Robert Hutton, Steve Brodie, Richard Loo, Sid Melton and Willie Chun as Short Round.

HELLCATS OF THE NAVY (Columbia 1957) Directed by Nathan Juran. Notable as the only theatrical teaming of Ronald Reagan and wife Nancy Davis (they did a handful of TV dramas), but also a palatable drama of submarine warfare in World War II, with Commander Reagan and crew assigned the task of detecting Japanese mines. The incident of the sub gliding through a mine net came from Warners' *Destination Tokyo* (1943). Filmed at San Diego Naval Training Center, with a prologue by Admiral Chester Nimitz, portrayed in the film by Selmer Jackson. Arthur Franz, Robert Arthur and Harry Lauter are crew members.
[Shown at The CoOp on the eve of the 1980 election, as a "Vote for Ronnie Special," with the comedy *The Girl From Jones Beach* (1949) and the Western *Tennessee's Partner* (1955).]

EDGE OF ETERNITY (Columbia 1959) Directed by Donald Siegel, who has a bit in a motel scene. Production titles: *Satan's Bucket* and *Rim of the Canyon,* with writer Marion Hargrove using the pseudonym Knut Swenson on the credits. Cornel Wilde made some above-average features as producer-director-star, and here is in the hands of auteurist Siegel for an exciting adventure yarn shot at the Grand Canyon, playing a deputy investigating deaths around an abandoned gold mine. When not romancing Victoria Shaw, he's coping with colorful villain Mickey Shaughnessy, who steals the film, as he usually did. The climax, in a dancing bucket or tram car high above the canyon, uses stunt people Guy Way, Chuck Couch and Rosemary Johnston doubling for Wilde, Shaughnessy and Shaw and provides a dazzling scene. In CinemaScope and Eastman Color by Pathe, Burnett Guffey's lensing also focuses on Edgar Buchanan, Rian Garrick, Jack Elam and Dabbs Greer on both sides of the law.

HELLCATS OF THE NAVY *(Columbia 1957) The only film in which the Reagans costarred shows that Nancy always looked up to Ronnie.*

ANGEL UNCHAINED (American International 1970) Directed by Lee Madden, who also co-produced and wrote the original story. A motorcycle movie with heart, as bikers and commune members team up to combat the marauding ranchers. Both Don Stroud and Luke Askew, who often played crazies and weirdos, are sympathetically cast, Stroud an ex-member of Larry Bishop's bikers and Askew as the hippie head. In the midst of a brawl, sheriff Aldo Ray and Bishop have a calm discussion of the problems at hand, adding a nice comedic touch. As an aged Indian with a supposed drug formula is veteran Pedro Regas, and the leading lady of the commune is played by a young (24) Tyne Daly, who impresses as a charming heroine in her first film lead. Shot in Arizona, Color by Movielab, with a good Randy Sparks score, this gives a fresh slant to a waning cycle.

THE HARD RIDE (American International 1971) Directed and written by Burt Topper. A plea for brotherhood disguised as a biker movie, involving a dead black, his white buddy and the Indian leader of a motorcycle gang. Several years before Dennis Hopper played a similar role in *Tracks* (1976), former Marine sergeant Robert Fuller accompanies his black friend Alfonso Williams' body home from Vietnam. Fuller encounters Williams' white girlfriend Sherry Bain and Tony Russel, the Indian leader of the dead man's motorcycle gang, in fulfilling the last requests. Fuller gives a sincere performance in this tragedy, with Marshall Reed as a priest and Biff Elliot as the cafe owner also giving strong characterizations. More story than in most films of its type, though not at the expense of action. Color by Movielab.

MS. .45 (Rochelle Films 1980) Directed by Abel Ferrara, from Nicholas St. John's script. Cult favorite is a change-of-gender *Death Wish* as repressed seamstress Zoe Tamerlis is raped twice in a short period of time, then goes about killing every Manhattan male in sight—eighteen, at least. A model and pianist at the time of the film's production, Tamerlis conveys the zombie-like catatonia which can drive one to kill. She uses an iron, symbolic of her work, to commit the first killing, on burglar-attacker Peter Yellen. Thereafter, she employs his gun to carry out her murders, always on men who might threaten her. At a party, she shoots every male in sight until stabbed in the back by co-worker Darlene Stuto. In dying, Tamerlis is unable to slay a female. Guaranteed to give feminists nightmares, this also offers a perverse tour of New York. Among the impressive scenes: pickup Jack Thibeau saving Tamerlis the trouble by committing suicide with her gun, Tamerlis kissing each bullet as she loads for the party slaughter. Keeping down the budget,

THE HARD RIDE *(American International 1971) Motorcyle action with an ethnic twist, as Tony Russel fights Robert Fuller (right).*

MS. .45 *(Rochelle Films 1980) Rapist Jimmy Laine (actually director Abel Ferrara) attacks Zoë Tamerlis in an alley; a cult favorite.*

Ferrara appears as the first rapist, billed as Jimmy Laine, while Yellen accompanies Sylvia Delia on the vocals. Color by Cineffects and naturally rated R, this was presented in 1980 at the Cannes and Milano Film Festivals before being released here in 1981.

HORROR, FANTASY AND SCIENCE FICTION

EVELYN ANKERS

ANNE GWYNNE

JAMIE LEE CURTIS *in* Halloween
(Compass International 1978)

MARSHALL REED

PEGGY SHANNON

AUDREY TOTTER

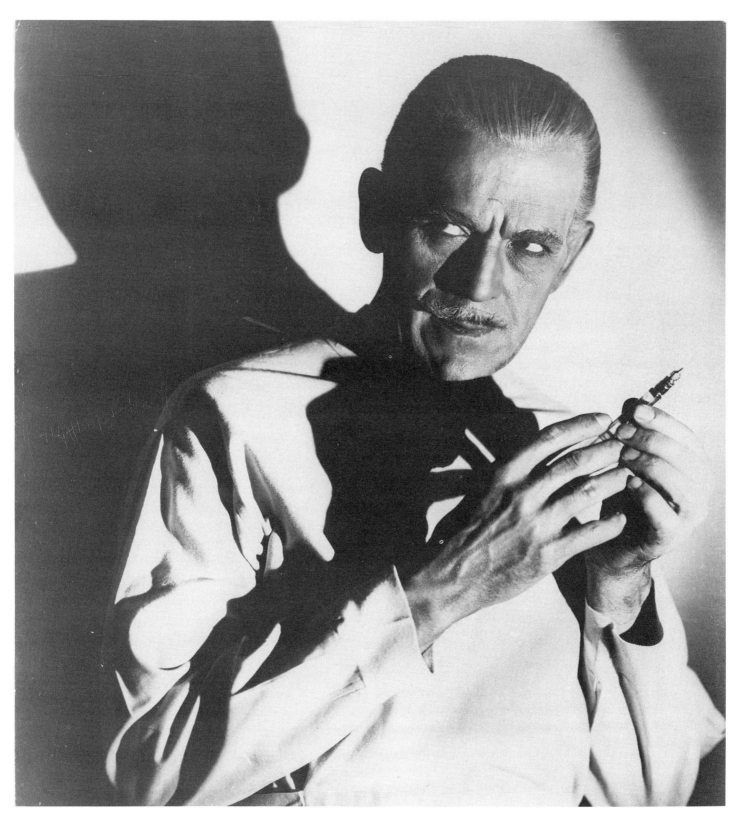

BORIS KARLOFF *in* Black Friday
(Universal 1940)

THE DRUMS OF JEOPARDY *(Tiffany 1931) Cousins Lloyd Hughes and Wallace MacDonald find that Broderick O'Farrell, a Secret Service operative, is a casualty of the drums. MacDonald was later a prolific Columbia producer.*

MURDER AT DAWN *(Big 4, 1932) A battle in the secret storeroom, between Jack Mulhall and Mischa Auer, whose comedy roles were a few years off.*

THE DRUMS OF JEOPARDY (Tiffany 1931)

Directed by George B. Seitz. Based on the 1920 novel by Harold MacGrath and the 1924 Truart silent, but actually different from both plotwise. Reissued as *Mark of Terror* by United Screen Attractions. Fanciful thriller with Warner Oland as a mad scientist, Dr. Boris Karlov (film was released nearly a year before actor Boris Karloff became a major name), who seeks vengeance on the Petroff family for the betrayal and death of daughter Florence Lake. The quest takes him from Petrograd to New York, where he sets up a lab and installs spies (one of whom is Mischa Auer). The drums are actually four rubies from a necklace, each given to a member of the Petroff family as a signal of death. Lloyd Hughes and cousin Wallace MacDonald, the treacherous one, attempt to escape the curse. Many striking camera shots, courtesy of photographer Arthur Reed, while Seitz's direction conjures up the serials he made in the silent days, also with Oland as villain. With June Collyer, Hale Hamilton and Clara Blandick, Oland's undoing.

HYPNOTIZED (World Wide 1932)

Supervised and directed by Mack Sennett, from a story by Sennett and Arthur Ripley. Few early talkies have the bad reputation of this comedy fantasy, last of the handful of features personally directed by slapstick king Sennett—and the one which, due to its failure, cost him his studio. Elephant trainer Wallace Ford wins $500,000 on a sweepstake ticket for the British Grand National horse race. Evil professor Ernest Torrence attempts to steal the ticket; he commands "Rigid!" and his subjects become completely immobile. Circus owner Charles Murray has the ability to bring the victims out of their trances as Ford courts tempestuous gypsy princess Maria Alba. Oddball but very funny, almost a black comedy. Blackface comics Moran and Mack are in and out, while Marjorie Beebe, Herman Bing, Alexander Carr, Luis Alberni, Harry Schultz and Hattie McDaniel supply mixed accents in support. Jackie the Lion runs loose in the manner of Numa in Sennett's silent epic *The Extra Girl* (1923).

THE MONSTER WALKS (Action Pictures/Mayfair 1932)

Directed by Frank R. Strayer. Old house mystery in which Vera Reynolds, accompanied by fiance doctor Rex Lease, faces death over her inheritance. Among the suspects are paralyzed uncle Sheldon Lewis, sinister housekeeper Martha Mattox, half-wit handyman Mischa Auer, family lawyer Sidney Bracy, and Yogi, the ape in the cellar; possibly all are guilty. Only frightened black chauffeur Sleep 'n' Eat (Willie Best) isn't directly involved. Of interest because this often-shown feature, once considered at least semi-serious, is now presented as a travesty due to its ineptitude.

MURDER AT DAWN (Big 4, 1932) Directed by Richard Thorpe. A rare non-Western from Big 4 Productions, soon to become the very short-lived Freuler Film Associates. Another old house mystery, with Martha Mattox and Mischa Auer once again as sinister housekeeper and strange son. Jack Mulhall and Josephine Dunn, accompanied by friends Eddie Boland and Marjorie Beebe, seek her father's consent to their marriage. Strictly baffling events occur at the estate of doctor Frank Ball, who has perfected the DXL Accumulator, to harness solar energy. However, Auer rigs the device so that Ball will die at the sun's first ray unless he reveals its formula. Some fascinating special effects by expert Kenneth Strickfaden compensate for some of the strained comedy early on. Rare sci-fi effort from a very prolific director, for years a major MGM helmsman.

BEFORE DAWN (RKO Radio 1933) Directed by Irving Pichel. Based on the story "Death Watch" (also the film's production title), the last written by prolific Edgar Wallace. Viennese physician Warner Oland journeys to the States to reclaim a million dollars hidden by dead gangster Frank Reicher. After dealing with Jane Darwell, Reicher's widow, and housekeeper Gertrude W. Hoffman, Oland is confronted by special investigator Stuart Erwin and clairvoyant Dorothy Wilson, known as Mademoiselle Mystera. A death mask and a deep well as a pit of horror are two effective ingredients of this Merian C. Cooper production, with fine atmospheric photography by Lucien Andriot, art direction by Van Nest Polglase, and music by Max Steiner. Dudley Digges and Oscar Apfel are also in the cast.

DELUGE (RKO Radio 1933) Directed by Felix F. Feist. Remarkable end-of-the-world production, a first feature for its director, based on a first novel by S. Fowler Wright. It was also the last KBS/Admiral co-production. Although over budget at nearly $171,000, the RKO release contains enduring footage of the destruction of New York City after atmospheric disturbances. Ned Mann, in charge of the special effects, spent as much on the miniature work as the cost of the average programmer. The earthquake was shot on a hill near the California desert, with eight cameras on tracks catching the action, in one take. The tidal wave was accomplished with the use of miniatures constructed at the Tiffany Studios, normal filming site of the KBS productions. The sensational results were used by Republic in several features and serials for almost two decades thereafter. Unfortunately, the destruction occurs at the beginning of the film. Thereafter, the main story predominates and never matches the impact of such a beginning. Bronson Canyon and Lake Sherwood are the principal locales for the survival portions. Sidney Blackmer, thinking he's lost wife Lois Wilson and children, takes up with swimmer

DELUGE *(RKO Radio 1933) Special effects magic, as New York City is destroyed by a tidal wave. For some reason, NYC audiences applaud this.*

Peggy Shannon, encountering Fred Kohler and a band of renegades. Shannon appears in bathing suit, or less, throughout and makes the most vivid impression. An original music score is heard throughout, unusual for an independent—even one released through a major company; Dr. Edward Kilenyi heads a list of nineteen different composers who contributed to the soundtrack. The cast also includes Matt Moore, Ralf Harolde, Samuel S. Hinds, Lane Chandler and the always welcome Edward Van Sloan.

[Lost for many years, *Deluge* was rediscovered in 1987, although in a dubbed Italian version. Its New York re-premiere, at the former Film Forum in the summer of 1988, attracted Blackmer's widow, Suzanne Kaaren. An English synopsis was provided to patrons.]

MURDERS IN THE ZOO (Paramount 1933) Directed by Edward Sutherland. A bound man stumbles out of a jungle, a closeup revealing that his lips have been sewn together, before he's devoured by animals. This scene, often cut on television, opens one of the most grisly of the horror features of the early Thirties. Lionel Atwill, owner of a zoo, is so jealous of his comely wife Kathleen Burke that he sets about to kill off any of her lovers, in various sadistic ways. The inhabitants of his zoo provide a cover for the crimes, particularly denizens of the crocodile pool. Randolph Scott and Gail Patrick are the romantic leads, but they tend to be overshadowed by the diabolical Atwill and by Charlie Ruggles as the zoo's always inebriated press agent. John Lodge and Jane Darwell are also on view in this deadly mystery, filmed under the title *Murder at the Zoo.*

NIGHT OF TERROR (Columbia 1933) Directed by Benjamin Stoloff. Production title, *He Lived to Kill.* From the story "The Public Be Damned" by Willard Mack. Whenever he appeared as a murder suspect, Bela Lugosi

was never guilty. Here, he's a sinister (no other kind) Hindu servant at the estate of professor Tully Marshall. A maniac (Pat Harmon) arrives there to do harm to those within, as scientist George Meeker is buried alive to test a fluid enabling him to live without breathing. When murders occur, a houseful of suspects cower—Wallace Ford, Sally Blane, Bryant Washburn, Gertrude Michael, Mary Frey (as Lugosi's equally sinister wife). At the end of this entertaining comedy thriller, The Maniac (now played by Edwin Maxwell) warns the audience not to reveal the ending. That epilogue is sometimes cut on TV. Meeker's experiment was inspired by that of a European scientist who'd claimed to have developed a means of drug-inducing suspended animation.

THE SIN OF NORA MORAN (Majestic 1933)
Directed by Phil Goldstone. From the play *Burnt Offering* by Willis Maxwell Goodhue. Produced under the title

NIGHT OF TERROR (*Columbia 1933*) Bela Lugosi stares down Wallace Ford's weapon, yet he isn't as menacing as he appears.

THE SIN OF NORA MORAN (*Majestic 1933*) Henry B. Walthall, Alan Dinehart and Paul Cavanagh at Zita Johann's bier in a fantasy sequence from one of the strangest films of the Thirties; also one of the best.

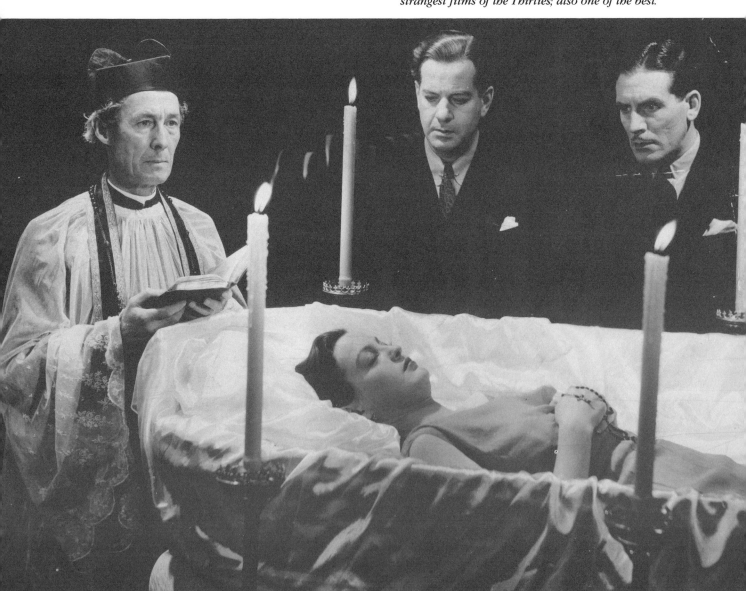

The Woman in the Chair, it was reissued by Independent-International in 1980 as *Voice From the Grave,* toned. By any name, it is a completely bizarre, fascinating, stream-of-consciousness presentation, the best independent feature of the Thirties. Unrelenting in its tragedy, it depicts the story of orphaned Zita Johann, kept by Governor Paul Cavanagh, prosecuted by his district attorney brother-in-law Alan Dinehart, and condemned to the electric chair for a murder she really didn't commit. Amazingly, this is the only sound era directorial credit for a producer of Westerns and few other features. Claire DuBrey, Henry B. Walthall and Cora Sue Collins lend support.

TERROR ABOARD (Paramount 1933)
Directed by Paul Sloane. Even more terrifying than *Murders in the Zoo* because the killings are committed by a supposedly civilized man. John Halliday was popular for his portrayals of witty, sophisticated gentlemen who looked upon strenuous activity with disdain. Here, he's the terror who murders almost everyone aboard a liner. Halliday's motives seem trivial and his methods are so gruesome that the film had trouble getting play-dates. He locks Verree Teasdale in a freezer and casually thrusts captain Thomas Jackson onto a spike. Bookending the story is a *Beau Geste* opening and resolution. Potential victims include Charlie Ruggles (from *Murders in the Zoo*), Neil Hamilton, Shirley Grey and Jack LaRue.

THE VAMPIRE BAT (Majestic 1933)
Directed by Frank R. Strayer. Filmed at Universal and produced by *Nora Moran's* Phil Goldstone, this emerges as one of the best independent horrors of the time. A top cast does wonders with the material, in spite of most suffering from an over-identification with their roles. Lionel Atwill is the scientist creating life, Fay Wray and Robert Frazer his assistants and unwitting pawns, Dwight Frye the village idiot, and Melvyn Douglas the intrepid police inspector. Add Maude Eburne and George E. Stone and stir for the proper mix. Bronson Canyon locales add color to the European setting as a village is threatened by a vampire bat—or a human fiend.

AIR HAWKS (Columbia 1935)
Directed by Albert Rogell. Only feature appearance of around-the-world flyer Wiley Post. Three months after this film's release, he and Will Rogers were killed in a plane crash near Point Barrow, Alaska. Playing himself, Post bolsters a tale of the race for an airmail contract, with the bad guys using an infra-red ray to bring down the planes of the good guys. Henry Freulich's photography is quite good in this instance. Ralph Bellamy and Tala Birell, who also does a song, take top billing, with Douglass Dumbrille, Robert Allen, Billie Seward, Victor Kilian and Edward Van Sloan supporting. *Air Fury* was the film's production title.

THE VAMPIRE BAT *(Majestic 1933) Robert Frazer, Melvyn Douglas, fainted Maude Eburne, Fay Wray and Lionel Atwill find housekeeper Stella Adams murdered in her bed.*

CONDEMNED TO LIVE (Chesterfield-Invincible 1935)
Directed by Frank R. Strayer. Filmed at Universal, with use of standing sets and props. Set in middle Europe around 1900, this well-done thriller was written by Karen DeWolf and shows how a vampiric curse haunts a man all his life. The victim is kindly doctor Ralph Morgan, who commits his crimes unknowingly. Hunchbacked servant Mischa Auer then disposes of the victims, out of loyalty for his master. The doctor's fiancée Maxine Doyle comes to love Russell Gleason and to discover Morgan's secret. Bronson Canyon is used to add realism to the Maury M. Cohen production, rather than erecting sets for the mountain scenes. In the cast are Pedro de Cordoba, Barbara Bedford and Robert Frazer.

REVOLT OF THE ZOMBIES (Academy Pictures 1936)
Directed by Victor Halperin. With the success of their *White Zombie* (1932), the Halperin Brothers (Edward and Victor) cashed in on that with this fanciful tale. Victor Halperin, writer-director Howard Higgin and writer-actor Rollo Lloyd contributed an original screenplay dealing with the possibility of zombies as soldiers in World War I. At Angkor in Cambodia, the secret of the living dead is hidden and an expedition is sent to destroy it forever. However, Dean Jagger, a translator in the group, uses the zombies for his interests. A popular film of its type, once known as *Revolt of the Demons,* it isn't really the best of its kind. Part of the problem lies with Jagger's indifferent performance. Others involved are Dorothy Stone, Roy D'Arcy and George Cleveland. Filmed in Los Angeles, but with generous stock shots of the setting.

REVOLT OF THE ZOMBIES *(Academy 1936) Dean Jagger finds one of those secrets which man was not meant to know.*

REEFER MADNESS a.k.a. TELL YOUR CHILDREN, THE BURNING QUESTION, DOPE ADDICT, DOPED YOUTH, LOVE MADNESS (G & H Productions 1938) Directed by Louis Gasnier. In what category would you put this exploitation feature, possibly the best known of the type? The evils of marijuana are depicted through the stories of high school kids Kenneth Craig, Warren McCollum and Dorothy Short. Craig is tried for the accidental killing of Short, while McCollum becomes a hit-and-run driver—all while under the influence of the evil weed. When the film was reissued in 1972 by NORML/Roninfilm as a pro-drug message, every contemporary critic—apparently using firsthand information—declared it a travesty of the real effects of marijuana, and in so doing, helped to make it a camp classic. Thelma White, who plays Mae, mistress of pusher Carleton Young, claims that she'd been loaned by RKO in 1935 to make the film. It had been written by a religious group and shot in three weeks. Original story is credited to Lawrence Meade, with Arthur Hoerl and Paul Franklin contributing to the screenplay (all have other Hollywood credits); the sensational aspects of the plot—rape, murder, insanity—probably wouldn't be sanctioned by many religious groups. Others in the cast: Dave O'Brien, who goes insane (he was in real life wed to Short); Lillian Miles, who goes wild and commits suicide; and Josef Forte, who introduces the story.

REEFER MADNESS *(G & H Productions 1938) Dope pusher Carleton Young and addict Dave O'Brien watch Lillian Miles (left) and Thelma White introduce innocent Kenneth Craig to marijuana.*

MIRACLES FOR SALE (MGM 1939) Directed by Tod Browning. Based on the book *Death From a Top Hat* by Clayton Rawson, this last film of a master of the macabre concentrates on illusionists, clairvoyants, magicians and the tricks of the trade. Excellent backdrop for what becomes, essentially, a murder mystery. Robert Young, tops at the craft, investigates the killings of demonologist Frederick Worlock and card manipulator Harold Minjir. Involved are frightened Florence Rice, handcuff king Henry Hull (a Houdini type), scientist Walter Kingsford, mentalists Lee Bowman and Astrid Allwyn, mystic Gloria Holden, and Frank Craven, Young's bucolic father. Browning uses some of the illusions offhandedly and, although everything gets explained away—television is employed in one instance—*Miracles* has an undeniable air of the supernatural at work.

S.O.S. TIDAL WAVE (Republic 1939) Directed by John H. Auer. Topflight feature with various elements meshed into a tale of political corruption. TV reporter Ralph Byrd opposes corrupt Ferris Taylor and Marc Lawrence, candidate and political party boss. To frighten voters away on election day, Lawrence airs TV scenes of the inundation of New York by tidal wave as a hoax. This footage is from the RKO *Deluge* (see 1933 entry) and became Republic's exclusive property. Also showing up on the TV screen are scenes from Republic's *Army Girl* (1938). The Armand Schaefer production treats television as a common part of everyday life, a decade before that was true. With George Barbier, Kay Sutton, Frank Jenks, Dorothy Lee, Oscar O'Shea, Mickey Kuhn (he was Montgomery Clift as a lad in *Red River,* 1948) and Donald Barry.

BLACK FRIDAY (Universal 1940) Directed by Arthur Lubin. Basically a gangster film with science fiction overtones, thanks to the Curt Siodmak-Eric Taylor screenplay. Boris Karloff, a noted surgeon, saves college professor Stanley Ridges' life by transplanting part of the brain of a dead gangster. However, Ridges takes on the latter's personality and begins to avenge the criminal on rival gangster Bela Lugosi and mob. Several things lift this above the average Karloff-Lugosi teaming. For one, they have no scenes together, nor do they use horrific makeup. Ridges dominates the film and changes personalities more by attitude than anything else. Publicity was derived from the use of a hypnotist, Manly P. Hall, to put Lugosi into a trance so that he could realistically play a death scene, by suffocation. Lugosi reportedly damaged the closet in which he was confined, without being aware of his actions. British-born Ridges, a baritone in musical comedies, never betrayed his origins in his lengthy screen career. Anne Nagel and Anne Gwynne play, respectively, the bad and good heroines, and an unbilled James Craig is the reporter to whom Karloff

S.O.S. TIDAL WAVE *(Republic 1939) Oscar O'Shea and Ralph Byrd view the inundation of New York (actually stock from 1933's* Deluge*) on an early large screen television receiver.*

BLACK FRIDAY *(Universal 1940) Having transformed into a criminal, Stanley Ridges turns on his old friend, Dr. Boris Karloff.*

relates his story. Originally, Lugosi had the Karloff role and Karloff was cast in the part(s) played by Ridges. It was determined that Karloff wasn't believable as an American gangster, so the footage was scrapped. Siodmak used the brain transposing theme more than once. This film, incidentally, had as its production title *Friday the Thirteenth,* which in another era developed a life of its own.

THE DEVIL BAT a.k.a. KILLER BATS (PRC 1940) Directed by Jean Yarbrough. This studio's first horror effort was also Bela Lugosi's sole film for the company. Despite repeated shots of the bats leaving Bela's belfry, the closeups of the winged mammal are chilling indeed. The murders are treated somewhat casually as good doctor Lugosi takes revenge on the families of partners in the cosmetics firm he helped to make successful. Dave O'Brien alternates between play-

THE MUMMY'S HAND *(Universal 1940) Peggy Moran and Dick Foran in the tomb.*

SON OF INGAGI *(Hollywood Productions/Sack Amusement 1940) Doctor Laura Bowman is horrified when apeman Zack Williams reacts to her experimental drug; a one-of-its-kind feature.*

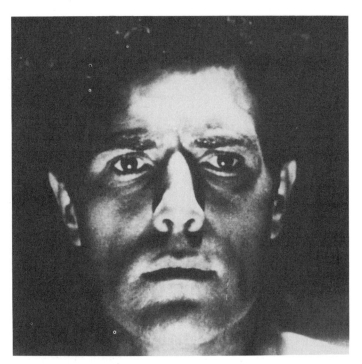

STRANGER ON THE THIRD FLOOR *(RKO Radio 1940) John McGuire finds himself in a nightmare, aided by imaginative special effects.*

ing for comedy or straight dramatics as the reporter on the case, while Arthur Q. Bryan (the voice of Elmer Fudd) subdues himself to perform as his editor. Leading ladies are Suzanne Kaaren and Yolande Mallott, later Yolande Donlan, major actress in British features. Ed Mortimer, a silent screen director who became a bit player and extra, is well cast as the head of Heath Cosmetics, and Donald Kerr supplies comedy relief as O'Brien's photographer. Sequel was *The Devil Bat's Daughter* (1946). The original was remade that year as *The Flying Serpent* with George Zucco, largely rewritten.

THE MUMMY'S HAND (Universal 1940) Directed by Christy Cabanne. First sequel to Boris Karloff's *The Mummy* (1932), from which it uses a generous excerpt, and the spawn for assorted sequels and remakes. George Zucco of the Cairo Museum is made to revive the 3,000-year-old mummy Kharis (Tom Tyler) by high priest Eduardo Ciannelli, Zucco's dying father, to protect the tomb of Princess Ananka, Kharis' long ago love. That tomb is uncovered by Zucco's associate, Charles Trowbridge, accompanied by adventurers Dick Foran and Wallace Ford, magician Cecil Kellaway and his daughter Peggy Moran. Lively doings in the giant tomb, which had been constructed for the larger budgeted *Green Hell* in 1939. Fluid photography by Elwood Bredell, editing by Philip Cahn and music directed by Hans J. Salter set the pace for the horrors to come.

SON OF INGAGI (Hollywood Productions-Sack Amusement Enterprises 1940) Produced and directed by Richard C. Kahn, who also wrote the story and continuity with featured actor Spencer Williams, Jr. Songs by The Toppers and Williams. Although the 1930 African documentary *Ingagi* has been revealed as a sham, consisting of pilfered footage and California-shot sequences, it was a huge hit and inspired, among others, this in-name-only all-black feature. *Son*, produced under the title *House of Horror,* emerges as the only all-black horror-musical-romantic comedy ever made. Scientist Laura Bowman is killed by the apeman (Zack Williams) she has brought back from Africa. Newlyweds Daisy Bufford and Alfred Grant inherit her mansion, unaware that the ape is loose or that $20,000 in gold is buried on the premises. Dumb detective Spencer Williams, Jr., is unable to prevent the mysterious happenings, including a fire. The latter was a writer, director, producer, editor and composer on many all-black films; in the early Fifties, he became famous as The Kingfish on the "Amos and Andy" TV series.
[Presented at The CoOp in 1980 as part of a Worst Film Festival, being well received; in 1988, a CoOp successor ran this with negative results. Had the audience grown up in the intervening years?]

STRANGER ON THE THIRD FLOOR (RKO Radio 1940)

Directed by Boris Ingster. Take a movie which has been called, accurately or not, the first *film noir;* a first time director; a star who hardly appears in the footage; and a story that really begins halfway through the 64 minutes. Result: one of the most bizarre, fascinating productions of its time. Reporter John McGuire helps convict cabby Elisha Cook, Jr., of murder on circumstantial evidence. Before Cook is executed, McGuire comes to believe that mysterious Peter Lorre could be the murderer. McGuire puts himself into Cook's position with a nightmare in which hated neighbor Charles Halton is killed and McGuire condemned for the crime. The surrealistic nightmare, special effects by Vernon L. Walker and photography by Nicholas Musuraca, turn an ordinary narrative into something unusual. From there, things come to a quick conclusion as McGuire is accused of Halton's death in actuality and sweetheart Margaret Tallichet tracks down Lorre as the killer in both cases. The leading lady would soon retire to become the wife of William Wyler and mother of their four children.

CRACKED NUTS (Universal 1941)

Directed by Edward F. Cline. Zany comedy with a mechanical man as a centerpiece. Stuart Erwin, a country lad (as he was usually cast), wins $5,000 in a contest (big money for the time) and becomes a target for confidence men. Ivan the Robot, designed to help in Erwin's fleecing, is modeled after featured actor Mischa Auer, but Ernie Stanton is credited with actually being in the costume. A great cast of studio farceurs—Una Merkel, William Frawley, Mantan Moreland, Shemp Howard, Astrid Allwyn, Marion Martin—adds to the nuttiness.

KING OF THE ZOMBIES (Monogram 1941)

Directed by Jean Yarbrough. Flyers John Archer and Dick Purcell and servant Mantan Moreland land on a Caribbean island, where doctor Henry Victor is creating zombies for use by the Axis powers. Archer falls for Victor's niece Joan Woodbury, while both Purcell and Moreland become zombies themselves. Fairly ordinary horror pic which becomes hilarious in the hands of black comic Moreland. With more than two decades of performing already behind him, he makes the picture his own by refusing to take any of it seriously. Marching his fellow zombies as soldiers, he manages to get off several funny lines. A good example of a routine film being turned into a better one through the efforts of its most talented performer. Oscar nomination to Edward Kay, Best Scoring of a Dramatic Picture.

MAN MADE MONSTER (Universal 1941)

Directed by George Waggner. Based on the story "The

CRACKED NUTS *(Universal 1941) Ivan the Robot, played by Ernie Stanton, is in Mischa Auer's image, prompting reactions from Astrid Allwyn and Una Merkel.*

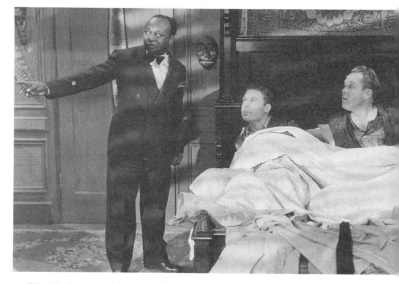

KING OF THE ZOMBIES *(Monogram 1941) Mantan Moreland scene steals as John Archer and Dick Purcell watch, hopelessly.*

Electric Man" by H. J. Essex, Sid Schwartz and Len Golos, this was produced under the title *The Mysterious Dr. R.* and reissued as *The Atomic Monster.* Lon Chaney, Jr., in his first true horror film, is Dynamo Dan, the Electrical Man, a carnival performer and sole survivor of a bus crash into a high tension pole. Doctor Lionel Atwill finds that Chaney is immune to electricity and uses him in experiments to create a race of superhumans run solely by electricity. Given the electric chair for killing Atwill's colleague, doctor Samuel S. Hinds, Chaney survives, his entire body glowing with deadly charges. A 59-minute classic, one of the best made by either Chaney or Atwill, both perfectly cast. Frank Albertson and Anne Nagel provide love interest as sympathetic observers. John Fulton's special effects and Charles Previn's musical direction are great assets.

FRANKENSTEIN MEETS THE WOLF MAN *(Universal 1942) Lon Chaney Jr. as The Wolf Man and Bela Lugosi as Frankenstein's Monster floor Ilona Massey.*

THE MONSTER AND THE GIRL (Paramount 1941) Directed by Stuart Heisler. Produced under the title, *D.O.A.*, this offers an excellent combination of horror and gangster themes with a daring plot twist. Ellen Drew is led by her seemingly nice young husband, Robert Paige, into a white slavery ring headed by Paul Lukas, who frames Drew's brother Phillip Terry for murder. Doctor George Zucco, however, puts Terry's brain into an ape that then sets about to exact revenge upon the gang. Charles Gemora, one of the best known portrayers of apes, actually puts pathos into his performance with only the use of his eyes. Rod Cameron emerges as the hero, although he's listed far down in a major cast: Joseph Calleia, Onslow Stevens, Marc Lawrence, Gerald Mohr, Willard Robertson, Cliff Edwards, Abner Biberman, Edward Van Sloan, Emma Dunn, Dave Willock.

FRANKENSTEIN MEETS THE WOLF MAN (Universal 1942 copyright, 1943 release) Directed by Roy William Neill. First instance of two film monsters meeting on the Universal lot is a well done affair. Lon Chaney, Jr., as Larry Talbot, The Wolf Man, finding that he can't die, tries to unearth doctor Frankenstein's records as a means of obtaining release from his affliction. He meets Bela Lugosi as The Monster (stuntman Eddie Parker doubling) and both undergo operations by doctor Patric Knowles. A complicated concept had Chaney slated to play both monsters; that and other twists were dropped. In general, each sequel picked up where the previous entry left off and Curt Siodmak followed that pattern here. A good cast, worth repeating, includes Ilona Massey, Lionel Atwill, Maria Ouspenskaya, Dennis Hoey, Dwight Frye, Adia Kuznetzoff, Jeff Corey, Doris Lloyd and Martha MacVicar (Martha Vickers).

CALLING DR. DEATH *(Universal 1943) Patricia Morison finally has a decent role as Lon Chaney Jr. hypnotizes her into revealing any knowledge of his wife's death.*

DEAD MEN WALK *(PRC 1943) George Zucco finds the crypt of his vampiric twin vacant; the actor is in familiar surroundings, as the set served as his estate in the swamp in* The Mad Monster *(1942).*

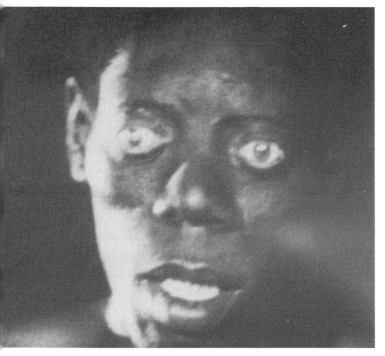

I WALKED WITH A ZOMBIE *(RKO Radio 1943) Darby Jones as the monster in question, who walks with Frances Dee.*

CALLING DR. DEATH (Universal 1943) Directed by Reginald LeBorg. First of six "Inner Sanctum" mysteries, all of variable quality from excellent to poor and all starring Lon Chaney, Jr. Each is introduced by a disembodied head (David Hoffman) who sets the stage for a strange tale. "Inner Sanctum" debuted on radio in January 1941, with the sound of a squeaking door and then a mysterious voice introducing the episode. In the first filmization, Chaney is a neurologist whose hated wife Ramsay Ames is killed, to the relief of his nurse Patricia Morison. Not happy about the death is Ames' lover, architect David Bruce, whose wife Fay Helm is a cripple. Inspector J. Carrol Naish suspects Chaney, since the latter is unsure that he didn't murder during a binge. In a well done dream sequence (special effects by John P.

Fulton), Chaney hypnotizes Morison into revealing what she knows of Ames' death. Isabel Jewell was a casualty of Norman A. Cerf's editing, which otherwise went smoothly.

DEAD MEN WALK (PRC 1943) Directed by Sam Newfield. Only one dead man walks as vampire Elwyn Clayton (George Zucco) returns from death at the hands of good twin Dr. Lloyd (Zucco with glasses and wig). Good reworking of an old tale, and one of PRC's best. Zucco underplays in both roles, as opposed to his histrionics as the mad doctor of *The Mad Monster* (1942) and tongue-in-cheek approach to *The Black Raven* (1943), another goodie. *Dead Men Walk* is interesting for its cast. Mary Carlisle, platinum blonde of the Thirties, lends beauty and charm to her last movie, at 31, while Dwight Frye in his last major horror role (he died later in 1943) belies his 43 years by looking haggard as the loyal, hunchbacked servant. Carlisle is a redhead while Frye, formerly blond, is dark haired. Juvenile lead Nedrick Young was later a screenwriter and authored Elvis' *Jailhouse Rock* (1957), and Al St. John, in a respite from the Buster Crabbe Westerns, has a bit. Zucco's estate from *The Mad Monster* serves as the crypt for the evil twin.

I WALKED WITH A ZOMBIE (RKO Radio 1943) Directed by Jacques Tourneur. Second of the nine horror pictures produced by Val Lewton between 1942 and 1946, and the only one which doesn't hold up as well as the others. Based on scientific information from articles by Inez Wallace, the Curt Siodmak-Ardel Wray screenplay is really a reworking of Charlotte Bronte's *Jane Eyre,* set in modern day Haiti. Nurse Frances Dee, summoned by Tom Conway to care for his catatonic wife Christine Gordon, finds that the patient's a zombie. One chilling scene has Dee encountering the giant zombie guard Darby Jones. *Zombie* was edited by Mark Robson, who directed four of the succeeding Lewton productions. With James Ellison, James Bell, Edith Barrett, Theresa Harris, calypso singer Sir Lancelot of the lilting voice, and dancer Jeni Le Gon.

SON OF DRACULA (Universal 1943) Directed by Robert Siodmak. Count Alucard—Dracula spelled backwards—arrives at the Southern plantation Dark Oaks to claim Louise Allbritton as a bride, to the distress of her fiancé Robert Paige and her sister Evelyn Ankers. Quite good thriller, the production title of which was *Destiny,* with Lon Chaney, Jr., adding yet another monster portrayal to his expanding repertoire—he was dubbed at the time "the screen's master character creator," character in this case meaning monster. In her only horror outing, Allbritton conveys the darker aspects of an obsessed woman who becomes a vampire. Although she and Ankers play sisters and both were blondes, Allbritton chose to wear a long dark wig for contrast; the explanation for this was that audiences would be confused between the two. Also in the cast: Frank Craven, J. Edward Bromberg and Samuel S. Hinds. Hans Salter's score borrows from his and Frank Skinner's music for *Seven Sinners* (1940).

BLUEBEARD (PRC 1944) Directed by Edgar G. Ulmer. After *Detour* (see 1945 Crime entry), this is considered to be PRC's best effort. John Carradine persuasively portrays a 19th century Parisian artist who is compelled to murder his models. Jean Parker nearly becomes a victim, but is saved by police inspector Nils Asther. A Punch and Judy show adds to the very gloomy atmosphere, with an admirable recreation of Grand Guignol settings and some unusual special effects. A

GILDERSLEEVE'S GHOST *(RKO Radio 1944) Gorgeous Marion Martin is about to be rendered invisible by doctor Frank Reicher, as assistant Joseph Vitale ponders the sense of it.*

DESTINY *(Universal 1944) Alan Curtis, a fugitive, is told by blind Gloria Jean that an abandoned and crumbling church is her Paradise.*

HOUSE OF FRANKENSTEIN *(Universal 1944) Time out from horror: Elaine Naish, 12, shows the jewelry willed to her by godmother Mrs. Leslie Carter, the famed stage actress, to father J. Carrol and Elena Verdugo between scenes.*

smallish cast includes veteran actors and fledgling actresses: Ludwig Stossel, George Pembroke, Iris Adrian, Teala Loring, Henry Kolker, Emmett Lynn, Patti McCarty and, as Renee, the soon-to-be Mrs. Carradine, Sonia Sorel.

DESTINY (Universal 1944)

Directed by Reginald LeBorg and Julien Duvivier. When *Flesh and Fantasy* was released in 1943, it was comprised of three main tales of the supernatural, rather than four. What would have been the first episode was expanded by LeBorg, adding sequences to Duvivier's original. This hybrid, released as *Destiny,* starred a non-singing Gloria Jean, then Universal's competition to its major star, Deanna Durbin. The film didn't make Jean a major star, and she did just a few others for the studio before moving on briefly to other companies. Here, she's a blind girl, daughter of Frank Craven, at whose farmhouse fugitive Alan Curtis suddenly appears. He falls for Jean and decides to do away with her father. Running from Curtis, she plunges into a stormy night. The powers of nature that protect her turn against Curtis and then… The quality of Duvivier's dark and brooding approach is in sharp contrast to LeBorg's sunnier surrounding. Yet, as presented, it does have a point, one well worth seeing. With Grace McDonald, Minna Gombell, Vivian Austin and Frank Fenton, all of whom contribute to Curtis' flight.

GILDERSLEEVE'S GHOST (RKO Radio 1944)

Directed by Gordon Douglas. The Great Gildersleeve originated on the "Fibber McGee and Molly" radio show before graduating to his own program in 1941. Similarly, the character evolved from the McGee movies at RKO to a short-lived series of his own. This, the last and best, is the only one with a science fiction plot. Harold Peary as Gildy is running for re-election as water commissioner of Summerfield. Two of his ancestors, now ghosts (both played by Peary), spy on doctor Frank Reicher's laboratory and find that he's discovered the secret of invisibility. A gorilla (Charles Gemora) becomes invisible and chorus girl Marion Martin can disappear at will. Martin, despite her limited footage, steals the show on cue and gets to whistle the popular "Wishing" (B. G. DeSylva) from *Love Affair* (1939). With Richard Le Grand, Amelita Ward, Freddie Mercer, Marie Blake, Joseph Vitale and Margie Stewart.

HOUSE OF FRANKENSTEIN a.k.a. DOOM OF DRACULA (Universal 1944)

Directed by Erle C. Kenton. Based on the story "The Devil's Brood" (also the film's production title) by Curt Siodmak. Nearly all of the famous movie monsters of Universal make appearances in this all-star extravaganza. Doctor Boris Karloff and his hunchbacked aide J. Carrol Naish seize George Zucco's traveling Chamber of Horrors and revive Dracula (John Carradine), the Wolf Man (Lon Chaney, Jr.) and the Frankenstein Monster (Glenn Strange), causing havoc everywhere. The lively doings resulted in some firsts. Karloff was appearing in his first Frankenstein film not playing the Monster, although some audience members thought he was doing both, via trick photography; Carradine was debuting in the Dracula part, which he would revive for decades after; and Strange was having his first turn at the Monster, playing it twice more. He had the help and support of both Karloff and Chaney in his characterization and wore the same costume that the latter had for *Ghost of Frankenstein* (1942)—Strange and Chaney being of the same build. Naish researched his role by finding a hunchbacked derelict and studying his walk and gestures while paying the man's expenses. Elena Verdugo, of Spanish descent, hides her blonde tresses under a dark wig and does a gypsy dance. Others of the all-stars: Anne Gwynne, Peter Coe, Lionel Atwill, Sig Ruman, Frank Reicher. Later meetings of the monsters were made as travesties.

JOHNNY DOESN'T LIVE HERE ANYMORE (Monogram 1944)

Directed by Joe May (his last directorial credit). A King Brothers production. Reissued as *And So They Were Married*. In crowded wartime Washington, French Canadian Simone Simon leases Marine William Terry's apartment and finds that all of his buddies have keys. Both Terry and his sailor pal James Ellison fall for Simon, while Chief Petty Officer Robert Mitchum (described in the dialogue as looking like a movie star which he certainly was soon to be) wants the place for a rendezvous, with his wife. Placing this in the fantasy category is the inclusion of a gremlin (midget Jerry Maren) to upset Simon's plans. Also, the epilogue occurs in the future, 1949, and features Alan Dinehart, who died one month after the film's release. Very engaging comedy, with quite a cast; also: Minna Gombell, Chick Chandler, Gladys Blake, Grady Sutton, Dorothy Granger, Janet Shaw, Douglas Fowley and horror man Rondo Hatton as a scary undertaker.

THE LADY AND THE MONSTER (Republic 1944) Directed by George Sherman. Production titles, *Monster and the Lady* and *The Monster.* Reissued in 1950 as *Tiger Man.* First film version of Curt Siodmak's novel *Donovan's Brain* and the first straight dramatic role for Vera Hruba Ralston. At an Arizona mansion, doctor Erich von Stroheim and his assistant Richard Arlen develop a machine which keeps the brain alive after death. Ralston, ward of von Stroheim and daughter of a late colleague, falls in love with Arlen. When the brain of dead financier W. H. Donovan, from a nearby plane crash, takes control of Arlen, the scientist is driven to commit crimes on its behalf. One of Republic's infrequent forays into horror and a good one. With Mary Nash, Sidney Blackmer, Helen Vinson, Juanita Quigley and, as a grandmother, Josephine Dillon, Clark Gable's first wife. Remade, officially and otherwise, various times.

THE SOUL OF A MONSTER (Columbia 1944) Directed by Will Jason. Good work from a director usually associated with comedy and music, using all of the gimmicks: a foreword and epilogue, angled shots, a sequence in negative. As humane doctor George Mac- ready lies near death, his wife Jeanne Bates calls on any power, good or evil, to save him. Strange Rose Hobart, who is unhurt when run over by a car, does so, but Macready changes completely and turns into a cold blooded, unfeeling monster (without makeup). In the smallish cast: Jim Bannon, Erik Rolf, Ida Moore and Clarence Muse, who provides one of the many musical interludes by playing boogie woogie on piano.

WEIRD WOMAN (Universal 1944) Directed by Re- ginald LeBorg. An "Inner Sanctum" mystery, based on the novel *Conjure Wife* by Fritz Leiber, Jr. College professor Lon Chaney, Jr.'s superstitious wife Anne Gwynne uses voodoo from the South Seas to further his career. Jealous ex-girlfriend Evelyn Ankers blames her crimes on Gwynne. Which is the weirder woman? John Fulton's special effects enhance Virgil Miller's fine pho- tography, as do Ralph Morgan, Lois Collier, Elizabeth Russell, Phil Brown and Elisabeth Risdon. Remade in England as *Burn, Witch, Burn (Night of the Eagle,* 1962) and in the U.S. as *Witches' Brew* (1980), a comedy.

JOHNNY DOESN'T LIVE HERE ANYMORE *(Monogram 1944) Defense worker Simone Simon finds many people have keys to her rented apartment, as she chats with Janet Shaw and Marine Sergeant Dick Rich; a comedy fantasy.*

THE LADY AND THE MONSTER *(Republic 1944) Di- rector George Sherman reported that stars Erich von Stroheim and Vera Hruba Ralston were cooperative dur- ing the making of the thriller, as this on-set party indicates.*

BEWITCHED *(MGM 1945) No relation to the TV series: Edmund Gwenn and Phyllis Thaxter examine her split personalities.*

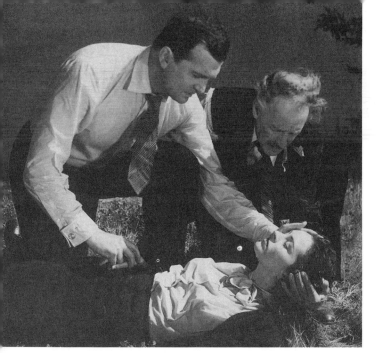

THE WOMAN WHO CAME BACK *(Republic 1945)*
John Loder and Otto Kruger aid Nancy Kelly, suspected of being a witch.

BEWITCHED (MGM 1945) Directed and adapted by Arch Oboler from his radio play *Alter Ego,* which was the film's production title. The few Arch Oboler films have been unusual, for the most part, and this, his first, was no exception. Sweet Phyllis Thaxter hears a voice which appeals to a baser self and leads her to New York, where she's attracted to lawyer Horace (Stephen) McNally. When her former fiancé Henry H. (Hank) Daniels, Jr., arrives to return her home, Thaxter stabs him. Psychiatrist Edmund Gwenn attempts to save her from execution by alienating the other self. Audrey Totter excels as the voice from within, but Thaxter plays that self in a brief scene near the end. Only a few false notes mar the overall quality of Oboler's best work. Music by the talented (and later Oscar-winning) Bronislau Kaper is also quite good.

FOG ISLAND (PRC 1945) Co-produced and directed by Terry Morse. Based on the play *Angel Island* by Bernadine Angus. Off the Florida coast is Fog Island, built by pirates and owned by once wealthy George Zucco. Having served time for embezzlement, he invites those responsible for his downfall and his wife's death to join him and stepdaughter Sharon Douglas. Accepting because they believe he has a buried treasure are Lionel Atwill and Jerome Cowan, who framed Zucco; ex-secretary Veda Ann Borg; psychic Jacqueline de Wit; and young John Whitney, who loves Douglas. Former Zucco cellmate Ian Keith also turns up and quickly disposes of butler George Lloyd, another ex-convict, while the various "guests" go about disposing of one another. Morse has overcome the stage limitations of the plot and uses Ira Morgan's cinematography and Paul Palmentola's art direction to good advantage—for one of PRC's last really good horror films.

A GAME OF DEATH a.k.a. DANGEROUS ADVENTURE (RKO Radio 1945) Directed by Robert Wise. Based on Richard Connell's short story "The Most Dangerous Game," which was also the title of RKO's original version in 1932, with Joel McCrea, Fay Wray, Leslie Banks and native Noble Johnson, who is visible in the stock shots. First official redoing of a classic, with many more versions to come. Edgar Barrier is the madman who hunts humans for sport, John Loder and Audrey Long are his main targets. Best of all the later editions, the most famous being *Run for the Sun* (1956) with Richard Widmark and Jane Greer.

THE PHANTOM SPEAKS (Republic 1945) Directed by John English. The phantom is Tom Powers, executed for the murder of his wife's lover, Ralf Harolde. Before the execution, though, doctor Stanley Ridges—who has been experimenting with the theory that he can communicate with the dead—tells Powers that his will is strong enough to return. Later, Powers takes over Ridges' mind and has him kill his lawyer Joseph Granby, the unfaithful burlesque dancer Marion Martin, and witness Garry Owen. Reporter Richard Arlen, who loves Ridges' daughter Lynne Roberts, suspects that something is not right. As he did in a similar role in *Black Friday* (see 1940 entry), Ridges dominates with his portrayal of a man under the spell of another, powerful personality. Derivative, but well done.

STRANGLER OF THE SWAMP (PRC 1945) Directed by Frank Wisbar. Screenplay by Wisbar and Harold Erickson, from Wisbar and Leo McCarthy's story. Remake of the German film *Fahrmann Maria (Ferryman Maria,* 1936). German director Wisbar took an old legend and made it twice, improving upon it despite an extremely low budget. Rosemary La Planche operates a ferry service through a thick swamp which is haunted by the spirit of strangler Charles Middleton, who was hanged. The strong presence of Robert Barrat, one of the locals, helps to defeat the strangler and save the life of his son, Blake Edwards—playing his first major role as an actor, having just a few more parts before switching to producing, directing, writing, etc. When run back to back on the same bill by Bill Everson, the lowly PRC proved to be more exciting than the stylish but slow original.

THE WOMAN WHO CAME BACK (Republic 1945) Produced and directed by Walter Colmes. Originating from an idea by writer and later producer Philip Yordan, this intriguing tale concerns Nancy Kelly's return to her New England town, where she's suspected of being a witch. Doctor John Loder and reverend Otto Kruger attempt to help, while Ruth Ford spreads lies.

The supernatural elements are logically explained, for the most part, but still leave lingering doubts. As any good film of this type should.

THE BRUTE MAN (Universal/PRC 1946) Directed by Jean Yarbrough. Known as The Monster Without Makeup, Rondo Hatton suffered from acromegaly, a nervous disease in which the head, hands and feet are swollen. His grotesque features made him ripe for horror roles, but these parts came very late in his film career, which started in 1930 with a bit in *Hell Harbor*. Universal began casting him as The Creeper in the mid-Forties and *The Brute Man* was to be his first starring role in that characterization. Unfortunately, he died of a heart attack, at just 50, before the film was released and so PRC took over its distribution. Hatton's character starts out as handsome young Fred Coby, whose face is scarred by acid, turning him into The Creeper. He avenges himself on nemesis Tom Neal and finds comfort with piano teacher Jane Adams who is, naturally, blind. Under the circumstances, this is a poignant tale of what might have been, if Hatton had lived. Also in the cast are Jan Wiley, Peter Whitney and Donald MacBride. For once, Universal's famed makeup expert Jack Pierce, who worked on the film, couldn't improve on the real horror.

FEAR IN THE NIGHT (Paramount 1947) Directed and written by Maxwell Shane. Based on the short story "Nightmare" by William Irish (Cornell Woolrich). In his first film, DeForest Kelley stars as a man who has a nightmare in which he's attacked in a room filled with mirrors. After killing the attacker with an electric drill, Kelley finds his dream may be coming true. Brother-in-law Paul Kelly, a police detective, sister Ann Doran, and fiancée Kay Scott are with Kelley when he finds the mirrored room at a mansion where the four have taken refuge from a storm. The tortured Kelley makes a good impression for the studio at which, in the part of Dr. Bones McCoy of *Star Trek*, he'd find his greatest fame as an actor. The nightmarish quality is well sustained in a higher budgeted Pine-Thomas production helmed by their longtime scripter, Shane, also making his debut as a director. With them, he remade the film as *Nightmare* (United Artists 1956), starring Kevin McCarthy and Edward G. Robinson in the Kelley-Kelly roles, with equally impressive results. Frank Paul Sylos contributed his art direction to both films.

THE AMAZING MR. X (formerly THE SPIR-ITUALIST) (Eagle-Lion 1948) Directed by Bernard Vorhaus. A classic of stylization with dazzling effects throughout. Lynn Bari, a wealthy young Pacific Coast widow, is convinced by medium Turhan Bey that he can

FEAR IN THE NIGHT *(Paramount 1947) DeForest Kelley and Kay Scott. He was debuting at the studio which would one day make him immortal.*

contact her husband Donald Curtis, killed in an auto accident. Her sister Cathy O'Donnell and friend Richard Carlson are unbelievers, but Bari is convinced of Bey's powers. It develops that Curtis is alive and conspiring with the spiritualist to gain control of Bari's estate. Magician Harry Mendoza was technical adviser and appears as a former illusionist, now a detective, determined to expose Bey's trickery. Virginia Gregg is the only other prominent member of the small but, yes, spirited cast. Cinematographer John Alton takes great advantage of the settings to create a fantastic atmosphere. For one shot, he mounted an extreme wide angle lens in a crystal ball for effect. Others deserving credit for their contributions: Alex Weldon (special effects), George J. Teague (photographic effects), Jack R. Rabin (special art effects), Alexander Laszlo (music), even Leon S. Becker and Frank McWhorter (sound).

ROCKETSHIP X-M a.k.a. EXPEDITION MOON-(Lippert 1950) Produced, directed and written by Kurt Neumann. Assistant director, Frank Heath. At mid-century, filmmakers were already dreaming of space exploration and other worlds to conquer. What better way to do all this than to start a new trend, although Georges Méliès made his *A Trip to the Moon* in 1902, with color. As a nod to that, the Lippert release uses red tint for the scenes on Mars, filmed in Death Valley and Red Rock Canyon. Rocketship Expedition Moon, piloted by colonel Lloyd Bridges, is launched from White Sands, New Mexico. Aboard are designer-physicist John Emery, Swiss mathematician Osa Massen, navigator Hugh O'Brian and engineer major Noah Beery, Jr., from Texas. Meteorites accelerate the ship's speed and throw it off course, landing instead on Mars, whose inhabitants prove to be primitive. An unexpected ending makes this first effort of the Fifties even more out of the ordinary. As an indicator of things to come, one of the correspondents is played by Judd Holdren, who starred in the

GLEN OR GLENDA *(Screen Classics 1953) Fantasy scene with narrator Bela Lugosi and transvestite Tommy Haynes. This film was once presented by the Syracuse Cinephiles at its Worse Than Bad Film Festival.*

IT CONQUERED THE WORLD *(American International 1956) Police Chief Taggart Casey is about to be blowtorched by Lee Van Cleef, a misguided scientist under control of a Venusian force.*

futuristic serial *Captain Video* (1951). *Rocketship X-M* was reissued in 1978 with new footage made by film-maker-distributor-buff Wade Williams.

BELA LUGOSI MEETS A BROOKLYN GORILLA a.k.a. THE MONSTER MEETS THE GORIL-LA (Realart 1952)

Directed by William Beaudine. TV title, *The Boys From Brooklyn.* With a title like that, you'd think it was funny, and you'd be right. In their film debuts, Duke Mitchell and 18-year-old Sammy Petrillo do

on-target takeoffs on Dean Martin and Jerry Lewis, while Bela does his standard mad scientist in the jungle. Intentionally making a monkey out of Mitchell, Lugosi gets his revenge on the singing half of the duo. Mitchell uses "'Deed I Do" (Walter Hirsch-Fred Rose) as his theme song, to prove to Petrillo that he's really a man-made ape. Mitchell appeared in a few other films and died at 55 in 1981; Petrillo, who once played Lewis' baby son on TV, later became a TV producer. The cast also includes Charlita, Muriel Landers and Ray Corrigan as a gorilla.

GLEN OR GLENDA (Screen Classics 1953)

Directed and written by Edward D. Wood, Jr. Also known as *Glen or Glenda, Which Is It?; I Led 2 Lives; I Changed My Sex; He or She,* and *Transvestite.* By any other name, one of the most incoherent films of all time. Bela Lugosi as the scientist warns "Bevare!" as he describes what evils lurk for the transvestite. Universally regarded as a poor director, Ed Wood, in his filmmaking debut, uses the name Daniel Davis as he plays the title roles, opposite Dolores Fuller (Wood's wife at the time), also making her debut, as his fiancée. A then-daring scene has Fuller removing her angora sweater for Davis to wear, revealing her foundation garment. Lots of stock shots and surrealistic scenes place this in the fantasy category—if any category can be deciphered. Timothy Farrell tries to explain to inspector Lyle Talbot—both Wood regulars—the stories of men who prefer to wear women's clothing. Among those handling more than one function is the producer, George Weiss, who shows up as the janitor. Not released in New York until 1963, this was actually reissued in 1981 by Paramount, unsuccessfully, as *I Led 2 Lives,* after its cult status had been established. As Bela says, "So many people. Going so many places," which is where this film could drive you.

INVASION OF THE BODY SNATCHERS (Allied Artists 1956)

Directed by Don Siegel. Assistant directors, Richard Maybery and Bill Beaudine, Jr. Based on Jack Finney's *Collier's* magazine serial and 1955 novel *The Body Snatchers,* one of the film's production titles (the other: *They Came From Another World*). An agitated Kevin McCarthy shouts to anyone who'll listen, "They're here!" He's referring to the alien pods which are cloning citizens as unfeeling creatures. This remains one of the best known science fiction features, with a plot that has been interpreted as a manifestation of the Cold War, an attack on McCarthyism or just good moviemaking. Making it believable are: Dana Wynter, Carolyn Jones, King Donovan, Larry Gates, Jean Willes, Whit Bissell, Virginia Christine and Sam Peckinpah—who contributed to the screenplay with Daniel Mainwaring (a.k.a. Geoffrey Homes). Originally in SuperScope and Perspecta Sound; remade by United Artists in 1978, with McCarthy in a cameo, reprising his original situation, if not the role itself (now played by Donald Sutherland). Influential, but not a big favorite in this corner.

IT CONQUERED THE WORLD (American International 1956) Produced and directed by Roger Corman, who also worked on Lou Rusoff's script. First really good AIP sci-fi/monster pic, making much use of Griffith Park locales. Misguided scientist Lee Van Cleef directs an invasion of earth by Venus, feeling that the creatures can only improve matters on his planet. Accompanying a Venusian creature are swift bat-like creatures that turn a colleague's wife into a zombie. The colleague kills the zombie-wife and Van Cleef discovers his own murdered by the creature, which he then destroys with a blowtorch, dying in the process. Odd casting has Van Cleef, normally a villain, as the scientist and Beverly Garland as his wife, rather than that of nominal star Peter Graves (sweet Sally Fraser is his spouse). The creature is played by Paul Blaisdell in a marvel of economy, since he also did the special effects. Corman regulars Dick Miller and Jonathan Haze are featured, while Garland emerges as a sensuous and tough woman, who attempts to finish the creature by herself. Remade for TV as *Zontar the Thing From Venus* (1966) with genre veteran John Agar.

I WAS A TEENAGE WEREWOLF (American International 1957) Directed by Gene Fowler, Jr. Important horror film in that it successfully combined themes of wayward youth and monster movies. First starring film for Michael Landon, who made remarkably few features, and initial directorial credit for Fowler, during a brief respite from editing and writing chores. Analyst Whit Bissell, in treating teenager Landon for antisocial behavior, uses drugs and hypnosis to regress the youth back to a primitive animal. On a killing spree, Landon murders Dawn Richard in the gym—the transformation scene, from her perspective upside down on parallel bars, is the film's highlight. Rounding out the cast: Yvonne Lime, Vladimir Sokoloff and Guy Williams, TV's "Zorro." Originally released with the comic *Invasion of the Saucer Men*.

THE BLOB (Paramount 1958) Directed by Irvin S. Yeaworth, Jr. One of the most famous sci-fi pictures of the Fifties, made for just $240,000 in Valley Forge, Pennslyvania, has several notable firsts. It was the maiden production of Jack H. Harris, who later produced and distributed other films of this type; it was director Yeaworth's initial credit; and it was the first leading role for star Steve (then Steven) McQueen. In DeLuxe Color, the low budgeter is among the most naturalistic of its type, because of the low budget, fresh locations and cast and realistic dialogue by first time screenwriters Theodore Simonson and Kate Phillips. McQueen and his girl

I WAS A TEENAGE WEREWOLF *(American International 1957) Dawn Richard can't escape Michael Landon in a horror hit of its day.*

THE BLOB *(Paramount 1958) Olin Howlin becomes first victim of the blob, as teens Aneta Corseaut and Steve McQueen and doctor Stephen Chase discover.*

Aneta Corseaut discover that a mass from outer space is able to absorb any object in its path. Elderly Olin Howlin (a.k.a. Howland) is the first victim, his arm being devoured initially, in one of the film's most effective sequences. Another good scene has teens enjoying a horror movie at a theater, when the blob attacks the projection booth and makes its presence felt on the screen. McQueen, then 28, is a bit difficult to accept as a teenager, but his natural style overcomes that problem. Stephen Chase, Vince Barbi and Robert Fields are among the few cast members to have a later career of any note. Title song, by newcomer Burt Bacharach and veteran Mack David became a hit, further enhancing the indelible image on the consciousness. Actually, how many horror films can boast of having a hit title song? Revamped by Harris as *Beware! The Blob* (1972), a sequel directed by Larry Hagman. The original was remade in 1988 much more elaborately by Tri-Star as *The Blob*.

I BURY THE LIVING *(United Artists 1958)* Richard Boone fears he has the power of life and death as his cemetery begins filling.

I MARRIED A MONSTER FROM OUTER SPACE *(Paramount 1958) Effective thriller with newlyweds Tom Tryon and Gloria Talbott and uninvited guest.*

I BURY THE LIVING (United Artists 1958) Co-produced and directed by Albert Band. Businessman Richard Boone, taking over as chairman of the local cemetery, discovers that when he places black pins on a large map of the plots, the owners die. Boone then comes to think he has mystical powers over the living, and the dead. Intriguing premise, well executed—so to speak. Nice camerawork by Frederick Gately creates the proper mood. With Theodore Bikel as the elderly caretaker, Peggy Maurer, Robert Osterloh, Glen Vernon and Cyril Delevanti. In the Seventies, Band's son Charles continued the family filmmaking tradition by turning out thrillers of his own.

I MARRIED A MONSTER FROM OUTER SPACE (Paramount 1958) Directed by Gene Fowler, Jr. As the critics said, almost universally, don't be misled by the title—this is a good sci-fi effort, produced and directed by a former editor for Fritz Lang and Sam Fuller. After marrying Tom Tryon, Gloria Talbott discovers that he isn't the man she loves but his clone, an unfeeling monster from outer space. He and fellow clones have taken over the bodies of local townsmen, for the purpose of repopulating their own planet. The enigmatic personality of Tryon, later a best-selling author, is for once entirely appropriate to his character. Valerie Allen, who plays the bar girl, recalls her demise as waiting for an off-camera gun to be fired and then reacting as if she'd been shot before falling to the ground. Special effects made it appear that she was hit by a ray and then disintegrated. Old friends on the production crew include John P. Fulton (special photographic effects) and Charles Gemora (makeup). With Ken Lynch, John Eldredge, Maxie Rosenbloom, Alan Dexter, Ty Hungerford (Hardin) and Mary Treen.

MACABRE (Allied Artists 1958) Produced and directed by William Castle. The first of Castle's nonstop thrillers and his initial gimmick pic, with moviegoers given a $1,000 life insurance policy from Lloyds of London, to be paid if they died of fright from watching the film. The story revolves around William Prince, a small-town doctor whose female relatives seem to be dying off. Most of the excitement occurs in a cemetery as a search for his daughter Linda Guderman takes place. Ellen Corby, Jacqueline Scott and Philip Tonge are co-starred and another interesting piece of casting is that of Jim Backus in the non-comic role of the sheriff. Robb White's fanciful script was based on the novel *The Marble Forest* by Theo Durrant, a pseudonym for twelve different authors, the best known of whom was Anthony Boucher—critic, editor, Sherlock Holmes adaptor, and detective and sci-fi writer. (The annual Bouchercon, a convention for mystery writers and devotees, is named in his memory.)

NIGHT OF THE BLOOD BEAST (*American International 1958) Ed Nelson in high tension danger, part of a sci fier about a pregnant man.*

NIGHT OF THE BLOOD BEAST a.k.a. THE CREATURE FROM GALAXY 27 (American International 1958) Directed by Bernard L. Kowalski. Touted as being the first film about a pregnant man, true science fiction. Considering that premise, though, this is a good feature. Major Michael Emmet returns from space with foreign cells placed in his body by an alien being (Ross Sturlin). Eventually, the cells will produce similar beings, but Emmet decides not to be a breeder. Small cast—Angela Greene, Ed Nelson, John Baer, Tyler McVey, Georgianna Carter—but of major interest. Gene Corman produced and wrote the original story, while brother Roger was executive producer.

TERROR FROM THE YEAR 5000 a.k.a. TERROR FROM 5000 A.D. and THE GIRL FROM 5000 A.D. (American International 1958) Produced, directed and written by Robert J. Gurney, Jr. Probably the most remarkable thing about *Terror* is that the title role is played by Salome Jens, who is screen credited but unlisted in any other source at the time of the film's release. Her official debut was a few years later in the highly regarded *Angel Baby* (1961). Via a time machine, she is transported from the radioactive future to the present. Horribly disfigured and able to hypnotize with her fingernails, she attempts to bring lab assistant John Stratton back with her to start an uncontaminated breed. Ward Costello and Joyce Holden have top billing but Salome dances away with the honors. An early credit for editor Dede Allen.
[Seen on a triple bill in San Francisco in the Sixties, Jens' name coming as a surprise.]

CURSE OF THE UNDEAD (Universal-International 1959) Directed by Edward Dein, who also wrote the script with Mildred Dein. Production titles, *Affairs of a Vampire* and *Mark of the West*. In the Forties, Universal made countless Westerns and horror pictures. As U-I, it produced one of the few horror films in a Western setting. Gunman Michael Pate is hired by Kathleen Crowley, unaware he's a vampire immune to bullets. He bites her neck in time honored fashion and has her in his power. Preacher Eric Fleming is able to stop Pate with a bullet on which is imbedded a miniature crucifix. Good reworking of the old themes, with two interesting leads. Fleming, in a rare film appearance (he died while on location in 1966 at 41, in a Peruvian river), reached fame on TV's "Rawhide" series with the lesser known Clint Eastwood costarring. Pate, a forceful actor for many years, returned to his native Australia, where he began to produce and write films. Also with John Hoyt, Bruce Gordon and Edward Binns.

PLAN 9 FROM OUTER SPACE (Distributors Corporation of America 1959) Produced, directed, written and edited by Edward D. Wood, Jr. One of the most famous movie titles of all time and at the same time one of the most inept films ever; its fame once extended to a mention in the "Dick Tracy" comic strip. Even more fascinating than the film itself is its history. Wood had only a rough idea for a horror movie when he began filming old friend Bela Lugosi in his Dracula cape for a feature to be known as *The Vampire's Tomb*. After four days of lensing in and around a cemetery and outside Tor Johnson's home in Sylmar, California, Lugosi died suddenly, on August 16, 1956. Wood then wrote a script called *Grave Robbers From Outer Space* and obtained

PLAN 9 FROM OUTER SPACE *(DCA 1959) Living near a cemetery in San Fernando, Mona McKinnon and Gregory Walcott try to make sense of the plot.*

THE TINGLER *(Columbia 1959) Vincent Price isn't attempting to kill wife Patricia Cutts, he merely wants her tingler.*

backing from J. Edward Reynolds and a group of Baptist businessmen, on the proviso that all members of the production be baptized (so far, it sounds like one of Wood's plots). To utilize Lugosi's footage, a double was necessary and he was found in the person of Dr. Tom Mason, a chiropractor who was young, tall and thin. For his scenes, he held up a cape to hide his face.

Lugosi was billed as The Ghoul Man, a widower killed by offscreen device and resurrected from the dead. With almost no sets to speak of, Wood saved money at every conceivable level. The flying saucers have been identified as auto hubcaps. Some of the non-actors were chosen because they just happened to be in close proximity to the production. Paul Marco, who plays Patrolman Kelton in several of the Wood films, had as house guests John Breckinridge and his secretary David DeMering. Breckinridge was cast as the overripe Ruler, while DeMering received the smaller role of the co-pilot,

Danny. Meanwhile, Wood's wife Norma McCarty played stewardess Edie. Another old Wood friend, supposed psychic and showman Criswell, did the overemphatic prologue and epilogue. Reynolds and associate producer Hugh Thomas, Jr., were given the parts of the grave diggers.

The plot, as nearly as can be deciphered, concerns aliens Dudley Manlove and Joanna Lee, who come to earth to prevent development of the Solaronite Bomb, which could harm the universe. Eight failed attempts to achieve this goal lead to their ninth plan (hence the title), to bring back to life and control the recently departed. Investigating police inspector Tor Johnson is killed and revived, attacking Mona McKinnon, who lives near the cemetery with husband Gregory Walcott, a pilot who had earlier seen the hubcaps from outer space. Others involved—mainly Wood regulars—are Lyle Talbot, Duke (James) Moore, Ben Frommer, Conrad Brooks, guest star Vampira (Maila Nurmi). While this is cited as Lugosi's last film, few have noted that it also marked the final appearance of cowboy star Tom Keene. Previewed in 1958.

THE TINGLER (Columbia 1959) Produced and directed by William Castle. In black-and-white Percepto. Castle and writer Robb White again team with Vincent Price (following *House on Haunted Hill*, 1958) to create a gimmicky but vastly entertaining chiller. Price and assistant Darryl Hickman perform experiments regarding a tingler, which forms on the spine of a person being frightened to death and snaps the spine unless released by the potential victim's screaming in fright. One victim is Judith Evelyn, a deaf mute unable to scream. Her widower Philip Coolidge runs a silent-movie theater. Castle gets things underway by introducing the proceedings in his usual gleeful manner. One sequence shows a bathtub filling with blood—red tinted, on a black-and-white background. When the film played in movie houses, Percepto was used twice during the action. The screen went black and certain members of the audience felt a slight electrical shock. This was the tingler, achieved by the use of vibrating motors in a small box under selected seats in the auditorium. Once during each showing, the film stopped, the house lights were turned on and a woman who had fainted (a plant) was carried out while Price's voice over the speaker calmed the audience. In the silent-movie house, generous clips are shown from the classic *Tol'able David* (1921) with hero Richard Barthelmess and villain Ernest Torrence in evidence. As Price's treacherous and unfaithful wife is Patricia Cutts, a British actress also known as Patricia Wayne, in one of her last films. One of the longer lasting but not permanent effects of the film was the union of juvenile lead Hickman and ingenue Pamela Lincoln. (For years, they lived in New York City with her mother, Verna Hillie.)

THE LITTLE SHOP OF HORRORS *(Filmgroup 1960) At the dentist's office, masochist Jack Nicholson tells Jonathan Haze how he enjoys pain.*

THE LITTLE SHOP OF HORRORS a.k.a. THE PASSIONATE PEOPLE EATER (Filmgroup 1960) Produced and directed by Roger Corman. At this point, Corman was receiving favorable critical attention and was making the most of minuscule budgets. As a joke, he bet that he could make a film in two days. Charles Griffith fashioned a script in a bit more time than that and *Little Shop* was completed in two and a half days for only $22,500. It proved to be one of Corman's favorite films and to have an afterlife of note. Corman regular Jonathan Haze adores co-worker Jackie Joseph at Mel Welles' flower shop in a rundown section of the city. After discovering that a hybrid plant thrives on human blood, Haze feeds it with his own and then does in lowlifes from the vicinity for their blood. The plant, named after Joseph, grows to enormous size and brings attention to the shop. Most memorable scene, however, belongs to young Jack Nicholson as a masochistic dental patient. Shown out of competition at the 1961 Cannes Film Festival, the film emerged as one of Corman's most enduring efforts. The musical version, off-Broadway in the Eighties, by Howard Ashman and Alan Menken, led to the huge budgeted 1986 Warner Bros. musical, filmed in England. Corman told author Ed Naha that the term B movie was inaccurate and not used in the industry when he was making such low budgeters as this. If that's true, then this is a C picture. The filmmaker's attitude notwithstanding, *Little Shop* is one of the funnier and most bizarre quickies of all time. It originally was released with *The Last Woman on Earth*.

HOMICIDAL (Columbia 1961) Produced and directed by William Castle, uniting him again with his favorite screenwriter, Robb White. The results this time are quite good and Castle was always proud of the fact that *Time* magazine, more apt to pun a film to death than praise it, stated that it was better than *Psycho*. It isn't, but rather a worthy second best. Blonde Jean Arless pays bellhop Richard Rust to marry her and then proceeds to stab justice James Westerfield to death. Afterwards she takes her place as the wife of Patricia Breslin's half brother. Breslin alerts sweetheart Glenn Corbett that Eugenie Leontovich, the paralyzed deaf mute nurse, is attempting to tell them something. Three minutes before the film's end, Castle—who also introduced the proceedings—announces a 45-second "Fright Break" for patrons too frightened to continue. At this point, they could request a ticket refund without staying for the terrifying conclusion. As with most Castle gimmicks, it provided a welcome outlet from the tension. In the small cast are Alan Bunce, best known for his TV series "Ethel and Albert," and silent-screen comic Snub Pollard in one of his last appearances, as an over-age bellboy.

HOMICIDAL *(Columbia 1961) Strange Jean Arless has plans for Eugenie Leontovich, in the wheelchair—unfortunately, both lose their heads.*

NIGHT TIDE a.k.a. GIRL FROM BENEATH THE SEA (Filmgroup/American International 1961) Directed and written by Curtis Harrington. Mermaids are usually presented in a comical-fantasy vein. In his first mainstream feature, experimental filmmaker Harrington uses a blend of fantasy and reality for a dark and mysterious view. Sailor Dennis Hopper is attracted to Linda Lawson, who works as "The Girl in the Fish Bowl" at a boardwalk concession owned by Gavin Muir, retired sea captain. Luana Anders, a merry-go-round operator, tells Hopper that men attracted to Lawson have died suddenly, and Muir admits that Lawson is a descendant of the Sea People, who kill under the spell of the full moon. Hopper then learns what this pseudo-mermaid really is and what she's doing to him. Only an unsatisfactory ending and Hopper's portrayal of a too-naïve seaman detract from the overall effect. California's Venice proves to be the ideal location and David Raksin's eerie score, featuring Chaino on bongos, is properly moody. This was released by AIP in 1963 after a 1961 presentation at the Venice Film Festival, and remains one of the few films of its striking leading lady, Lawson, who came from the TV.

TRAUMA *(Parade 1962) In the pre-credits sequence, crippled Lynn Bari and Lorrie Richards, her niece, discuss a death shortly before Bari's drowning in the pool.*

CARNIVAL OF SOULS (Herts-Lion International 1962) Directed by Herk (Harold) Harvey. For years, the most famous unseen low budget thriller of its time. Made for only $30,000 in Lawrence, Kansas, and at Salt Lake City's strange-looking Saltair amusement park, it has a cast and crew which, for the most part, never made another commercial feature. One exception is star Candace Hilligoss (later in *Curse of the Living Corpse*, see 1964 entry), surviving a drowning to wander in a half-life. There's much talk of the soul in John Clifford's script (from an original by Harvey and Clifford), as it becomes clear that she doesn't possess one and is unable to relate to those around her. She has lapses during which no one can see or hear her, while always, the apparition of a ghoulish man (Harvey again) is near. As a church organist, Hilligoss is repelled by fellow boarder Sidney Berger (a University of Kansas drama teacher), the coarse laborer who unwittingly offers her last chance at redemption. By making Hilligoss the only glamorous, therefore otherworldly, figure among very ordinary looking people, Harvey cleverly conveys the theme of alienation. Excellent atmosphere and black-and-white photography by Maurice Prather. Despite its British name, the original distributor was a Hollywood-based company of short duration. A 1989 release by Panorama Entertainment signified the film's cult status, mostly among those who'd never seen it. Ubiquitous Harvey also produced this one-of-a-kind entertainment.

PANIC IN YEAR ZERO! a.k.a. SURVIVAL (American International 1962) Directed by and starring Ray Milland. Reissued in 1965 as *End of the World*. Ray

Milland and Jean Hagen leave Los Angeles on vacation with their children Frankie Avalon and Mary Mitchel, then learn that the city has been destroyed in a nuclear attack. With Milland's resourcefulness, the family survives against those who give in to animal instincts and metes a harsh justice to marauders Richard Bakalyan, Rex Holman and Neil Nephew. Good sci-fi drama, with emphasis on the human element rather than special effects. Notable as having two ingenue leads, Mitchel and Joan Freeman, who are raped, as well as being in black-and-white wide screen, a fact not exploited at the time of release or recorded by any reference books.

TRAUMA (Parade Films 1962) Directed and written by Robert Malcolm Young. Young amnesiac Lorrie Richards, sole heir to the family fortune, marries older John Conte, her guardian. Conte was involved with her crippled aunt, Lynn Bari, who was murdered in the pool, thereby triggering Richards' condition. Interesting role for singer-TV personality Conte, while Bari makes her presence felt despite her role being limited largely to flashbacks. It adds up to a good psychological thriller with a cast that also includes Warren Kemmerling and David Garner.

THE HAUNTED PALACE (American International 1963) Produced and directed by Roger Corman. In Panavision and Pathé Color. Based on the 1941 story "The Case of Charles Dexter Ward" by H. P. Lovecraft. In the Sixties, the Corman adaptations of Edgar Allan Poe tales were so popular that the title of an 1839 poem was used for this film, the story taken from a Lovecraft piece in two consecutive issues of *Weird Tales* magazine. Vincent Price is an 18th century warlock burned at the stake by ungrateful denizens of his New England village. He's also his own great-great-grandson, arriving there 100 years later with beautiful wife Debra Paget. Shunned by the local folk and menaced by the mutants whose ancestors had been cursed by the warlock, Price begins to take on his ancestor's personality. Two practitioners of the craft, Lon Chaney, Jr., and Milton Parsons, join Price in his quest for family vengeance and conjure up Cathy Merchant, the warlock's assistant. One of Corman's best non-humorous horror works, with a cast of his regulars—Leo Gordon, Barboura Morris, Bruno Ve Sota—and old favorites—Elisha Cook, Jr., I. Stanford Jolley and John Dierkes. The memorable trailer for this feature restored the Jr. to Chaney's screen name and pointed out his continuance in the horror tradition.

SHOCK CORRIDOR (Allied Artists 1963) Produced, directed and written by Samuel Fuller. Reporter Peter Breck, anxious to receive a Pulitzer Prize, contrives to be committed to an insane asylum to investigate a murder. Gene Evans, James Best and Hari Rhodes represent the most interesting inmates, while stunt man Chuck Roberson appears to be a sympathetic attendant. Constance Towers is Breck's girl, a stripper, posing as his sister (that could drive one insane). Fuller's most outrageous effort, finding special effects in a hospital corridor (some scenes in Technicolor) and having the hero attacked by nymphomaniacs. A cult film, not overly appreciated in its day. Production titles: *Straitjacket* and *The Long Corridor.*

X—THE MAN WITH X-RAY EYES *(American International 1963) Paying the price for heightened vision, Ray Milland repents.*

X—THE MAN WITH X-RAY EYES a.k.a. THE MAN WITH THE X-RAY EYES (American International 1963) Produced and directed by Roger Corman. Production title, *X*. In Spectarama and Eastman Color. The man is Ray Milland and the picture is one of the most intelligent of science fiction features. As Dr. Xavier, he experiments with vision in an attempt to see beyond normal sight. At first, he can see through clothing, which proves both amusing and delightful. Then, he penetrates skin to correctly diagnose a patient. After inadvertently causing the death of associate doctor Harold J. Stone, Milland seeks refuge in a carnival, where barker Don Rickles exploits him as Mentalo, The Man Who Sees All. Doctor Diana Van Der Vlis attempts to help Milland, who eventually can see beyond the heavens at the cost of his normal sight. A Biblical quotation, "If thine eye offend thee, pluck it out," ends this most impressive

THE CURSE OF THE LIVING CORPSE *(20th Century-Fox 1964) A screaming Candace Hilligoss discovers a body, unaware that Roy Scheider will strike again.*

THE STRANGLER *(Allied Artists 1964) Sizing up each other, strangler Victor Buono and potential victim Diane Sayer.*

presentation. Rickles is properly slimy, Milland has one of his best later roles, and John Hoyt and John Dierkes supply other good work.

THE CURSE OF THE LIVING CORPSE (20th Century-Fox 1964, with a 1963 copyright) Produced, directed and written by Del Tenney. A neglected horror thriller notable for at least three reasons: as the other film of Candace Hilligoss of *Carnival of Souls* (see 1962 entry), the movie debut of Roy Scheider, and the first pre-rating American horror feature with nudity. Just above the frame line in the bath, Margot Hartman is strangled to death. The wife of Tenney, she felt that it was a daring and important thing to do. Her father's estate in Stamford, Connecticut, provided the filming site. Plot takes a thrust from Poe's *The Premature Burial* and concerns murders in the family of a tyrant who may have been buried alive. Some of the principals were working in the theatre in New York and were surprised when the film opened locally and caused problems because of its violence. The period piece broke box office records in Texas. Top billed was Helen Waren (her only credit), with Robert Milli and Dino Narizzano also cast.

THE STRANGLER (Allied Artists 1964) Directed by Burt Topper. Obese Victor Buono likes dolls and hates his mother Ellen Corby, so he takes out his frustrations by strangling other women. After killing his mother's nurse, Jeanne Bates, he causes Corby's fatal heart attack by informing her of the crime. Buono then turns his attentions to sexy Diane Sayer and sweet Davey Davison, operators of a concession in an amusement park; the former becomes his last victim and the latter the object of perverted affections. David McLean is the police lieutenant certain of Buono's guilt. Buono seemed poised to take over the roles that Laird Cregar had portrayed two decades earlier. They were alike in girth and age; Cregar died at 28, Buono was just 24 when he was *The Strangler*. However, Buono's later roles merely exploited his eccentric personality or cast him in very cheap horror films. He aged considerably and died at 43 on New Year's Day of 1982. *The Strangler* is a tribute to what could have been.

NIGHT OF THE LIVING DEAD (Continental 1968) Directed, written, photographed and edited by George A. Romero. Screenplay by John A. Russo. Production titles: *Night of the Flesh Eaters* and *Night of Anubis*. Classic chiller in which radiation from atomic testing causes the dead to rise and seek the flesh of the living. Claustrophobic atmosphere is well sustained by barricading the leading actors in a farmhouse, where they attempt to withstand the onslaught of the vampiric zombies. A resourceful black, Duane Jones, is the only

one responsible enough to take charge. Most terrifying scene has a dead child, Kyra Schon, attacking and devouring her parents. Karl Hardman and Marilyn Eastman, the doomed parents, also supplied the makeup, while Hardman and Russell Streiner—who plays heroine Judith O'Dea's brother—served as producers. The Pittsburgh-based Romero took time from making industrial films to do this low budgeter (under $200,000) in Evans City, Pennsylvania, with far reaching results. Somehow the gore and a touch of nudity were included in the theatrical release just prior to the ratings system (uncut versions play late night TV, in the original black-and-white or colorized). Constant TV reports throughout the film, an unfamiliar cast and settings, and the poverty-stricken budget add up to a very realistic, unique and terrifying piece. Romero's personal sequels came much later: *Dawn of the Dead* (1979) and *Day of the Dead* (1985).

TARGETS a.k.a. BEFORE I DIE (Paramount 1968) Directed by Peter Bogdanovich, also producer, screenplay writer and—with then-wife Polly Platt—story writer. In Pathecolor. The last great and the first great effort, respectively, of its star Boris Karloff and its maker, Bogdanovich. Financed by Roger Corman, for whom Bogdanovich and Karloff had worked, the $130,000 wonder incorporates footage from Corman's *The Terror* (AIP 1963) and Howard Hawks' *The Criminal Code* (1930) to show Karloff at various stages of his sound-film career. To cut costs even further, Bogdanovich more or less plays himself, a director-writer, while Karloff is cast as a horror film actor who feels that everyday violence has made his work look ridiculous. As Karloff prepares to attend a drive-in theater premiere of his latest feature (*The Terror*), a disturbed youth—Tim O'Kelly—begins shooting people, starting with wife Tanya Morgan and mother Mary Jackson. The O'Kelly rampage finally takes

NIGHT OF THE LIVING DEAD *(Continental 1968) Zombies and fire in a horror classic.*

HELLO DOWN THERE *(Paramount 1969) Life on the ocean floor: Lou Wagner, Kay Cole, Janet Leigh, Gary Tigerman and Richard Dreyfuss.*

LET'S SCARE JESSICA TO DEATH *(Paramount 1971) In a pensive moment, Zohra Lampert reflects upon the horrors at hand.*

him to the drive-in where Karloff on the giant screen and Karloff in actuality confront the confused killer. Originally released with a gun control message, the film gained its reputation upon re-release, after Bogdanovich had earned his. The sniper angle was inspired by the 1966 killings committed by Charles Whitman at the University of Texas after murdering his wife and mother. A later TV movie, *The Deadly Tower* (1975), cast Kurt Russell in the role of Whitman (called Bobby Thompson in the Los Angeles-based *Targets*).

HELLO DOWN THERE (Paramount 1969) Directed by Jack Arnold; underwater sequences directed by Ricou Browning. In Eastman Color. G-rated science fiction comedy with music and quite a few familiar faces. The sea mammals, dolphins and seals, however, create much interest. Hungarian-born producer Ivan Tors, who loved animals and sea life, made this in Florida and at his North Miami studios. Inventor Tony Randall creates an undersea home, the Green Onion, and tries to convince employer Jim Backus of its usefulness. Randall agrees to live in it, ninety feet under the sea, with wife Janet Leigh and children Gary Tigerman and Kay Cole. So that the teens can rehearse with their rock band, Richard Dreyfuss and Lou Wagner accompany them. Ken Berry, a Randall rival, sabotages the experiment and causes the house to tilt. The Navy also becomes involved. Moving things along is Jeff Barry's song fest; he composed such appropriate numbers as "Glub," "Hey Little Goldfish," and the title song. Apart from Dreyfuss in one of his earliest roles, the players include Merv Griffin (as himself), Roddy McDowall, Charlotte Rae, Henny Backus (Jim's wife), Harvey Lembeck and Arnold Stang, farceurs all. Reissued for children's matinees as *Sub-A-Dub-Dub*.

LET'S SCARE JESSICA TO DEATH (Paramount 1971) Directed by John Hancock. In DeLuxe Color. Filmed in rural Connecticut: Chester, Essex, Old Saybrook; the Dickinson home, built in 1913 in Essex, is a principal location. Before directing the baseball drama *Bang the Drum Slowly* (1973), John Hancock made his feature debut with a gothic horror piece. Zohra Lampert, out of a mental hospital, travels by hearse to Old Brookfield, a farm purchased by husband Barton Heyman and friend Kevin O'Connor. She encounters voices, ghostly Gretchen Corbett and farm inhabitant Mariclare Costello, along with hostile locals, who may be vampires. Excellent nightmarish thriller, in the is-it-real-or-is-it-mental vein. Electronic music by Walter Sear, eerie photography by Bob Baldwin add to the atmosphere. Debuting producer Charles B. Moss, Jr., of the famed theater chain family, got the idea for the film from a mountain climbing expedition; scriptwriters Norman Jonas and Ralph Rose shaped their tale of the supernatural around the concept of a community's hostility towards outsiders. The outstanding opportunity for star Lampert, best remembered as the kooky Eve in the Garden of Eden for Cranapple Juice in the TV commercials. Made for $180,000 and rated GP.

THE RETURN OF COUNT YORGA (American International 1971)

Directed by Bob Kelljan. Produced by Michael Macready and Kelljan. Screenplay by Kelljan and Yvonne Wilder. "I'm *so* proud of my work" said the effervescent Mariette Hartley, facetiously describing her film career. True, except for her very first film, the classic *Ride the High Country* (1962), she doesn't have too much moviewise to excite anyone; in fact, she's made few theatrical films. Among the best, however, is the sequel to *Count Yorga, Vampire* (1970), one of AIP's hits. Again starring Robert Quarry as the Count, with Edward Walsh as the warped aide Brudah, the sequel reunites Macready and Kelljan as the principal filmmakers and proves to be even better than the original. Quarry and followers, mainly female, reside in a Santa Ana chateau near Westwood Orphanage. Reverend Tom Toner, who heads the orphanage, and assistant Hartley host a fund-raising masquerade party, at which Quarry appears without causing unnecessary concern. He's immediately attracted to Hartley, in spite of the presence of her fiancée doctor Roger Perry (in a different role from the one he had in the first *Yorga*). Thereafter, an orgy of blood ensues as Quarry pursues Hartley and she remains loyal to Perry, who has a final surprise for her. Funny and frightening, with a good cast, including Walter Brooke, Craig Nelson and co-scripter Wilder as a deaf mute. George Macready, father of the co-producer and an old hand at such matters, makes his final screen appearance in a campy cameo as an addled expert on all sorts of vampires. In keeping with the tongue in cheek (or neck) approach, there's a shot on the TV from the British *The Vampire Lovers* (a 1970 AIP release of a Hammer Production) in which Ingrid Pitt kills Ferdy Mayne, dubbed in Spanish.

SSSSSSS a.k.a. SSSSNAKE (Universal 1973)

Directed by Bernard L. Kowalski. A monster movie with quite a lineage, this was the first Richard D. Zanuck-David Brown Production (*The Sting* and *Jaws* followed) and the only feature to be co-produced and written by Dan Striepeke, who helped create the makeup for *Planet of the Apes*. Hal Dresner did the screenplay for director Kowalski's last feature. Strother Martin experiments with transforming humans into snakes, believing that cold-blooded species will eventually survive. Student Dirk Benedict becomes a successful example, to the distress of Martin's daughter Heather Menzies, who helps run a snake farm. Doctor Richard B. Shull, a jealous colleague, is made a victim of a giant python. John Chambers and Nick Marcellino, associates

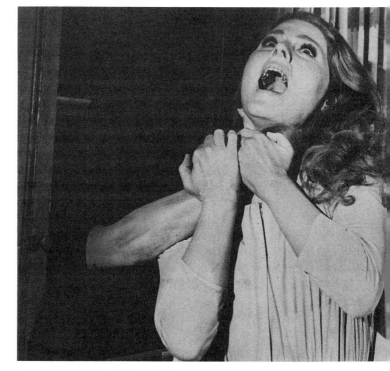

THE RETURN OF COUNT YORGA *(American International 1971) A reaction to Mariette Hartley's lack of enthusiasm about her film career.*

of Striepeke, collaborated on the impressive makeup work. Jack Ging, Tim O'Connor and Felix Silla as the seal boy contribute to the PG-rated Technicolored release. Don't say it—hiss it, advised the ads. It was released on a double bill with *The Boy Who Cried Werewolf*. Universal expert David Barnes has suggested that *Sssssss* seems to be a reworking of *The Mad Ghoul* (1943).

THE TEXAS CHAINSAW MASSACRE (Bryanston 1974)

Produced and directed by Tobe Hooper, who also wrote the screenplay with Kim Henkel and the music with Wayne Bell. The true classic of its kind, this avoids the gory contents of its sequels by concentrating on the terror and not the visuals. Marilyn Burns leads a luckless group of youths encountering slaughterhouse workers who literally bring home their jobs. Teri McMinn makes the grisly discovery of how they furnish their home before becoming a victim. A no-name cast—Allen Danziger, Paul A. Partain, William Vail—adds to the realism. Only Gunnar Hansen as the dreaded Leatherface makes a real impression, despite the handicaps of his role. Last shot of him swinging the chainsaw is a memorable one, obviously ideal for sequelizing. TV's John Larroquette has admitted doing a voiceover for this in his hungrier days. Color by CFI, rated R.

SQUIRM (American International 1976)

Directed and written by Jeff Lieberman. Worms, not just a can of them but millions, provide the menace and reduce the cast considerably in this tight little thriller. The foreword states that this was based on a true incident in Fly Creek, Georgia, in 1975. Shot in Port

THE TEXAS CHAINSAW MASSACRE (*Bryanston 1974*) *At the climax, Gunnar Hansen as Leatherface chases Marilyn Burns as she escapes from the farm-slaughter-house.*

Wentworth, Georgia, it tells of downed electrical power lines driving volts into the ground and stirring up the local worm populace. Some gruesome effects creep into the R-rated proceedings as the worms begin eating away at the human element. Don Scardino stars as a New York lawyer romancing Patricia Pearcy, who lives with pot-smoking sister Fran Higgins and their mother Jean Sullivan. This was only the fourth film for Sullivan, who'd starred briefly at Warner Bros. in 1944-45. Later the co-manager of Manhattan's South Street Theatre, where she has produced many stage offerings, she took the *Squirm* assignment on the understanding that it would be a much better role before Brian Smedley-Aston's editing reduced it. With R. A. Dow, Peter MacLean, and makeup by Rick Baker. Color by Movielab.

HAUNTS a.k.a. THE VEIL (Intercontinental 1977) Directed by Herb Freed, who also produced with Bert Weisbourd and did the screenplay with Anne Marisse. Small-town mores are well depicted in this offbeat horror item, detailing what happens when murders are committed in the vicinity. May Britt as the farm woman who is haunted by homicidal visions, is a likely victim. Sheriff Aldo Ray and her uncle Cameron

Mitchell may or may not be part of her nightmares. Probably the best role for Britt, whose career was spotty at best and overshadowed by her marriage to Sammy Davis, Jr. In Eastman Color and rated PG.

ATTACK OF THE KILLER TOMATOES (Four Square Productions-NAI Entertainment 1978) Directed by John De Bello, also co-producer with Steve Peace and co-writer with Costa Dillon and Peace. Even the credits are silly, claiming that the story is based on "The Tomatoes of Wrath" and that The Royal Shakespearean Tomatoes appear. This is the camp classic in which tomatoes grow to huge sizes and begin devouring people. When it is discovered that loud music can shrink them back to normal size, one giant wears ear muffs to combat the counterattack. Songs by Gordon Goodwin and Paul Sundfor punctuate the action. Deliberately bad, with cramped sets, poor acting and genuinely funny situations. Color by CFI and rated merely PG, with a cast of nonentities, including David Miller, George Wilson, Sharon Taylor, Jack Riley, Rock Peace, Eric Christmas. De Bello also directed the sequel, *Return of the Killer Tomatoes* (1988).

HALLOWEEN (Falcon International/Compass International 1978) Directed by John Carpenter, who

wrote the screenplay with its producer Debra Hill and composed the music. In MetroColor and Panavision, rated R. For 19-year-old Jamie Lee Curtis, her film debut in this was a stepping stone to better things. Actually, it led to enough horror films for her to be typecast for some time. Made for only $300,000, it was a huge hit and had countless sequels. On Halloween night in 1963, six-year-old Will Sandin becomes a killer. Fifteen years later, as Tony Moran, he escapes a mental institution and concentrates on baby sitters in the vicinity—Curtis, Nancy Loomis, P. J. Soles. Pursued by his wild-eyed psychiatrist, Donald Pleasence, he proves to be difficult to kill as Curtis uses every sharp instrument at her disposal to stab him and Pleasence shoots him six times. Scenes from the sci-fi classics *The Thing* and *Forbidden Planet* on the TV give the impression of an actual Halloween. Dean Cundey's shots of the deserted streets add to the mood. Curtis and Pleasence also starred in the far higher-budgeted sequel, *Halloween II* (Universal 1981).

PIRANHA (New World 1978) Directed by Joe Dante. The best ripoff of *Jaws* ever, with a genuinely amusing script by John Sayles (story by Richard Robinson and Sayles). Under the guidance of executive producer Roger Corman, who could have done this himself, the Piranha Production starts with a good premise. Teen backpackers Roger Richman and Janie Squire swim in the pool of an abandoned military research center. They are devoured by piranha fish which had been bred by Doctor Kevin McCarthy as a weapon in the Vietnam War and are now in the nearby waters. Bradford Dillman plays a great nonheroic hero, and Barbara Steele manages to look as sinister as possible for no particular reason. Heather Menzies is the sometimes annoying female lead, while smaller roles are handled by Keenan Wynn, Dick Miller, Bruce Gordon, Paul Bartel and the tragic Barry Brown in his last film. Special effects are by a team from *Star Wars*—Jon Berg, Phil Tibbet, Rob Bottin, Adam Beckett. Filmed mainly in San Marcos, Texas, in Metrocolor, rated R, *Piranha* is that rare shocker which never once shows the objects of death in lingering closeup. The 1981 sequel, an Italian/U.S. coproduction, was called *Piranha II: The Spawning*.
[Made with the help of a few who could be called Friends of The CoOp—director Dante, producer Jon Davison and actor Brown, acquaintance of mine until his suicide. Dante contributed a wanted poster with the likeness of friend Pierre Guinle, one of Europe's most dedicated film buffs and a true CoOp devotee.]

TILL DEATH (Cougar 1978) Produced and directed by Walter Stocker. Two of the stars of the notoriously bad *They Saved Hitler's Brain* (1963), Walter Stocker and Marshall Reed, make up for it—somewhat—with an

HALLOWEEN *(Compass International 1978) Nick Castle as the killer in the original in the series with a debuting Jamie Lee Curtis, typecast for some time afterward.*

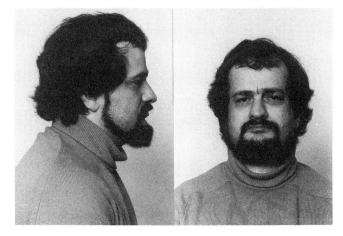

PIRANHA *(New World 1978) Mug shots of Pierre Guinle, used for a wanted poster in a horror comedy (Courtesy of Pierre Guinle).*

intriguing depiction of love after death. Stocker stays behind the cameras, while Reed, a talented actor-producer-director-writer-etc., has a small part and worked on the production end as well. Newlyweds Keith Atkinson and Belinda Balaski have an auto accident on their honeymoon, killing her and seriously injuring him. After

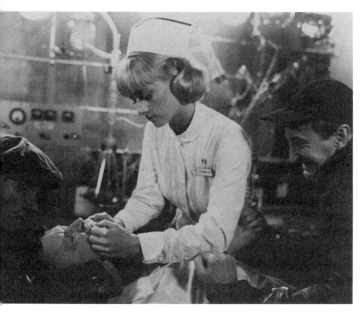

DEAD & BURIED *(Avco Embassy 1981) Patient Joe Medalis receives special attention in Potter's Bluff, from Michael Pataki, Lisa Blount and Robert Englund.*

recovering from his injuries, the grieving groom visits his wife's crypt and miraculously finds her alive and well—seemingly. The Gregory Dana script then becomes a duologue as she attempts to persuade him to join her on the other side. No budget whatsoever, but effective despite that. Bert Freed is also in the cast. Rated PG.

DEAD & BURIED (Avco Embassy 1981) Directed by Gary A. Sherman. Made for a reported $6 million, this one has the murky look of a real B thriller. The look is intentional, as the Ronald Shusett Robert Fentress production was shot in gloomy Mendocino, California, on the coast in the foggy offseason, as well as at the Goldwyn Studio. Coroner-undertaker Jack Albertson (in his last screen performance) has the ability to reconstruct and resurrect the dead, an unsettling fact. Sheriff James Farentino investigates some brutal local killings and finds that his wife, teacher Melody Anderson, is involved. The screenplay by Shusett and Dan O'Bannon, who also wrote the huge hit *Alien* (1979), is definitely strange and unpredictable. An energetic cast includes Dennis Redfield, Lisa Blount, Bill Quinn, Linda Turley (Mrs. Shusett, as a waitress), Michael Pataki—who knows his way around such films—and a pre-Freddy Krueger Robert Englund. Marvelous makeup by Stan Winston; the R-rated feature is in Technicolor, prints by CFI, shot with Panavision lenses.

MIDNIGHT (Independent-International 1981) Directed and written by John Russo, from his novel *Congregation*, which was also the film's production title. The scripter of *Night of the Living Dead* (see 1968 entry) makes his directorial debut with a less explicit thriller shot also in Pennsylvania: Kaylor, Lewisburg and Pittsburgh. Lawrence Tierney forces himself on stepdaughter Melanie Verliin, who then runs off. Lying to wife Doris Hackney about what happened, Tierney is filled with remorse as he uses his skills as a policeman to locate Verliin and bring her home. She unfortunately becomes involved in robbery, then capture by a group of sadistic policemen who prove to be cultists anxious to sacrifice her to the devil at midnight on Easter Sunday. John Amplas, who starred in George Romero's vampire feature *Martin* (1979), is one of the cultists. Tierney's good work highlights the horror. Tom Savini did the makeup. Eastman Color, processed by Precision Film Laboratories. Rated R.

NIGHT OF THE COMET (Atlantic 1984) Directed and written by Thom Eberhardt. A Paramount TV release. A nice reputation surrounds this quirky sci-fi comedy, which has elements from such efforts as George Romero's *Dawn of the Dead* (1979). The basic plot can be traced to Terence Fisher's British *The Earth Dies Screaming* (1964) as zombies menace the few survivors of a California wipeout. A comet comes near earth during the Christmas season and reduces inhabitants to a reddish-orange powder. To underscore this, a poster from *Red Dust* (1932) is seen. Movie usherette Catherine Mary Stewart (who is not Mary Stuart Masterson), cheerleader sister Kelli Maroney and Hispanic trucker Robert Beltran are the resourceful leads, while mom Sharon Farrell is an early casualty. Genre favorite Mary Woronov and Geoffrey Lewis are scientists at a research center and need the kids' uncontaminated blood to survive. Both exciting and funny, and hip except for the sparse special effects by Court Wizard (!). Naturally, it has references to other films, as all good pix of this kind do. Rated PG-13.

A NIGHTMARE ON ELM STREET (New Line Cinema 1984)

Directed and written by Wes Craven. As with many horror series, the first is the freshest and best. This introduction to the man of your nightmares cost $1.7 million to make and grossed $26 million. Robert Englund as hideous Freddy Krueger was a neighborhood child killer, operating in the boiler room of a school. He was burned to death by angry parents and has now returned to do harm to teenagers in their dreams. The film twists and turns as one teen, Amanda Wyss—seemingly the heroine—escapes death but is eventually murdered by her nightmare. Then Heather Langenkamp, daughter of police lieutenant John Saxon and Ronee Blakley, becomes the next intended victim. Great special effects by Jim Doyle and makeup by David Miller turn a bed into a pool of blood and each dream into a dark reality. Blakley, so good in Robert Altman's *Nashville* (1975), is surprisingly weak while others convey the horrors around them. She plays a major part in the climax, a startling orgy of revenge. Rated R, naturally, in DeLuxe Color, and featuring the forgotten theme song "Nightmare" (Martin Kent-Steve Karshner-Michael Schurig). Despite the ever-increasing success of the series, Englund really didn't become a star on his own until 1989, when the fifth installment was released.

NEAR DARK (DeLaurentiis 1987)

Directed by Kathryn Bigelow. Screenplay by Eric Red and Bigelow. The last outstanding horror film of the Eighties, this rewrites the vampire legend in a sardonic and sanguinary fashion. The cult includes Lance Henriksen, Jenette Goldstein, Bill Paxton, Jenny Wright and Joshua Miller (the first three actors were also in the sensational *Aliens* in 1986). At one point, Henriksen reveals that he's been around for a long time when he admits, "I fought for the South." Basically a love story between normal Adrian Pasdar and vampire girl Wright, the film rises to classic dimensions while not neglecting its abilities to shock. The director appeared with her film at a showing at New York's Museum of Modern Art, as a prelude to its becoming a cult favorite. In Technicolor and Ultra Stereo, rated R, it has an excellent score by Tangerine Dream.

MIDNIGHT *(Independent-International 1981) Lawrence Tierney as avenger in a tale of virgin sacrifice.*

A NIGHTMARE ON ELM STREET *(New Line Cinema 1984) As the heroine of Freddy's nightmares, Heather Langenkamp survived to reprise her role in a sequel,* A Nightmare on Elm Street 3: Dream Warriors *(New Line Cinema 1987).*

NEAR DARK *(De Laurentiis 1987) A family of vampires
in an untypical thriller—Lance Henriksen, Joshua Miller,
Jenette Goldstein, Bill Paxton.*

LUPE VELEZ

BOB CROSBY

EDDY DUCHIN

SIDNEY FOX

JOHN PAYNE

JOY HODGES

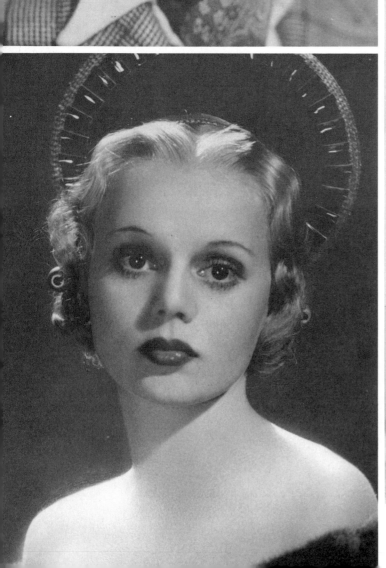

MARIE WILSON

PAINTED FACES *(Tiffany 1929) On the midway, Helen Foster and her adopted father Joe E. Brown the clown. The beloved comedian was a true clown, as he proved in dozens of films, this being a musical drama.*

DANGEROUS NAN McGREW *(Paramount 1930) Frank Morgan and Helen Kane forget boop-oop-a-doop for the time being, at a costume party.*

PAINTED FACES (Tiffany 1929) Directed by Albert Rogell. Story by Frances Hyland, screenplay by Frederic and Fanny Hatton. For one of his first film appearances, Joe E. Brown goes dramatic in a serious musical offering. He plays a Dutch-born clown who is the sole juror holding out for the innocence of dancer Barton Hepburn in a murder. It develops that Brown knew the dead man, singer Lester Cole, and he proceeds to tell his fellow jurors what really happened. Apart from a lengthy jury scene and the long arm of coincidence being unduly stretched, *Painted Faces* has an absorbing plot and a good Joe E. performance. Broadway musical star Cole, when not playing a rotter with leading ladies Helen Foster and Dorothy Gulliver, manages to introduce to the screen "Somebody Just Like You" (Abner Silver) and the enduring "If I Had You" (James Campbell-Reginald Connolly-Ted Shapiro). The film's ending reflects pre-Code attitudes about justifiable homicide. Sojin, a Japanese actor who was the last to portray Charlie Chan in silents, has a small part, while Richard Tucker, Purnell Pratt and William B. Davidson have other non-singing roles. Production title: *The Midway.*

THE TALK OF HOLLYWOOD (Sono Art-World wide 1929) Produced and directed by Mark Sandrich. Story by Sandrich and Nat Carr, its star. One of the first of the independent musicals was made by Prudence Pictures, a successor to the silent company Excellent Pictures (as in, "If it's a good picture—"). Intentionally or not, this is one of the most hilarious pictures of its era, largely due to the generally inept New York cast. Shining like a beacon in this sea of mediocrity is Nat Carr, who portrays movie producer J. Pierpont Ginsburg. After stating that "talking pictures are in their infantry," he proceeds to put all of his savings into a big budgeted musical while daughter Hope Sutherland is involved in a romance with Carr's Gentile lawyer Sherline Oliver. Although easily stealing the film with his Yiddish-accented pronouncements, Carr manages to be effective in one or two dramatic moments and in a straightforward presentation of the song "Sarah." International star Fay Marbé, however, fails to live up to her billing (she plays film star Adore Renée, a pun on the name of MGM star Renée Adorée). Although reportedly a sensation in Paris, she employs a transparent French accent and insufficient charm to accompany her rendering of "Good Night, My Lovey Dovey." Her brother Gilbert Marbé is cast as a gay caricature of a leading man. One gag concerns projectionist Tom O'Brien's switching of the sound disks so that the images don't match the dialogue and sound effects at the screening of Carr's finished film—an idea later used brilliantly by Comden and Green for *Singin' in the Rain* (1952). Al Goodman and His "Follow Thru" Orchestra plus the Leonidoff Ballet provide musical moments, while a large percentage of the cast never made another film. One exception is Sam Levene, spotted briefly as one of the film buyers in the screening room sequence; he became one of Hollywood's—and Broadway's—best character actors. Sandrich and Carr also used the Ginsburg character for a series of comedy shorts which they made for RKO in 1929-30. Carr and Sandrich, both of whom died in the mid-Forties, went on to greater fame in Hollywood, the former as a character man at Warners and the latter as director of some of the great Astaire-Rogers musicals for RKO. They were able to overcome *The Talk of Hollywood* and its promotion as a "100% Singing, Talking, Laughing Burlesque Drama— The First Laughing Exposé of the Talkies." Songs by Nat Carr, Al Piantadosi and Jack Glogau.
[Revived at the American Museum of the Moving Image, Astoria, New York in 1989; it may stand as one of that institution's greatest contributions to culture.]

DANGEROUS NAN McGREW (Paramount 1930) Directed by Malcolm St. Clair. Notable as the only starring film of Helen Kane, the Boop-Oop-a-Doop singer, and for being so terrible. She stars in a medicine show for Victor Moore (making his talkie debut) and performs as a singer and sharpshooter. In the Canadian

Northwest, they encounter bank robber Frank Morgan (an odd casting), Mountie James Hall (a long way from *Hell's Angels*) and myopic Stuart Erwin, whose portrayal has to stand as one of the most annoying of the decade. Only Kane's rendering of the title song (by Don Hartman and Al Goodhart) and her usual exuberance give the film any lift. Hard to believe that St. Clair directed this and that such tunesmiths as Richard A. Whiting, Leo Robin, Irving Kahal and Sammy Fain contributed their talents.

SWEETHEART OF SIGMA CHI (Monogram 1933)

Directed by Edwin L. Marin. At last, a college musical, one of Monogram's bigger and better efforts of the time. Co-ed Mary Carlisle is pursued by Buster Crabbe and Charles Starrett (both Western stars of later vintage). Rowing team star Crabbe is the more down to earth of the two, and as the star, wins Mary's heart. Comedy leads are two lesser known relatives of famous actors, Florence Lake (sister of Arthur of "Dagwood" fame) and Eddie Tamblyn (father of Russ). Ted Fio Rito's Orchestra features young Betty Grable and Leif Erickson, then a singer, while specialties are performed by The Three Midshipmen and Three Blue Keys—former UCLA co-eds. The memorable title song was provided by Byron D. Stokes and F. Dudleigh Vernor, while George Waggner—who wrote the original story—collaborated with Eddie Ward on the other numbers, "It's Spring Again" and "Fraternity Walk." Remade as an even bigger but not necessarily better Monogram musical in 1946, with Phil Regan and Elyse Knox. As of 1990, only five of the nearly thirty Sigma Chi men in the cast were still living. (Crabbe, a 1931 Sigma Chi inductee, died in 1983.)

DOWN TO THEIR LAST YACHT (RKO Radio 1934)

Directed by Paul Sloane. This once was considered to be the worst film made by RKO, although the company certainly distributed much less entertaining pictures, particularly some of the dramas of the Thirties. In retrospect, it's just good, silly fun, although it originally cost producer Lou Brock his job (previously, he'd been responsible for *Flying Down to Rio*, the first Astaire-Rogers teaming). If anyone cares, the story is a blueprint for the decades-later TV series "Gilligan's Island," with millionaires stranded on a remote island when their yacht is destroyed. If any credit is due, it goes to Herbert Fields and Brock for the original story, Marion Dix and Lynn Starling for the screenplay. Resisting or giving in to the temptation to go native are Sidney Blackmer (male), Sidney Fox (female), Mary Boland, Ned Sparks, Polly Moran, Sterling Holloway, Marjorie Gateson, Tom Kennedy and, in her debut, Marie Wilson. One of the singers is an unbilled Felix Knight, shortly thereafter to costar with Laurel and Hardy in *Babes in Toyland* (1934), also with Wilson. Ann Ronell contrib-

SWEETHEART OF SIGMA CHI *(Monogram 1933) Ted Fio Rito, minus his orchestra, accompanied by Mary Carlisle, on loan from MGM.*

uted a majority of the songs, collaborating with Max Steiner on "South Sea Bolero." The featured song, by Sidney Mitchell and Cliff Friend, is "There's Nothing Else to Do in Malakamokalu But Love" (of course, after pronouncing that name, there isn't time for much else). Dave Gould contributed the campy choreography, in keeping with the zany antics. In the Thirties, all bad musicals were measured against this *Yacht*.

KING KELLY OF THE U.S.A. (Monogram 1934)

Directed by Leonard Fields. A spoof of Ruritanian romances, which shouldn't have been taken too seriously in the first place. Guy Robertson, a theatrical producer, trades places with efficiency expert Franklin Pangborn when both fall in love—not with each other, that is. For one of the rare times in his screen career, Pangborn is allowed a romantic interest, this time with showgirl Joyce Compton. Robertson, meanwhile, has eyes only for Irene Ware, who proves to be the Princess of Belgardia. Once in her kingdom, Robertson uses his singing voice to stimulate the economy in selling its biggest asset, mops. It's about as silly as it sounds, but played for maximum laughs by Edgar Kennedy and especially Ferdinand Gottschalk as the bemused king. Hattie McDaniel has a bit as one of the mop customers. Stage star Robertson, in his only film, sings three pleasant but unmemorable songs by Bernie Grossman and Joe Sanders: "Right Next Door to Love," "Believe Me" and "There's a Love Song in

KING KELLY OF THE U.S.A. *(Monogram 1934) Ferdinand Gottschalk, Irene Ware, Guy Robertson and Edgar Kennedy in the Ruritanian country of Belgardia. Robertson has just been given one of the king's medals by princess Ware, accounting for the varying reactions.*

the Air." A highlight is an animated sequence during the shipboard portion of the story, when Robertson becomes a literally animated hero while crooning "Believe Me" to Ware.

THE LOUDSPEAKER (Monogram 1934) Directed by Joseph Santley. The title is a pun and refers to the conceited radio star played by Ray Walker. Arriving in New York from Burlap, Pennsylvania, he lands a job as comical emcee on Spencer Charters' pancake program. Walker's conceit—he addresses the audience as "My lucky public"—helps him win and lose Jacqueline Wells (later Julie Bishop), who works in the Automat (remember?). Before the hero learns humility, the proceedings manage to spoof Ed Wynn as well as the Boswell Sisters by a black trio and offer such melodies as "Who But You" and "Doo Ah, Doo Ah, Doo Ah Know What I'm Doing?" (both by Lew Brown and Harry Akst). No comment on

THE LOUDSPEAKER *(Monogram 1934) Drunk with success, Ray Walker mistreats sweetheart Jacqueline Wells (later Julie Bishop) and associate Lorin Raker.*

the latter song. Charley Grapewin and Noel Francis also are in the cast, with Lorin Raker as a sympathetic love rival for Wells' affections.

BROADWAY HOSTESS (Warner Bros.-First National 1935)

Directed by Frank McDonald. Notable as the only starring film of the charming Wini Shaw—known to everyone as having introduced the Oscar-winning "Lullaby of Broadway" in *Gold Diggers of 1935*. In the title role here, she is a small-town lady who becomes a big-town nightclub chanteuse. Some minor dramatic flourishes revolve around the fortunes of Lyle Talbot, as her manager. Phil Regan, soon to be a mainstay of Republic and Monogram musicals, joins in the singing. However, Wini's leading man in the featured "Playboy of Paree" number is Bill Elliott, still in his dress extra and bit player days. That song and most of the others were written by Mort Dixon and Allie Wrubel, one other being "Who But You"—not the earlier tune of that name featured in *The Loudspeaker* (see previous entry). Oth-

BROADWAY HOSTESS *(Warner Bros.-First National, 1935) Stepping out: Phil Regan, Winifred (Wini) Shaw and Lyle Talbot. You know her from "Lullaby of Broadway."*

DOWN TO THEIR LAST YACHT *(RKO Radio 1934)*
Going native in what was considered one of the worst musicals of the Thirties; remember, there's nothing else to do in Malakamokalu, but love.

CORONADO *(Paramount 1935) Jack Haley, Alice White, Andy Devine on location. Among the specialties are the dancing boy wonders the Nicholas Brothers.*

HARMONY LANE *(Mascot 1935) Adrienne Ames marries Douglass Montgomery, as Stephen Foster, but doesn't make the composer's life any happier than this.*

ers in the star-studded *Hostess* cast are Genevieve Tobin, Allen Jenkins, Spring Byington, Marie Wilson, June Travis, Dennis O'Keefe, and Ward Bond. Dances by Bobby Connolly, who was Oscar nominated as Best Dance Director for the "Playboy of Paree" number.

[Shaw, who was of Hawaiian descent, and husband Bill O'Malley were dedicated members of New York's Catholic Actors Guild for years before her death in 1982.]

CORONADO (Paramount 1935) Directed by Norman McLeod. Getting his due here is famed society orchestra leader Eddy Duchin, in a rare film appearance. His band backs the stars, Johnny Downs and Betty Burgess, in "You Took My Breath Away" and "How Do I Rate With You?" and Jack Haley on "All's Well in Coronado by the Sea" (all by Sam Coslow and Richard A. Whiting). Unfortunately, the Don Hartman-Frank Butler screenplay doesn't match the musical portions that feature dances by LeRoy Prinz. Singer Burgess and sister Alice White are the daughters of former acrobat Leon Errol, who won't allow sailor Haley near White until he gives her a ring. Downs is the son of motor tycoon Berton Churchill, but Burgess thinks he's a poor songwriter. Andy Devine and Jacqueline Wells (Julie Bishop) are also on hand. Location filming at the Hotel Del Coronado in Coronado helps. Leading lady Burgess, only 18 in her film debut, had a short career. *I Demand Payment* (1938) and *The Adventures of the Masked Phantom* (1939; see Westerns) comprise her only other credits.

HARMONY LANE (Mascot 1935) Directed by Joseph Santley, not Al Santell. Screenplay by Santley and Elizabeth Meehan, based on the life and songs of Stephen Foster, by Milton Krims. Elaborate retelling of the tragic story of American composer Stephen Foster, as played by Douglass Montgomery. Well thought of, the Nat Levine presentation shows Foster's influence by Negro spirituals and his work's acceptance and use by Christy's Minstrels. Rather than wed the woman he truly loves, Evelyn Venable, Montgomery unhappily marries Adrienne Ames and is miserable. His money spent, he becomes a drunk and spends his last days in New York. Foster favorites "Oh Susannah," "My Old Kentucky Home" and "Swanee River" are featured, most only in snippets or brief renditions. As E.P. Christy, William Frawley has the opportunity to sing, a talent always played for laughs much later in his career, particularly on "I Love Lucy." Joseph Cawthorn does his standard Dutch-German accent efficiently, while the always reliable Clarence Muse shows up briefly as a preacher. There seemed to be little stinting on the colorful production and the cast is especially big, with Lloyd Hughes, James Bush, Gilbert Emery, Florence Roberts, David Torrence and Cora Sue Collins featured. The Shaw Negro Choir is

seen and there are useful bits by such as Smiley Burnette, Joan Woodbury, Hattie McDaniel, Cornelius Keefe and Earle Hodgins as Mr. Bones. Montgomery does a thoughtful interpretation of the composer. Minor Hollywood mystery: all sources list Santley as director, but Santell receives sole screen credit mistakenly. In 1939, 20th Century-Fox made a more elaborate but less accurate adaptation of Foster's life, *Swanee River* with Don Ameche as the songwriter and Al Jolson as Christy. Republic, the successor to Mascot Pictures, produced an even more fanciful color version, *I Dream of Jeanie* (1952), featuring Ray Middleton as Christy and Bill Shirley as Foster.

MILLIONS IN THE AIR (Paramount 1935)

Directed by Ray McCarey. Amiable takeoff on radio's amateur hours, with some pleasant surprises among the large and lively cast and many musical numbers. Samuel S. Hinds hosts the show for sponsor George Barbier, whose daughter Wendy Barrie wants to compete. Incognito, she teams up with ice cream vendor John Howard for a duet. Willie Howard, from vaudeville, makes the first of just three features—sandwiched in between comedy shorts—as an amateur opera singer of some thirty years' standing; he's the kind of hopeful who'd be encouraged by Major Bowes' advice, "You're a real amateur." Joan Davis, also in a feature debut, does "You Tell Her Because I Stutter" (Billy Rose-Cliff Friend), while Eleanore Whitney—feature debuting at 18—performs the Moochie and is billed as the world's fastest tap dancer. Burly Paul Newlan (remembered as Lee Marvin's chief on the old "M Squad" TV show) serenades his babies with "Crooner's Lullaby" (Arthur Johnston-Sam Coslow), actually using Bing Crosby's voice, or a sound-alike. Robert Cummings, Benny Baker, Inez Courtney and Dave Chasen also are featured, while Paramount staff songwriters Leo Robin and Ralph Rainger contribute Howard and Barrie's "A Penny in My Pocket" and Cummings and Whitney's "Laughin' at the Weather Man." Cummings, Whitney and a group of bands do "Love Is Just Around the Corner" (Leo Robin-Lewis Gensler), from Crosby's *Here Is My Heart* (1934).

OLD MAN RHYTHM (RKO Radio 1935)

Directed by Edward Ludwig. The title, not necessarily a twist on "Old Man River," refers to George Barbier. He plays a wealthy businessman who enrolls in college as a freshman to keep an eye on son Charles "Buddy" Rogers, save him from the gold digging co-eds, particularly Grace Bradley, and marry him off to sweet Barbara Kent. Betty Grable, Eric Blore, Erik Rhodes and choreographer Hermes Pan take time from the Astaire and Rogers musicals to participate. Lucille Ball can be seen as one of the co-eds, while some of the college boys are played by such silent-screen offspring as Erich von Stroheim, Jr.,

OLD MAN RHYTHM *(RKO Radio 1935) Couples enjoying a dance include Grace Bradley, John Arledge, Margaret Nearing and Bill Carey; first named was the last wife of cowboy star William Boyd.*

Carlyle Blackwell, Jr., Bryant Washburn, Jr., and Claude Gillingwater, Jr. One of the film's writers, Lewis Gensler, teamed up with Johnny Mercer to produce the score. The affable Mercer, in his first of two films, joins in on such numbers as "There's Nothing Like a College Education," "Comes the Revolution, Baby," "Boys Will Be Boys" and "I Never Saw a Better Night." Barbier and Bradley do the title tune, while Rogers has just one duet, "When You Are in My Arms," with Bradley.

TO BEAT THE BAND (RKO Radio 1935)

Directed by Ben Stoloff. Enjoyably wacky musical madness, Johnny

TO BEAT THE BAND *(RKO Radio 1935) Roger Pryor (center), just wants to beat it, permanently, as Eric Blore and Hugh Herbert restrain his suicidal tendencies.*

THREE CHEERS FOR LOVE *(Paramount 1936)* Eleanore Whitney and Robert Cummings maneuver their way
through the library number, as exuberant youth do.

WALKING ON AIR *(RKO Radio 1936)* Gene Raymond
has a false mustache but real feelings for Ann Sothern.

Mercer's second and last screen appearance. Playboy
Hugh Herbert stands to inherit $59 million from his aunt
(also played by Herbert) if he weds a widow within three
days. Suicide-prone Roger Pryor is eager to assist by
marrying and then making his bride a widow. Fred
Keating is the orchestra leader who will inherit the
money if Herbert doesn't fulfill the terms of the will.
Helen Broderick and Eric Blore also star, with former
model Phyllis Brooks in her first lead, after some bit
parts. Singer Joy Hodges, dancers Sonny Lamont and
Nick Condos and The Original California Collegians help
to make things musical. Mercer, Keating and Evelyn Poe
do "I Saw Her at Eight O'Clock," one of the Mercer-Matty
Malneck songs in the score. Others: "Meet Miss America
1936" combined with "Time Marches On" for a lengthy
production number, "Eenie, Meenie, Minie, Mo," "If You
Were Mine" and "Santa Claus Came in the Spring"—not a
memorable musical lineup by any means.

HATS OFF (Grand National 1936) Directed by
Boris Petroff. Once called a film made out of thin air
because it was built around footage of the 1936 Texas
Centennial, this offers the first leading role for 24-year-
old John Payne, and also is the initial screen credit for
Sam Fuller. Edmund Joseph collaborated on the
screenplay of the Petroff production with Fuller, the
latter participating in his only film musical. Payne and
Mae Clarke are press agents for competing expositions,
she pretending to be a teacher, as Skeets Gallagher and
Franklin Pangborn supply their individually specialized
forms of assistance. Luis Alberni offers his ethnic humor,
while Helen Lynd—featured comedienne—does "Little
Odd Rhythm" and "Let's Have Another." The Three Radio
Rogues don't contribute their usual imitations, but do a
singing commentary on a boxing match. Publicity prom-
ises 75 Grand National Gorgeous Girlies, but a lot less
appear to be on view. Western regular Charles King plays
a character named Handsome, for a bit of silly casting.
Payne and Clarke use their own voices on the featured
song, "Twinkle, Twinkle, Little Star," which Gene Raymond popularized on records. Payne, who later became
a tough guy in 20th Century-Fox musicals, sings pleasantly, while Clarke—a favorite in this corner—does her
best. The Herb Magidson-Ben Oakland score includes
the title song for this, one of the more enjoyable B
musicals.

THREE CHEERS FOR LOVE (Paramount 1936) D-
irected by Ray McCarey. Robert Cummings, not everyone's favorite, surprises in this early effort with his
dancing ability, performing a number with Eleanore
Whitney on and around the furniture in a library, with
both later maneuvering a fencing routine set to music.
Danny Dare's choreography goes a long way in this one,
the plot of which revolves around William Frawley's

stranded show troupe mounting a production for Whitney's father, movie producer John Halliday. One shot uses that often repeated gag—"Miracle Studios. If It's a Good Picture, It's a Miracle." Roscoe Karns and Elizabeth Patterson hand the veteran leads some competition, while the other young talent includes Grace Bradley, Billy Lee, and in their film debuts, Olympe Bradna, Veda Ann Borg and dancer Louis Da Pron (later a choreographer). Boris Morros did the musical direction and Edward Dmytryk handled the editing. Mack Gordon and Harry Revel wrote "Learn to Be Lovely," while all other songs are by Ralph Rainger and Leo Robin, including "Where Is My Heart" and "Long Ago and Far Away" (not to be confused with the Jerome Kern-Ira Gershwin song for *Cover Girl*, 1944).

WALKING ON AIR (RKO Radio 1936) Directed by Joseph Santley. Based on Francis M. Cockrell's *Cosmopolitan* magazine story "Count Pete," the picture's original title. Considered one of the best of RKO's B musicals and a box office hit in its day, the Gene Raymond-Ann Sothern starrer is the second of five they did together for the studio—and the best. Beverly Hills heiress Sothern wants to marry divorced Alan Curtis, but her father Henry Stephenson and aunt Jessie Ralph object. In an attempt to change their minds, she hires Raymond to pose as her fiancé, a rude French count. Since his character aspires to be a radio singer, a glass enclosed broadcasting studio was constructed for the Edward Kaufman production. Charles Coleman, considered the screen's most perfect butler, has some fine comic moments and receives what may be his only screen kiss, from cook Fern Emmett. Raymond imitates Major Bowes of "Amateur Hour" fame, adding to the feel-good quality. Composers Bert Kalmar and Harry Ruby worked overtime, not only collaborating on the screenplay with Viola Brothers Shore and Rian James, but also writing the songs: "Cabin on the Hilltop," and with Sid Silvers, "My Heart Wants to Dance" and "Let's Make a Wish." Featuring George Meeker, Gordon Jones, Maxine Jennings, Anita Colby.

WAY OUT WEST (Hal Roach-MGM 1936; a 1937 release) Directed by James W. Horne, produced by Stan Laurel. Production titles: *Tonight's the Night* and *In the Money*. Granted, this may not be a musical, but it contains the single best number ever performed by Laurel and Hardy. The boys, standing in front of a process screen depicting a Western town, listen to the singing of The Avalon Boys. Led by a young and thin Chill Wills, the Avalons (also including Art Green, Walter Trask and Don Brookins) do "Commence to Dancing" (J. L. Hill). Stan and Ollie begin to move to the music and then break into a seemingly spontaneous, totally hilarious softshoe. Shortly thereafter, inside the saloon, Stan uses Wills' voice to sing "On the Trail of the Lonesome Pine" (Harry

WAY OUT WEST *(Hal Roach-MGM 1936) Lois Laurel and father Stan during the making of this musical comedy gem; its colorized version is one of the best.*

Carroll-Ballard MacDonald). Sharon Lynne and chorus perform "Won't You Be My Lovey Dovey?" (Seymour Furth-E.P. Moran, from the 1905 show *The Rollicking Girl*), and the merriment ends with Stan, Ollie and Rosina Lawrence warbling "We're Going Down to Dixie" ("Hold on Abraham," by William B. Bradbury, 1862). By golly, it *is* a musical. Apart from that, it's just about the best of all L & H features, as the two attempt to deliver the deed to a gold mine, intended for pretty Rosina, but get sidetracked by greedy saloonkeeper James Finlayson and his wife, singer Lynne. Somehow, the boys succeed. The film contains Hardy's classic line to fellow stage passenger Vivien Oakland: "A lot of weather we've been having lately." Oscar nomination to Marvin Hatley for Best Music Score.

THE GIRL SAID NO *(Grand National 1937)*

Produced, directed and written by Andrew L. Stone, screenplay by Betty Laidlaw and Robert Lively. Reissued as *With Words and Music*. The lilting and witty operettas of W. S. Gilbert and Arthur Sullivan have not been overly exposed on film and this Grand National release took credit as the first feature built around their music. In fact, the score includes just one original song, "Rhythm in My Heart" (Val Burton-Will Jason), performed by star Irene Hervey. The plot, quickly put out of the way, concerns bookie Robert Armstrong's efforts to produce a Gilbert and Sullivan presentation starring dance hall hostess Hervey who owes him a good deal of money. Luckily, veteran G & S performers are present—Frank Moulan, William Danforth, Vera Ross and Vivian Hart—

THE GIRL SAID NO *(Grand National 1937) Singing "Three Little Maids from School" from Gilbert and Sullivan's* The Mikado *are Irene Hervey as Peep-Bo, Carita Crawford as Yum-Yum, Vivian Hart as Pitti-Sing. Production cost was $70,000.*

A.S.

members of a real group initially called the Civic Light Opera Company—who had comprised part of the only American G & S company to tour the United States. Moulan, also the dance director, performs Ko-Ko in *The Mikado*, sings "Monarch of the Sea" *(HMS Pinafore)* and joins Delos Jewkes and Tudor Williams as well as Danforth on "Policemen's Song" *(Pirates of Penzance).* Hervey displays her musical talents as Peep-Bo, with Vivian Hart (Pitti Sing) and Carita Crawford (Yum-Yum), doing "Three Little Maids from School" *(The Mikado).* This was to be Moulan's only film, as the New York-based performer died at 63 in 1939. Also starring, but not singing, are Ed Brophy, Paula Stone, Richard Tucker, Bert Roach, Max Davidson and Gwili Andre. Long before he specialized in disaster epics in the Fifties and Sixties, Stone was making musicals of this calibre. With *Song of Norway* (1970), he returned to the genre on a much bigger and a lot less successful scale. *Girl* was Oscar-nominated for Best Sound Recording, A. E. Kaye.

IT CAN'T LAST FOREVER (Columbia 1937)

Directed by Hamilton MacFadden. Divergent elements make for a diverting picture. Theatrical agents Ralph Bellamy and Robert Armstrong promote drunken Raymond Walburn as a prophet, The Master Mind. When Bellamy has to substitute for Walburn, he becomes a radio sensation after his predictions come true. Then gangsters led by Ed Pawley move in on Bellamy, whose romance with reporter Betty Furness—not to mention his well-being—is threatened. Lee Loeb and Harold Buchman's radio spoof allows for two Ben Oakland-Herb Magidson songs, "Lazy Rhythm" and "Crazy Dreams." The specialty numbers really shine and there are musical

SING WHILE YOU'RE ABLE *(Ambassador-Conn-Melody 1937) Pinky Tomlin, as he did in real life, has eyes for Toby Wing, one of our favorite dumb blondes.*

SWEETHEART OF THE NAVY *(Grand National 1937) At her Snug Harbor Cabaret, Cecilia Parker wins over an unruly crowd by singing the title song, as Ray Teal leads the orchestra.*

turns by prima donna Barbara Burbank, The Blenders, The Morella Brothers and comedy adagio dancers Armanda and Lita. Outstanding are two sequences featuring future stars. The first, early in the film, offers The O'Connor Family, with 11-year-old Donald dancing up a storm between his tall and lanky brothers Willie and Jack. Later on, a street dance is performed by two young black teams, The Jackson Brothers—actually Eugene Jackson and Charles Bennett, and The Dandridge Sisters—really Dorothy and Vivian Dandridge and Etta Jones. Dorothy Dandridge, then only 14, went on to become a major black performer in musicals and dramas before her death in 1965.

SING WHILE YOU'RE ABLE (Ambassador-Conn-Melody 1937) Directed by Marshall Neilan. Singer-composer Pinky Tomlin, a sort of unsophisticated Kay Kyser, had a brief series of starring vehicles in which his musical talents and shyly appealing personality were exploited. Here, he's a country lad enamored of Toby Wing (as he was in real life) when he has a chance to sing on the radio. Before his first broadcast, Pinky gets kidnapped and then, worse, loses his voice. Suzanne Kaaren co-stars and Bert Roach has some telling moments as a booker. Soon-to-be Western star Jimmy Newell, The Brian Sisters and Prince Mike Romanoff have singing or comedy interludes. The song titles express the Tomlin philosophy, although he contributed just one: "I'm Just a Country Boy at Heart" (Tomlin-Paul Parks-Connie Lee), "I'm Gonna Sing While I'm Able" (Parks-Lee), "You're My Strongest Weakness" (Coy Poe-Al Heath-Buddy LeRoux).

SWEETHEART OF THE NAVY (Grand National 1937) Directed by Duncan Mansfield. After three films together at MGM and three more at Grand National, Eric Linden and Cecilia Parker were considered to be the top romantic team since the Janet Gaynor-Charles Farrell combination—or so the publicity stated. In their last time together on screen, Parker, naturally, has the title role and Linden is the sailor who falls in love with her. She wants him to fight fleet champion Jason Robards as a way of saving her debt-ridden Snug Harbor Cabaret. The Bennie F. Zeidman production starts out as a musical and has musical moments thereafter, but there's evidence of cutting to save the budget. The first number, "I Want You to Want Me" (Jack Stern-Harry Tobias) is interrupted and never repeated. Parker's rendering of the title number (Stern-Tobias) is the highlight, being joined by her sailor audience. Ray Teal, who went on to a long career as a character actor, is the sleek orchestra leader. Late in the film, a scene stolen from *Alice Adams* is played out. In that 1935 comedy, cook Hattie McDaniel helped to ruin Katharine Hepburn's dinner for Fred MacMurray. Grand National's version has Parker with commander Roger

Imhof, the twist being that the singing and imbibing cook here is Hattie's sister Etta. Bernadene Hayes and Cully Richards have other leading roles in this Parker-Linden swan song, silly, unsophisticated but endearing because of its stars.

SWING YOUR LADY (Warner Bros. 1937 copyright, a 1938 release) Directed by Ray Enright. Based on the story "Toehold on Artemus" by H. R. Marsh and the play *Swing Your Lady* by Kenyon Nicholson and Charles Robinson. Called Humphrey Bogart's worst film, *Lady* is actually a very funny feature mixing hillbillies and wrestling. Bogey promotes a match between his star wrestler Nat Pendleton and Kentuckian Daniel Boone Savage over muscular blacksmith Louise Fazenda. Penny Singleton, formerly Dorothy McNulty and soon to be "Blondie," is Bogey's true love, while The Weaver Brothers and Elviry—a hillbilly trio—make their debut. Frank McHugh, Allen Jenkins, Ronald Reagan and dancer Sammy White join in. Songs by Jack Scholl and M. K. Jerome are predictable: the title song, "Mountain Swingeroo" and the somehow haunting "Dig Me a Grave in Missouri," all performed by the Weavers, Singleton and/or White. Choreography by Bobby Connolly. The Weavers, vaudevillians, went on to star at Republic.

SWING YOUR LADY *(Warner Bros. 1937) Penny Singleton, just before becoming Blondie, seems uncertain of Humphrey Bogart's intentions. Romantic?*

SWISS MISS (Hal Roach-MGM 1938) Directed by John G. Blystone and Hal Roach. Production title: *Swiss Cheese.* Short version called *Alpine Antics.* The last really good Laurel and Hardy musical comedy. As failed mousetrap salesmen in the Alps, the boys are forced to work in a hotel under the stern watch of chef Adia Kuznetzoff (a Russian-born gypsy singer). Walter Woolf King and Della Lind are on hand to render such treasures as "Yo-Ho-Dee-O-Lay-Hee," "The Cricket Song," "Could You Say No To Me?" and "Mine to Love" (Arthur Quenzer-Phil Charig). Eric Blore, Charles Judels, Anita Garvin and Eddie Kane are also in evidence. There are two marvelous scenes with animals, one being Stan's efforts to take brandy from a St. Bernard and the other, the famous foot bridge scene with a gorilla, played by Charles Gemora, and a piano. Laurel and Roach also worked on the original story with Jean Negulesco (later a 20th Century-Fox director) and gagman Charles Rogers. Other assets: choreography by Val Raset and colorful settings, although mainly stagebound.

SWISS MISS *(Hal Roach-MGM 1938) Oliver Hardy and Stan Laurel demonstrate the correct manner of yodeling.*

DANCING ON A DIME (Paramount 1940)
Directed by Joseph Santley. Judging by the stars and some of the supporting cast, this seems to be a Universal musical that happened to get produced at Paramount. It's a backstage effort, so dear to the hearts of Universal screenwriters, concerning a musical troupe funded by the WPA (the governmental Works Project Administration). When the money isn't forthcoming, the discovery of a roll of counterfeit bills saves the show, at least until opening night. Amidst bickering, Robert Paige and Grace McDonald—both new to leading roles—promote a romance. Other talents: William Frawley, Peter Lind Hayes, Eddie Quillan, Frank Jenks, Lillian Cornell, Virginia Dale and Phillip Terry. Frank Loesser collaborated with Burton Lane on the songs "Dancing on a Dime," "Mañana" and "I Hear Music," and with Victor Young on "Lovable Sort of Person."

DANCING ON A DIME *(Paramount 1940) Sometime singer Robert Paige and often dancing Grace McDonald have a confrontation; both shortly went to Universal.*

HIT PARADE OF 1941 (Republic 1940) Directed by John H. Auer. Reissued in 1953 as *Romance and Rhythm*. Here is the blueprint for *Singin' in the Rain*: To save his radio station, Kenny Baker features Ann Miller as a vocalist. Since she can't sing, the voice of Frances Langford is substituted. Although he cares for Langford, Baker has to squire Miller for publicity purposes. Langford's friend Patsy Kelly exposes the deceit by switching the controls so that Miller's real voice is heard. Langford then goes on to become a star, with Baker as her beau. All of this is set against a television revolution which threatens to make radio obsolete. Credit for the screenplay goes to Bradford Ropes, F. Hugh Herbert, Maurice Leo, Sid Kuller and Ray Golden. In on the fun are Hugh Herbert (not the aforementioned writer), Mary Boland, Phil Silvers, Sterling Holloway, Franklin Pangborn, Six Hits and a Miss, and Borrah Minevitch and His Harmonica Rascals. Danny Dare did the choreography (Miller—naturally—can dance but not sing, as per the plot), while the new songs were concocted by Jule Styne and Walter Bullock: "Who Am I?" (which won an Oscar nomination as Best Song), "Swing Low Sweet Rhythm," "In the Cool of the Evening" (not the Oscar-winning song of 1951 which had an extra "Cool, Cool"). Musical director Cy Feuer (later the Broadway producer) was Oscar-nominated for Best Score. Sequel to the top-rated *The Hit Parade* (1937).

I CAN'T GIVE YOU ANYTHING BUT LOVE, BABY (Universal 1940) Directed by Albert S. Rogell. Based on the story "Trouble in B Flat" by James Edward Grant. Genuinely funny gangster comedy, one of Universal's many pictures built around a popular song of lengthy title. Comic mobster Broderick Crawford, searching for his grade school sweetheart, kidnaps composer Johnny Downs to help write a song expressing his feelings. The result: "Sweetheart of P. S. 59" (Paul Gerard Smith-Frank Skinner). The composers also contributed "Day by Day," with the title song written by Dorothy Fields and Jimmy McHugh, a pop standard and used in many films. Jessie Ralph is Brod's no-nonsense mother, Peggy Moran and Gertrude Michael are the romantic interests, Sunshine Sammy Morrison and Jeni LeGon contribute to the entertainment, and Warren Hymer, Horace McMahon and John Sutton are assorted hoods.

LET'S MAKE MUSIC (RKO Radio 1940) Directed by Leslie Goodwins. Production title, *Malvina Swings It*. Bob Crosby, complete with his orchestra and The Bobcats, makes his debut in this tuneful treat. Bing's younger brother, cast as himself, actually plays second fiddle to Elisabeth Risdon as the elderly music teacher who writes a hit song, a tribute to her school, "Fight on for Newton High" (actually by Dave Dreyer, Roy Webb and Herman Ruby), and sings it endlessly. Bob naturally romances her niece, Jean Rogers. Nathanael West's screenplay conveys some pointers as to how a novelty song becomes a hit, while one in that vein actually did: "Big Noise From Winnetka" (Gil Rodin-Ray Haggart-Ray Bauduc-Bob

Crosby). Other numbers: "Central Park" (Johnny Mercer-Matt Malneck), "You Forgot About Me" (Dick Robertson-Sammy Mysles-James Hanley). Also in the cast are Joseph Buloff, Joyce Compton, Bill Goodwin, Grant Withers, Benny Rubin, and drunk Jack Norton. Affable Crosby made few films, but had success as a singer/bandleader and led one of the best Dixieland groups ever.

ALL-AMERICAN CO-ED (Hal Roach-United Artists 1941) Directed by LeRoy Prinz, who also produced this Streamliner, running just 48 minutes. Slapstick and drag humor abound as Johnny Downs of Quinceton poses as a co-ed to compete in a beauty contest at Mar Brynn. When not in drag, he's romancing Frances Langford. Kent Rogers imitates such stars as Gary Cooper and there's still time for such numbers as "I'm a Chap With a Chip on My Shoulder," "The Farmer's Daughter" and "Up at the Crack of Dawn" (Walter G. Samuels-Charles Newman), as well as the Oscar-nominated ballad

HIT PARADE OF 1941 *(Republic 1940) Ann Miller and chorus in a story involving radio and televison; other Republic production numbers were a bit more elaborate.*

"Out of the Silence" (Lloyd B. Norlin). With Harry Langdon, Esther Dale, Allan Lane and lots of juniors as seniors—Noah Beery, Jr., Alan Hale, Jr., Joe Brown, Jr., Carlyle Blackwell, Jr. Plus, in her film debut, future femme fatale Marie Windsor. Edward Ward got an Oscar nomination for Best Scoring of a Musical.

BLONDIE GOES LATIN (Columbia 1941) Directed by Frank R. Strayer. For a change of pace, this entry in the long-running "Blondie" series is a musical, with a Latin accent. Blondie and Dagwood (Penny Singleton, Arthur Lake) go on a South American cruise and circumstances involve her with singer Tito Guizar and him with singer Ruth Terry. Lake also runs around in a dress (obviously a popular form of entertainment in 1941). The regulars, including Larry Simms as Baby Dumpling (later Alexander) and Jonathan Hale as Dithers, are joined by other musical talents as well, Kirby Grant and Harry Barris. The songs by Chet Forrest and Bob Wright salute the Americas—"You Can't Cry on My Shoulder," "You Don't Play a Drum—You Beat It," "Querida." For the singing and dancing comedienne Singleton, this was one of her last opportunities to display all of her talents for the cameras, and she proves to be well matched with Mexican entertainer Guizar.

ALL-AMERICAN CO-ED *(Hal Roach-UA 1941) Harry Langdon, nearing the end of his career, isn't moved by the charms of Marie Windsor, at the start of hers.*

BLONDIE GOES LATIN
(Columbia 1941) Tito Guizar serenades Penny Singleton in a musical entry of the long running series (1938-50).

SWEETHEART OF THE CAMPUS *(Columbia 1941) A musical with a boogie beat, as Ruby Keeler steps out—for the last time— with Ozzie Nelson and His Orchestra.*

TIME OUT FOR RHYTHM *(Columbia 1941) Time out for romance (?) with two comedy groups: Larry Fine, Blanche Stewart, Moe Howard, Elvia Allman and Curly Howard, aka The Three Stooges and Brenda and Cobina.*

SWEETHEART OF THE CAMPUS (Columbia 1941)

Directed by Edward Dmytryk. Ruby Keeler bowed out of musicals in this let's-save-the-college story. She's a singer in Ozzie Nelson's band and they all enroll in school to prevent a takeover by trustee Kathleen Howard. At the time, Ozzie was really a popular bandleader and quite naturally wins singer (and real-life wife) Harriet Hilliard. Gordon Oliver, Don Beddoe, The Four Spirits of Rhythm are in it and this time the juniors are football players—Fred Kohler, Jr., Alan Hale, Jr. Songs, mainly by Eddie Cherkose and Jacques Press, include "Tap Happy" and "Zig Me Baby With a Gentle Zag." Louis Da Pron choreographed the dances, with director Dmytryk and cinematographer Franz Planer experimenting with split screen and angled shots as Ruby tap dances to a boogie beat.

TIME OUT FOR RHYTHM (Columbia 1941)

Directed by Sidney Salkow. Another Forties musical with Ann Miller set against a television background. Rudy Vallee, Richard Lane and Allen Jenkins, producing shows for TV, utilize such new talent as singers Miller and Joan Merrill. When Lane tries to use Rosemary Lane (no relation) as a star, however, friction develops. Glen Gray and His Casa Loma Orchestra participate in the highlight number, when the musicians disappear into a black background so that only their instruments are seen—an idea perfected some years earlier by Busby Berkeley. Here, LeRoy Prinz takes credit as the choreographer. The Sammy Cahn-Saul Chaplin score features the title song, "Obviously the Gentleman Prefers to Dance," "As If You Didn't Know," "Boogie Woogie Man," and "Did Anyone Ever Tell You?" Merrill, 21, a singer from Washington, was making her debut in the company of such acts as Six Hits and a Miss, Eddie Durant's Rhumba Orchestra and The Three Stooges teamed with Brenda and Cobina (Blanche Stewart, Elvia Allman) from Bob Hope's radio show. How three men could wind up with two women is best left unanswered.

BEHIND THE EIGHT BALL (Universal 1942)

Directed by Edward F. Cline. Based on Stanley Roberts' story "Off the Beaten Path" (the film's production title was *Off the Beaten Track*). In just an hour, this Ritz Brothers comedy squeezes in plot, gags and nine Don Raye-Gene de Paul songs. One, "Mr. Five by Five," was already popular when the film was released. The boys here are The Jolly Jesters, aspiring performers who land jobs in a musical called "Fun for All," trying out at a straw-hat theater in the Berkshires owned by Carol Bruce and Dick Foran. The only problem is that the new performers are being killed off by German spies, certainly a topical plot. Bruce, Grace McDonald, Johnny Downs and Sonny Dunham and His Orchestra join the

Ritzes—Harry, Al and Jimmy—on such numbers as "You Don't Know What Love Is," "Atlas Did It" and the touching lost-love tribute "Wasn't It Wonderful?" Eddie Prinz did the choreography. One of the last, but among the best, Ritz riots.

GIVE OUT SISTERS (Universal 1942) Directed by Edward F. Cline. If any singing group epitomized World War II, it was the Andrews Sisters. Maxene, Patty and LaVerne thought that their Universal musicals would team them with the studio's handsomest leading men. Instead, they were cast with The Ritz Brothers or Abbott and Costello. On their own in *Sisters*, the girls are surrounded by a wealth of talent both old—Charles Butterworth, Walter Catlett, William Frawley—and new—Dan Dailey, Grace McDonald, Donald O'Connor, Peggy Ryan, Jivin' Jacks and Jills; all in the newer group danced. The plot revolves around the sisters' efforts to make a star out of McDonald, over the objections of her spinster aunts—Edith Barrett, Marie Blake and Fay Helm. The sisters Andrews do some nice tongue-in-cheek

acting when they pose as the elderly ladies. They perform a nostalgic number, "You're Just a Flower From an Old Bouquet" (Gwynne and Lucien Denni), and the whole cast joins in on the rousing finale, "Pennsylvania Polka" (Lester Lee-Zeke Manners), one of the most enduring Andrews Sisters numbers. Choreography by John Mattison.

PRIORITIES ON PARADE (Paramount 1942) Directed by Albert S. Rogell. Production title: *Priorities of 1943*. Popular World War II tunefest which didn't hit it off with the critics and seems fairly ordinary today. However, it has a topical plot, Jack Donohue's zesty dance numbers, entertaining songs and an appealing cast. New talent Johnnie Johnston, who later did a couple of major MGM musicals, takes his place alongside Ann Miller (no, she wasn't in most of the best B musicals, it just seems so), Jerry Colonna, Betty Rhodes and Vera

BEHIND THE EIGHT BALL *(Universal 1942) Jimmy, Harry and Al Ritz demonstrate how Charles Atlas' body building has helped them in the "Atlas Did It" number.*

PRIORITIES ON PARADE *(Paramount 1942) Jerry Colonna, Ann Miller, Betty Rhodes and Johnnie Johnston in a popular WWII entertainment.*

GIVE OUT SISTERS and PRIVATE BUCKAROO *(both Universal 1942) The Andrews Sisters were very popular that year: Maxene (top), LaVerne and Patty.*

Vague. Art Arthur and Frank Loesser's original screenplay shifts from swing to swing shift as a musical group goes to work at an aircraft plant and puts on a show for the workers' morale. Loesser and Jule Styne contributed "You're in Love With Someone Else But I'm in Love With You," while Styne and Herb Magidson supplied the other songs. With Harry Barris (an ex-Rhythm Boy, along with Bing Crosby), Eddie Quillan (somehow away from Universal), Dave Willock, Rod Cameron and The Debonairs.

PRIVATE BUCKAROO (Universal 1942) Directed by Edward F. Cline. The plot, what there is of it, is often sacrificed for the wealth of songs—twelve in all. When Harry James and His (entire) Orchestra are drafted, they and the Andrews Sisters put on a USO show. Self-centered recruit Dick Foran falls in love with Jennifer Holt, who wants him to learn discipline and devotion to duty. Sergeant Shemp Howard romances Southern Mary Wickes and indulges in some strained comedy. The Andrewses give out with their hits "Don't Sit Under the Apple Tree" (Lew Brown-Sammy Stept-Charles Tobias) and "Three Little Sisters" (Irving Taylor-Vic Mizzy). Joe E. Lewis, of the nightclubs, makes a rare screen appearance and sings "I Love the South," while Foran does the Charles Newman-Allie Wrubel title number. Helen Forrest offers the standard "You Made Me Love You" (Joseph McCarthy-James Monaco) with Harry James and the boys, amidst a wealth of patriotic tunes. Choreography by John Mattison. Lots of engaging Universal talent on view, too: Donald O'Connor, Peggy Ryan, Huntz Hall, The Jivin' Jacks and Jills, as well as Ernest Truex.

THE GIRL FROM MONTERREY (PRC 1943) Directed by Wallace Fox. A tribute to Hollywood's Good Neighbor Policy towards South America, this exuberant boxing comedy with music stars Armida, an authentic Mexican, born in Sonora, in an otherwise non-Mexican cast. American Indian actor Jay Silverheels (later Tonto to "The Lone Ranger"), has a small part as a Mexican fighter. The action is set mainly in New York, where Armida manages brother Anthony Caruso's boxing career and falls in love with his closest rival, likeable Terry Frost. Singer Veda Ann Borg tries to compromise Caruso but ends up in love with him; she and Armida have a brief and frantic wrestling match, better than anything staged on "Dynasty." Edgar Kennedy and Jack LaRue also star. The Louis Herscher-Harold Raymond score has Armida doing "Jive Brother Jive" with an accent.

HIT PARADE OF 1943 (Republic 1943) Directed by Albert S. Rogell. Reissued in 1949 as *Change of Heart.* Top Republic musical in which Susan Hayward ghost-writes for composer John Carroll, whose charm overcomes his character's many faults. In fact, some observers feel that Carroll's easygoing style influenced Dean Martin's personality. Making this entry unusual is the emphasis on black talent, topped by Count Basie and His Orchestra with Dorothy Dandridge of Harlem niteries. Jack Williams, known as The Harlem Sandman, and dancers Pops and Louie (Albert Whitman and Louis Williams) also perform. Plus The Golden Gate Quartet, Chinita Marin and the orchestras of Freddy Martin and Ray McKinley. In the cast: Gail Patrick, Eve Arden, Walter Catlett, Melville Cooper, Mary Treen, Wally Vernon, Astrid Allwyn, Sunshine Sammy Morrison, Tim Ryan—quite impressive. Most of the seven songs were written by Jule Styne and Harold Adamson, including Oscar-nominated "Change of Heart," "Harlem Sandman," "That's How to Write a Song" and "Tahm-Boom-Bah." Walter Scharf got an Academy Award nomination for Best Scoring of a Musical.

REDHEAD FROM MANHATTAN (Columbia 1943) Produced by Wallace MacDonald. Directed by Lew Landers. In her last Hollywood film (she made only one further picture, in her native Mexico), Lupe Velez played a dual role, did some good imitations, and dropped her accent to prove her versatility. The picture "guaranteed to knock you for a Lupe" has the former Mexican Spitfire as both a Broadway musical star and her hot-blooded cousin, the latter substituting for the former when the star is expectant. The undistinguished Walter G. Samuels-Saul Chaplin score, including "Let's Fall in Line," "I'm Undecided" and "The Fiestango," didn't prevent Lupe from going out in good fashion. Michael Duane, Tim Ryan, Gerald Mohr and Lewis Wilson (who originated the role of Batman in the 1943 serial) costar, while Larry Parks, Adele Mara and Richard Talmadge have bits. Good, unpretentious fun.

TWO SEÑORITAS FROM CHICAGO (Columbia 1943) *Starlets with a beat are Leslie Brooks, Ann Savage, Jinx Falkenburg and Ramsay Ames.*

HIT PARADE OF 1943 *(Republic 1943) Susan Hayward is about to find that John Carroll has his own hit parade; he's in a position many of her later costars may have enjoyed. These two were briefly engaged before she wed Jess Barker.*

MINSTREL MAN *(PRC 1944) Backstage, watching Benny Fields perform with daughter Judy Clark, are Alan Dinehart and Gladys George (it's a backstage musical).*

SILVER SKATES (Monogram 1943) Directed by Leslie Goodwins. As Vera Hruba Ralston proved at Republic, ice skating epics weren't the sole domain of Sonja Henie. However, only Henie's films enjoyed really top budgets. Monogram had a good bet in Belita, who performs here quite ably—she was also an accomplished dancer. A screenful of stars also take to the skates: Frick and Frack, little Irene Dare, Danny Shaw and Eugene Turner. Belita becomes the object of singer-bandleader Kenny Baker's attentions, as he doesn't want her to leave "Silver Skates," the ice show produced by his sweetheart Patricia Morison. The latter, who has said that she was dubbed on the few occasions she was called upon to sing for the cameras, has a duet with Baker, "A Girl Like You and a Boy Like Me." Baker solos on "Love Is a Beautiful Song," as Belita and Turner waltz on ice. Most of the tunes are by Dave Oppenheim and Roy Ingraham, with Dave Gould staging the production numbers. Joyce Compton, Frank Faylen, Henry Wadsworth and Ted Fio Rito and His Orchestra also play in this extravaganza on ice.

TWO SEÑORITAS FROM CHICAGO (Columbia 1943) Produced by Wallace MacDonald. Directed by Frank Woodruff. Five leading ladies, beginning with Joan Davis, share top billing in a comedy about two aspiring actresses—Jinx Falkenburg and Ann Savage—posing as Portuguese damsels to land roles in a Broadway musical. The script is provided by Davis, maid in a Chicago hotel, who sells it to producer Emory Parnell. All goes well until jealous Leslie Brooks and Ramsay Ames reveal the deceit, but Parnell's assistant Bob Haymes (yes, Dick's brother) substitutes another script and the show goes on. Nick Castle staged the dances for this all-starlet musical. Songs and composers are best left unmentioned.

CAREER GIRL (PRC 1944) Directed by Wallace W. Fox. It's said that the only ism in which Hollywood believed was plagiarism (nepotism obviously goes without saying). Scripted by Dave Silverstein, Stanley Rauh and Sam Neuman, *Career Girl* is a blatant rewrite of RKO's *Stage Door* (1937). Frances Langford resides in Barton Hall, New York hotel for aspiring actresses (she's a more sympathetic Katharine Hepburn). Outgoing Iris Adrian (the Ginger Rogers role) organizes Talent Inc., a company to manage Langford's career and produce the show "Manhattan Rhythm." Sweet Ariel Heath (in the Andrea Leeds part) finds that she lacks talent and, dejected, is seriously injured. The original ending had Heath dying and Langford triumphing on her behalf on opening night. Released version ends with the final number at rehearsal of the all-girl show, Heath still alive for an upbeat if abrupt conclusion. In the male leads are nice guy Edward Norris and stuffy Craig Woods, who resembles Kirk Alyn as Clark Kent; they more or less divide the Adolphe Menjou role. Lorraine Krueger even dances a la Ann Miller. Songs by Morey Amsterdam, Tony Romano, Sam Neuman and Michael Breen.

MINSTREL MAN (PRC 1944) Directed by Joseph H. Lewis. In his only starring film, vaudevillian and one-time minstrel Benny Fields reprises his career in pleasant fashion. When wife Molly Lamont dies in childbirth, Fields gives his infant daughter to fellow minstrel Roscoe Karns and his wife Gladys George. Years later, after he's thought to be long dead, Fields returns to join now grown daughter Judy Clark onstage. The oldie "My Melancholy Baby" (George A. Norton-Ernie Burnett) leads off a set of originals by Paul Francis Webster and Harry Revel, including "Remember Me to Carolina." Nominated for an Academy Award, the song caused a dispute with Walter Donaldson, who thought it was too close to his "Did I Remember?" from MGM's *Suzy* (1936) and settled out of court. Revel was associate producer and Martin Mooney, one of the writers, functioned as assistant to the producer and as supplier of the footage of the burning of the ship *The Morro Castle*. Interior footage of the burning boat is stock from *Whom the Gods Destroy* (Columbia 1934). Dance director Johnny Boyle and technical adviser Lee "Lasses" White also appear onscreen; White was more prominently a sidekick in Westerns. Production designer was the ubiquitous Edgar G. Ulmer, and the small cast includes the recently-deceased Alan Dinehart, plus Jerome Cowan, Gloria Petroff and later Broadway star John Raitt. For Best Scoring of a Musical, Leo Erdody and Ferde Grofe also received Oscar nominations.

MURDER IN THE BLUE ROOM (Universal 1944) Directed by Leslie Goodwins. Based on the story "Secrets of the Blue Room" by Erich Philippi. Evolution of a plot: in 1933, Universal produced *Secret of the Blue Room*, a murder mystery set in a castle. A seriocomic remake, *The Missing Guest*, was turned out in 1938. The World War II version is a musical mystery with comedy and a touch of fantasy, supplied by Robert Cherry as a ghost. The original has been embellished by I. A. L. Diamond and Stanley Davis into the story of theatrical manager John Litel and new wife Nella Walker reopening the old house in which her previous husband was murdered. New crimes occur as The Three Jazzibelles—Grace McDonald, June Preisser, comedienne Betty Kean—sing and dance to relieve the tension. The hit of the show is "The Boogie Woogie Boogie Man" (Milton Rosen-Everett Carter), of course. Anne Gwynne and Donald Cook command top billing (someone had to), while Regis Toomey and Bill Williams—credited as Bill MacWilliams in his film debut—are in support. Other

MURDER IN THE BLUE ROOM *(Universal 1944) Frank Marlowe, Ian Wolfe, John Litel, Regis Toomey, Anne Gwynne, Nella Walker and Bill Williams' body, in the Blue Room.*

numbers: "One Starry Night" (Don George-Dave Franklin), "A-Doo-Dee-Doo-Doo" (Teepee Mitchell a.k.a. F. J. Tablepocter-Leo Erdody-Lew Porter). Note: "The Boogie Woogie Boogie Man" is not the same song written by Ted Koehler and Burton Lane for Paramount's splashy *Rainbow Island* that same year.

ROSIE THE RIVETER (Republic 1944) Directed by Joseph Santley. Based on the *Saturday Evening Post* story "Room for Two" by Dorothy Curnow Handley. Introducing the popular title song by Redd Evans and John Jacob Loeb, the film can be considered the definitive wartime musical about defense plants. Four workers on the swing shift are forced to share a room—at different hours—in Maude Eburne's boarding house. The men, Frank Al-

ROSIE THE RIVETER *(Republic 1944) Jane Frazee receives a telegram from fiancé Frank Fenton, who's arriving unexpectedly, as Carl "Alfalfa" Switzer and Vera Vague watch. Goldie Hawn's* Swing Shift, *anyone?*

bertson and Frank Jenks, eventually fall for the women, Jane Frazee as Rosie (Rosalind) and Vera Vague (a.k.a. Barbara Jo Allen). Other songs point up some wartime romantic problems: "I Don't Want Anybody at All" (Herb Magidson-Jule Styne) and "Why Can't I Sing a Love Song" (Sol Meyer-Harry Akst). Carl "Alfalfa" Switzer and Lloyd Corrigan are featured, with Kirby Grant and dancer Joe McGuinness lending their musical talents. Coincidentally, production wound up on a December 7, in 1943.

SWING HOSTESS (PRC 1944)
Directed by Sam Newfield. Significant, since it depicts jukeboxes as being operated by a hostess at a record company. She plays platters on request, rather than the records spinning automatically within the machine. A poor singer (Betty Brodel) takes credit for a recording by a good one (Martha Tilton). Ironically, Brodel, real-life sister of star Joan Leslie, really could sing and performed with Hal Kemp and Bob Crosby's orchestras. The popular Liltin' Miss Tilton—as she was known—sang with Benny Goodman and as part of Three Hits and a Miss. Score by Jay

Livingston, Ray Evans and Lewis Bellin includes the good "Say It With Love" and the funny "I'll Eat My Hat." Iris Adrian provides laughs, and the leading men chores are handled by Charles Collins (star of RKO's *The Dancing Pirate,* 1936) and double-talker Cliff Nazarro.

TAKE IT BIG (Paramount 1944)
Directed by Frank McDonald. A Pine-Thomas Production. Entertainer Jack Haley's performer pals put on a benefit show to help save his dude ranch from bankruptcy. Sandwiched in between the Western settings are numerous numbers, both old and new. Jerry Seelen and Lester Lee provided the new songs, including the title tune and "I'm a Big Success With You." Ozzie Nelson and Harriet Hilliard appear in their last movie musical together, performing "Sunday, Monday and Always" (Johnny Burke, James Van Heusen and special lyrics by Ozzie) with his orchestra, the soon-to-be standard that Bing Crosby introduced in *Dixie* (1943). Frank Forest and even Richard Lane and Fritz Feld get to sing; among those who don't are Mary Beth Hughes, Arline Judge, Lucile Gleason, Fuzzy Knight, Pansy the Performing Horse, dancers Rochelle and Beebe. Musical numbers were staged by Carlos Romero.

SWING HOSTESS (PRC 1944) *The boys meet the girls at Bosco's Cafe: Cliff Nazarro and Iris Adrian, friends of singer Martha Tilton and bandleader Charles Collins.*

EVE KNEW HER APPLES (Columbia 1945) Produced by Wallace MacDonald. Directed by Will Jason. Absolutely the *last* Ann Miller musical for consideration herein. The story and the songs are borrowed from elsewhere, as the star portrays a radio singer who needs a rest and meets a reporter, William Wright, who somehow gets the impression that she's an escaped killer. It doesn't sound that way, but the Rian James-E. Edward Moran plot is actually a reworking of *It Happened One Night*. Miller doesn't dance, but she does sing (agreeably) such recycled hits as "I'll Remember April" (Gene de Paul-Don Raye-Patricia Johnston, from Universal's *Ride 'Em Cowboy*, 1942); "I've Waited a Lifetime" (Eddie Brandt, from Columbia's *She's a Sweetheart*, 1944); and "I've Got the Blues for Someone to Love" (Robert Warren, from PRC's *Follies Girl,* 1943). See it and believe.

SING YOUR WAY HOME *(RKO Radio 1945) Glen Vernon does that, as Colleen Townsend peeks over his left shoulder. The singer-actor was later the West Coast advertising manager for* Boxoffice *magazine.*

TAKE IT BIG *(Paramount 1944) Jack Haley's singing leaves something to be desired by Ozzie Nelson and Harriet Hilliard.*

HIT PARADE OF 1947 *(Republic 1947) Eddie Albert, from the music department of Hyperion Picture Corporation, presents his latest song, "You Said a Mouthful" (not in the film), to uninterested producer Bill Goodwin.*

SING YOUR WAY HOME (RKO Radio 1945)

Directed by Anthony Mann. The war was over and the title seemed to be good advice for those still returning from it. Principal photography was actually completed at the end of 1944, but the released version has Jack Haley as a war correspondent sailing home after victory was won; in his charge, a group of young entertainers who had been unable to leave Europe because of the conflict. He and singer Anne Jeffreys get romantic between complications. The engaging William Bowers screenplay allows for an optimistic score by Herb Magidson and Allie Wrubel: Oscar-nominated "I'll Buy That Dream," "Heaven Is a Place Called Home," plus a rendering of "The Lord's Prayer" (music by Albert Hay Malotte) by 15-year-old Donna Lee with chorus. There's a funny number with chorus girls dancing in the showers, Frank Redman's camera discreetly concentrating on their feet. Lots of young talent on view: Glen Vernon, Marcy McGuire, James Jordan, Jr., Colleen Townsend, Lawrence Tierney (who would shortly costar with Jeffreys), plus three who were overshadowed by their relatives: Robert Clarke of The King Family, Paul Brooks (Jeanne Crain's husband Paul Brinkman) and Bill Williams (husband of Barbara Hale, father of William Katt). Numbers staged by Charles O'Curran.

SONG OF THE SARONG (Universal 1945)

Directed by Harold Young. Odd mixture of comedy, melodrama, music and religion, written by producer Gene Lewis. Flying to the South Seas in search of fortune in pearls, footloose pals William Gargan, Eddie Quillan and Fuzzy Knight find love and salvation. The three play and sing two Jack Brooks songs, "Ridin' on the Crest of a Cloud" and the swinging "The Pied Pipers From Swingtown, U.S.A." Lovely Nancy Kelly, as the island princess, both hulas and sings—being doubled and dubbed—"Lovely Luana" ("Song of the Sarong," Don Raye-Gene DePaul) and wears Maria Montez castoffs from *South of Tahiti* (1941) and *Cobra Woman* (1944). Some of the hula footage is from Abbott and Costello's *Pardon My Sarong* (1942). The original choreography is by Carlos Romero. With George Dolenz, George Cleveland, Larry Keating, Jay Silverheels and big Mariska Aldrich in the cast, it's charming in its way.

HIT PARADE OF 1947 (Republic 1947)

Produced and directed by Frank McDonald. TV title: *High and Happy.* Songwriter Eddie Albert forms a quartet with singers Constance Moore and Joan Edwards and comic Gil Lamb. Calling themselves The Tune Toppers, they achieve success in Manhattan clubs until Albert insists on using more sophisticated material. When Moore is tapped by Hollywood, she becomes a movie star and asks that her fellow Toppers be hired. Realizing what's happened, the other three attempt to find fame on their own. The original story by Parke Levy, screenplay by Mary Loos, seems to have been inspired by the group called The Revuers, which launched the careers of Judy Holliday, Adolph Green and Betty Comden in Manhattan clubs in the late Thirties. This act spoofed the current scene, movies in particular, in song and dance and sketch. Edwards, who makes her film debut here, had been a member of the radio edition of "The Hit Parade." The Jimmy McHugh-Harold Adamson score, featuring many reprises, offers "Couldn't Be More in Love," "The Cats Are Goin' to the Dogs," "I Guess I'll Have That Dream Right Now," "The Customer Is Always Wrong," and even a number for guest stars Roy Rogers and The Sons of the Pioneers, "Is Anyone Here From Texas?" Spotted throughout are Woody Herman and His Orchestra, featuring Red Norvo on the xylophone. Fanchon was dance director and the stellar cast includes Bill Goodwin, William Frawley, Richard Lane, Janet Warren and Mary McCarty. There's even a tour of Republic Studios. Albert finally has a chance to demonstrate his singing and piano playing skills, some things he later performed in posh supper clubs with his wife Margo.

LADIES OF THE CHORUS (Columbia 1948)
Directed by Phil Karlson. Can the only reason for the inclusion of this one be that it's the first leading role for Marilyn Monroe? Yes.

SQUARE DANCE JUBILEE (Lippert/Screen Guild 1949) Directed by Paul Landres. Almost nonstop Country and Western tunes as television talent scouts Don Barry and Wally Vernon look for acts to book on Spade Cooley's show. Barry, who also produced with Ron Ormond, manages to clean up a gang of modern day cattle rustlers. The fact that nothing is to be taken too seriously is evidenced by Barry and Vernon's discussion of a Don "Red" Barry Western (the two also made a few oaters for Lippert release). Mary Beth Hughes sings "Gotta Soft Spot in My Heart" (by husband David Street, along with Sam Freedman-Jules Fox). Cooley starts things humming by introducing the June Carr-Ray

LADIES OF THE CHORUS (Columbia 1948) Rand Brooks, Marilyn Monroe and Adele Jergens. The other lead is Eddie Garr, Teri's father.

SQUARE DANCE JUBILEE *(Lippert/Screen Guild 1949) Spade Cooley and His Band perform in a musical package for the Country and Western fan.*

MEET ME AT THE FAIR *(Universal-International 1952) Diana Lynn and Dan Dailey at a medicine show; one of Irving Wallace's last screenplays before becoming a novelist.*

ALL ASHORE *(Columbia 1953) Mickey Rooney, Jody Lawrance and Dick Haymes on the dance floor prove that three is indeed a crowd.*

Broome title song, even before the credits begin. In the large cast are John Eldredge, Thurston Hall, Max Terhune, Tom Tyler, Britt Wood, Marshall Reed and such specialties as Cowboy Copas, Herman The Hermit, The Tumbleweed Tumblers and The Elder Lovlies (sic)—a group of square dancing grannies, as silly as can be imagined.

G.I. JANE (Lippert 1951) Directed by Reginald Le Borg. Pleasant nonsense in which TV producer Tom Neal, staging a show with WACs, gets his induction notice and dreams of bringing WACs to a remote desert radar command where he encounters cute Jean Porter (the Jane of the title) and tough lieutenant Iris Adrian. Jimmy Dodd sings two of his own compositions, "Gee I Love My G.I. Jane!" and "I Love Girls" while Porter counters with "Baby, I Can't Wait" (Dian Manners-Johnny Clark). Fact that there were no new dances to exploit then is evidenced by a musical sequence in which "truckin'" is shouted as a prelude to that dance, introduced in the late Thirties. Also with Jimmy Lloyd, Mara Lynn, Michael Whalen and Bobby Watson, now in the American Army after playing Hitler throughout the war years and after.

MEET ME AT THE FAIR (Universal-International 1952) Directed by Douglas Sirk. Based on the novel *The Great Companions* by Gene Markey. Screenplay by Irving Wallace, adaptation by Martin Berkeley. Usually associated with meatier material, Sirk and Wallace concern themselves with crooked politics and an orphanage in a nostalgic Technicolored musical, set in 1904. Dan Dailey is the amiable medicine man who helps runaway orphan Chet Allen, while Diana Lynn plays the social worker who comes to love both, forsaking her fiancé, crooked district attorney Hugh O'Brian. Latter has a real character part and plays for laughs, and Allen impresses with his beautiful voice. Only 13, the boy was hired through Columbus Boychoir School of Princeton, New Jersey. This was the only film for Allen, who had a difficult later life. He solos on Schubert's "Ave Maria" and joins Dailey and Scatman Crothers with "I Was There" (F. E. Miller-Crothers). Title song (Milton Rosen-Frederick Herbert) is delivered by Carole Mathews, actually dubbed by Joanne Greer. Lots of oldtimers in supporting roles.

ALL ASHORE (Columbia 1953) Directed by Richard Quine, who did the screenplay with Blake Edwards. Story by Edwards and Robert Wells. The kind of a Technicolor musical in which the story is slight, the complications predictable, the songs tuneful, and the characters have daffy names—Francis "Moby" Dickerson (Mickey Rooney), Gay Knight (Peggy Ryan). It all adds up to nothing but entertainment. Rooney, Dick Haymes and

Ray McDonald are penniless sailors on leave, who, while supporting themselves as waiters and entertainers, find romance in the respective persons of Barbara Bates, Jody Lawrance and Peggy Ryan. The dancing of Ryan and McDonald, married in real life, is a highlight (choreography by Lee Scott), so is Haymes' singing. Songs by Robert Wells and Fred Karger practically tell the story: "All Ashore," "Heave Ho, My Hearties," "You'll Love Catalina," "Boy Meets Girl," "I'm So Unlucky," "Who Are We to Say," "I Love No One But You."

CRUISIN' DOWN THE RIVER (Columbia 1953)

Directed by Richard Quine, written by Blake Edwards and Quine. Another Technicolored entry with Dick Haymes (his last starrer). The onetime crooning idol here is a New York singer who inherits a riverboat from his old grandpappy in Alabama. Haymes is also seen as his ancestor, a Gaylord Ravenal type, in the prologue. The film makes some use of the distinctive talents of singers Billy Daniels and Connie Russell, who were never fully exploited by films. Audrey Totter plays a good girl for a change and Cecil Kellaway and Johnny Downs (from Thirties and Forties film musicals) play her grandfather at different ages. Douglas Fowley is along for the cruise in both eras, a prologue establishing the elder Haymes' winning both the boat and Russell from Downs. The songs are all nostalgic, from the title evergreen by Eily Beadell and Nell Tollerton on down. Daniels really cooks with his versions of "Sing You Sinners" (Sam Coslow-W. Franke Harling) and "I Never Knew" (Tom Pitts-Ray Egan-Roy K. Marsh).

SHAKE, RATTLE AND ROCK! (American International 1956)

Directed by Edward L. Cahn. The very first AIP musical wasn't a portent of things to come, as the "Beach Party" epics of the next decade were much slicker, more entertaining and faster moving. In effect, this was a cashing in on a trend as the studio's average release had been a Western or a horror feature. Even the title is derivative and shouldn't be confused with "Shake, Rattle and Roll," one of the seminal rock songs. The specialty acts are well integrated and the kids in the cast serve little purpose other than to dance. In fact, the last-billed team of Rosie and Carlos takes center stage in most of the dance scenes. There's more plot than usual as Touch (Michael) Connors plays a Dick Clark-type disk jockey who champions the teens who happen to like rock and roll. Via his TV show, he begins a drive to erect a Teen Town where the kids can pursue useful activities and stay away from gangster Paul Dubov's influence. Old snob Douglass Dumbrille, meanwhile, organizes a group to have rock and roll banned. Complicating matters is the fact that Connors' fiancée Lisa Gaye is the niece of Dumbrille supporters Margaret Dumont and Raymond Hatton. Fats Domino, the major name of note,

CRUISIN' DOWN THE RIVER *(Columbia 1953) Johnny Downs, Connie Russell and Dick Haymes, all musical talents, in a flashback to riverboat days.*

SHAKE, RATTLE AND ROCK! *(American International 1956) Rosie (right) and Carlos dance to "Rockin' on Saturday Night," sung by Annita Ray.*

performs three of his own compositions (written with David Bartholomew), "Honey Chile," "Ain't That a Shame" and "I'm in Love Again." Joe Turner does two of his own numbers, "Feelin' Happy" and "Lipstick, Powder and Paint," while Annita Ray, the only featured female rocker, offers "Rockin' on Saturday Night" (George Matola-Johnny Lehman). Veteran director Cahn and

MISTER ROCK AND ROLL *(Paramount 1957) Lionel Hampton and Alan Freed, representing two kinds of pop music, find a common ground.*

JUKE BOX RHYTHM *(Columbia 1959) Brian Donlevy and his family, Marjorie Reynolds and Jack Jones, share the leads in a prophetic rock feature.*

scripter Lou Rusoff have the older actors overact, knowing too well that teens preferred to see grown-ups, especially authority figures, behave foolishly. Sterling Holloway's hipster (complete with subtitles) proves that rock lingo hadn't taken over from jive talk. Connors gives the best performance, Gaye looks incredibly beautiful and Clarence Kolb presages Judge Wapner by engagingly presiding over a TV trial. Originally released with *Runaway Daughters* on a double bill.

MISTER ROCK AND ROLL (Paramount 1957)

Directed by Charles Dubin. Here, almost at the dawn of rock, is the leading disk jockey of his day, Alan Freed, in a very crudely done feature, playing himself. He attempts to refute columnist Jay Barney's charge that he's a "Pied Piper for illicit adolescent emotion." Freed explains that he "just happened to be there when the breeze started blowing up a storm" and shows that the young rockers are worthwhile kids by having them donate money for a heart fund drive. Scenes of a Freed rock show at the legendary New York Paramount are included, those concerts having passed into music lore. The popular Teddy Randazzo offers "Kiddio," "Next Stop Paradise" and, with ex-boxer Rocky Graziano, "Rocky's Love Song." Lionel Hampton and His Band are on hand to show the origins of rock in rhythm and blues, while genuine rockers also putting in appearances include the ageless Chuck Berry, Little Richard, Frankie Lymon and The Teenagers, LaVern Baker, Clyde McPhatter, Brook Benton, Ferlin Husky, The Moonglows and Shaye Cogan. Among the non-rockers: Lois O'Brien and the non-comedy team of Al Fisher and Lou Marks. Freed was the major DJ whose career was destroyed by the payola scandal of the early Sixties—the bribing of platter spinners by record companies to have their product played on the air. Freed, who died not long after that, was played, brilliantly, by the late Tim McIntire in *American Hot Wax* (1978, also Paramount), but this feature offers the real thing.

JUKE BOX RHYTHM (Columbia 1959)

Directed by Arthur Dreifuss. Sam Katzman's production contended that, in 1959, Brian Donlevy, as a supposedly intelligent Broadway producer, could successfully mount a rock and roll show. It would take another decade for such productions as *Hair* and *Grease* to prove that this wasn't just a quaint notion. As Donlevy's son, Jack Jones (Allan Jones and Irene Hervey's offspring) romances Jo Morrow, a princess whose participation could make the musical a hit. Hans Conried steals the proceedings as a junk dealer turned fashion designer. Veterans dominate the cast: Frieda Inescort, Marjorie Reynolds, Edgar Barrier, Karin

CINDERELLA 2000 *(Independent-International 1977) Eddie Garetti as Roscoe the Robot and chorus in the "Mechanical Man" number of this futuristic musical.*

Booth, Fritz Feld; the newcomers are confined mainly to the featured acts in Donlevy's show, "Juke Box Jamboree." That song, written by Richard Quine, Fred Karger and Stanley Styne, is performed by Jones and the Earl Grant Trio. Johnny Otis and Band do "Willie and the Hand Jive," a hit in its day (honestly). The Treniers offer "Get Out of the Car," and George Jessel gets into the act with "Spring Is the Season for Remembering," which he wrote with Ben Oakland.

HOW TO STUFF A WILD BIKINI (American International 1965) Directed by William Asher. One of the Beach Party group, but with Frankie (Avalon) and Annette (Funicello) separated. In the Naval Reserve, Frankie is afraid that Dwayne Hickman will replace him in Annette's heart, so witch doctor Buster Keaton uses Beverly Adams and the bikini of the title to keep Hickman occupied. As silly as it sounds, but lots of fun and actually one of the best of the AIP musicals. Brian Donlevy and Mickey Rooney (a truly unlikely musical duo) are around to spoof big business and sing "Madison Avenue." Motorcycle gang leader Harvey Lembeck and his Rat Pack offer "Follow Your Leader," Annette pines for "The Perfect Boy," and the beach gang does "That's What I Call a Healthy Girl." Songs by Guy Hemric and Jerry Styner; choreography by Jack Baker. Pathecolor-Panavision photography is by the great Floyd Crosby. There's even animation by Jack Kinney and some deft special effects by Roger George and Joe Zomar, photographic effects by Butler-Glouner. And of course, there's the title song.

THE FIRST NUDIE MUSICAL (Paramount/Northal Film Distributors 1976; originally scheduled for 1975 release by Westamerica) Directed by Mark Haggard and Bruce Kimmel. Screenplay and songs by Kimmel, who also stars as the inept novice director. When porno filmmaker Stephen Nathan finds that stewardesses and nurses are out as subjects, he's persuaded by secretary Cindy Williams to make the first porno musical, "Come, Come Now." Virtually one of a kind as the only mainstream feature of its type. Lots of frontal views of the performers, mainly female, and although it's R rated, Paramount passed on distribution rights to an independent after having acquired it from another indie. Williams, who had just started her TV series "Laverne and Shirley" at this time, believed in the film and promoted it extensively. It managed to acquire a cult status. Diana Canova (Judy's daughter) was one of the few cast members to make an impact. "The Lights and the Smiles," a good number, was given screen credit as being sung by Annette O'Toole, dubbing for Leslie Ackerman, who performs it onscreen. Many of the songs can't be mentioned here. Choreography by Lloyd Gordon, who appears as one of the (clothed) chorus boys.

THE FIRST NUDIE MUSICAL *(Paramount/Northal Film Distributors 1976) Cindy Williams, of TV, and Stephen Nathan are a sophisticated, and fully clothed, couple in this uninhibited release.*

CINDERELLA 2000 (Independent-International 1977) Produced and directed by Al Adamson. Although rated X and inspired by the hardcore feature *Rollerbabies* (1976), this co-production of Sam Sherman and Dan Kennis is rather harmless, for all its sexy intent. In the year 2047, Erwin Fuller as The Controller outlaws sex except by computer. Catharine Erhardt is the 21st century Cinderella, one of her stepsisters (Bhurni Cowans) being black and her Fairy Godfather (Jay B. Larson) living up to his designation. The Sparky Sugarman score includes "2000 A.D.," "Doin' Without," "Cinderella, Why Can't I Be You?" and "We All Need Love," all agreeable. Choreography is by John Appleton and Eddie Garetti, both of whom appear. Garetti plays Roscoe the Robot and, with a small chorus, performs "Mechanical Man" with an ineptness boarding on the hilarious. Erhardt was actually Catharine Burgess, also a model, TV soap opera actress and porno star. Before the film's release, she was known briefly as Barbara Southern. Vaughn Armstrong portrays her Prince, this time forced to make love to all the pretenders of the realm who claim to be Cinderella.

INDEX
(Italicized number refers to photo)

Gordon, C. Henry, 54